The beginning point of true transformati  for the change promised in the gospel and simistic view of the human condition, Dr. . is possible and goes on to show how. He be ...ie reality of the divine indwelling the human s ... implications for you. But the implications of the divi ...yond transformation: it is also the secret to effective living and powe ...ss. This book is practical, thoroughly biblical and easy to read. I highly recommend it.

— Bulus Silas Bossan
International Vice-President, The Navigators;
Colorado Springs, Colorado, USA

Three things happen to me every time I read *The Indwelling*: First, I gain a deeper revelation of the person of Jesus and grow in amazement at the work He accomplished on the cross to bring me into oneness with the Godhead. Second, I become dissatisfied with my present level of manifesting His glory and long to know His living presence within me even more. Third, I eagerly pray that many more will be able to access these awesome truths and encounter the living reality of Jesus dwelling in us. The more I read *The Indwelling*, the more I am convinced that God's plan and design for the redeemed life boils down to this one simple fact: He lives in me so that He may work through me to accomplish His eternal purpose on earth. To the degree to which I align my entire being with His indwelling presence, the greater the victory I enjoy, the fruit I produce, and the glory I experience. I highly recommend this book with the confidence that in the years to come it will rank among other great literary classics penned by men such as A. W. Tozer, E. W. Kenyon, Andrew Murray, and others.

— Mark Kolo
Director and Lead Catalyst,
Global Activation Ministry, Nairobi, Kenya

The Indwelling powerfully reassures us that the requisite empowerment to accomplish great things for the kingdom is already resident inside every believer. Every child of God needs a new revelation of the conviction that this indwelling is able to quicken every area of our lives towards successful witnessing and Christian living, even as we hopefully anticipate our soon coming King. Dr. Nweke's expository gifting, epitomized by his logical, Bible-based approach, laced with real life applications of the Word of God, is as always clearly manifest in this book. It is a welcome addition to the many materials through different media that God is sending to His people through Dr. Nweke, with an urgency indicative of the imminence of His appearing. I most enthusiastically recommend this book to all God's laborers, with a solemn prayer that the *dunamis* of this Indwelling will enable us to accomplish the unthinkable for our Father in heaven.

— Dr. Prosper Okonkwo
CEO, APIN Public Health Initiatives

Dr. Ferdinand Nweke dissects the Bible with the savvy, skill, and passion of an anatomy surgeon. I am amazed at his ability to teach the Bible and his creative approach and commitment to social media age evangelism. He takes his game one step higher in this new book, which I have no doubt will impact many on the things of God and what is expected of man. I endorse this book and believe it will reach the ends of the earth spreading the Good News.

— MIKE AWOYINFA
Author, columnist, and pioneer Managing
Director and Editor-in-chief of The Sun (Nigeria)

After receiving Jesus Christ as Lord and savior, a Christian's next greatest miracle, besides the desire to make heaven, is walking in His divine nature through the transformative action of God's Word on his/her life. In *The Indwelling,* Dr. Nweke has shown us how meditating on the Word of God (through the cycles of truth assimilation and the attendant elevation to different levels in wisdom and *dunamis* power), moves a believer towards the image of Christ, which is the desire of God (Romans 8:28). With a razor-sharp scientific mind, he has dissected for us the processes by which the Word of God becomes flesh in us, hence elevating us in leadership responsibility as a light to our environment. The concepts explained in this wonderful book are not just theories. I have personally experienced both the transformative and the promotional nature of the Word in my life, by applying the principles prescribed in this book. This book is a jewel that can be given to our families and friends to help them understand and experience God's power in their lives. Thank you, Dr. Ferdinand, for this treasure.

— VINCENT ANIGBOGU, PHD
Director General, Institute for
National Transformation

Dr. Ferdinand is not only a preacher of the gospel but a teacher; even a layman can understand the message of the *The Indwelling* with the basic analogy and illustrations he has provided. I highly recommend this book to every believer. It will bring healing as you read through it. You will find answers to the silent questions and yearnings of your heart. You will also understand how to practically explore "the exceeding greatness of God's power at work in you." This will not only help you to walk in victory but will also aid your work as an ambassador of Christ. Be blessed as you embark on this journey of self-transformation.

— GIDEON PARA-MALLAM (REVEREND)
Ambassador WA 2019
International Fellowship of Evangelical
Students(IFES)

The Indwelling is a divine revelation; it is the mystery and wonder of the Christian faith made plain. God's original plan for man is the Indwelling; as Dr. Ferdinand puts it, *from being FOR us, He came to be WITH us, so that He could be IN us!* Any effort to live the Christian life apart from the Indwelling will end in failure simply because that is how it was designed to work! I highly commend this work with prayers that it will be a great tool in the hand of God to equip and propel His people into their divinely assigned tasks in these last days.

— 'ABUCHI EMMANUEL OHIA
Coordinator, Eternity Ministries,
United Kingdom

THE INDWELLING

*The Exceeding Greatness
of God's Power at Work in You*

FERDINAND NWEKE

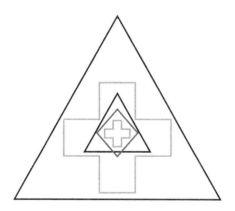

Published in the United States by Credo House Publishers,
a division of Credo Communications LLC, Grand Rapids, Michigan
credohousepublishers.com

Visit eternityministries.org for more on the author's ministry.
He can also be contacted at eternitymin@yahoo.com.

ISBN   978-1-62586-144-3

Cover and interior design by Klaas Wolterstorff
Cover illustration: Fresco in Žiča, 13th-century Serb Orthodox monastery,
    Wikimedia Commons
Editing by Donna Huisjen

*This book is dedicated to the next great move of God—
an era of ordinary believers filled with all the fullness of God,
walking in all redemption rights and privileges, and revealing God to
the world from their varied platforms—resulting in earth being filled
with the knowledge of the glory of the Lord, as the waters cover the sea.*

Contents

Foreword

Allowing God to express his love through our lives is one of the most important assignments we will be provided in this one life. The fulfillment of the Great Commission is at stake, which makes our understanding of hosting his precious presence our primary concern.

I've watched Dr. Ferdinand Nweke teach multitudes through print, media, and preaching this most prized truth for more than a decade. He has inspired me as a leader to strive for the fullness of the finished work accomplished at Calvary, which is available for every follower of Jesus. And now, *The Indwelling* brings us a comprehensive action guide on how to experience the wholeness of the gospel and to minister in the power of Christ.

If you are ready to be deeply challenged by some of the most profound elements of discipleship, you must read *The Indwelling*. Dr. Nweke has an infectious approach to keep you captivated as he leads you on this journey. As you absorb this book, you'll begin to understand more thoroughly and intimately the critical value of a Spirit-led inner life.

This book is loaded with Scripture and loving commentary that is a tribute to the author's personal passion and devotion to our Lord. The gentle dissection of and insight into the Word of God will bring you a fresh revelation of your ability to live and minister like Christ.

Among the powerful chapters, I found the idea of agreeing with

God (chapter 15) highly motivating. We are challenged to value the process of agreement with God while listening to his voice. As we do, the eternal promises of the Word of God are unlocked and made available. Glory to God!

I'm making *The Indwelling* mandatory reading for my staff, board members, and field workers. It will be a regular gift to friends and family members. My desire is for the truth and insights from my dear friend to be a catalyst for kingdom impacting transformation all over the world. May that be your testimony as well as you invest your life in the pages of this book.

GREG KELLEY
CEO World Mission |
Host, Great Commission Update podcast

Introduction

The very premise of this book—that God would actually, personally, and presently indwell believers—is mindboggling and unthinkable. But if words mean anything, that is exactly what the Bible teaches—not in an isolated verse or two but in an overwhelming array of passages— from different authors!

The Indwelling: The Exceeding Greatness of God's Power at Work in You is a revelation of the believer's actual and current indwelling by the Father, the Son, and the Holy Spirit, and the astounding consequences of that priceless inheritance.

Every believer desires to live free of condemnation, to walk in sustained victory, and to be used greatly by God. This book shows *how.* In a very practical way, it shows how believers can stand firm in the fullness of the victory that is theirs in Christ. It brings believers into the astonishing realization that they are indwelt by the Godhead and challenges them to walk in the fullness of that reality by allowing the One who indwells them to live His life fully from within them and manifest His supernatural power through them.

The blessings of our being in Christ are many, but the infinite possibilities of Christ being in us—*indwelling us*—are largely unexplored. *The Indwelling: The Exceeding Greatness of God's Power at Work in You* is sent forth to help catalyze this exploration. You have heard a lot about who you are in Christ but in *The Indwelling,* you will discover who He is in you!

By reading and applying the message of this book, you will:

1. Come to partake of the divine nature and walk in the realities of that nature.
2. Become Spirit-ruled instead of flesh-ruled. You will learn to develop your inner life and to operate from inside—as God originally designed—rather than from externalities.
3. Lose every sense of unworthiness and condemnation as you discover what the finished work of Christ accomplished on your behalf.
4. Discover that God's supernatural power is the common heritage of every believer, not just of "big" men or women of God. You will learn that the same Spirit who worked in Christ, the apostles, and other great men and women of God is presently at work within you.
5. Experience joy and permanent freedom from realizing your true identity and priceless heritage in Christ. You will walk in the fullness of all redemption benefits, including forgiveness, healing, peace, boldness, joy, love, etc.
6. Experience transformation from one degree of glory to another, become more like Christ, and be empowered to minister as He did.
7. Gain an abiding consciousness of the divine presence. This will strengthen your faith to expect and manifest the supernatural power of God through the indwelling Holy Spirit.

In this book you will receive a revelation of the greatest blessing of the New Covenant: God's present and actual residence *inside* believers, and the unlimited possibilities of that indescribable inheritance. Your days of struggle will come to an end as you learn to allow the indwelling One to work in you to will and to do according to His good pleasure.

To facilitate detailed study, *The Indwelling* is divided into parts:

Part One establishes the reality of the Indwelling as a biblical fact, neither mythical nor figurative, but actual—to be experienced by faith.
Part Two discusses the believer's indwelling by the triune God;

since the Father, Son, and Holy Spirit are one, an indwelling by one equals indwelling by all.

Part Three unveils the consequences of the finished work of the Lord Jesus Christ, which are so central to experiencing and maximizing the revelation of the Indwelling.

Part Four explores the unquantifiable possibilities of a life that is filled with all the fullness of God.

Finally, Part Five shows how we can respond to, and maximize, the Indwelling. Chapter 18, titled "Embracing the Indwelling," provides clear steps to help readers practically apply the truths encountered in the book.

How to Get the Most out of this Book

The revelation of the Indwelling—our priceless heritage in Christ— is so astounding and mindboggling that it is necessary to outline certain principles that will help the reader maximize the information contained in this book. Attending to these principles will ensure transformation from one degree of glory to another by the application of the truths that will be encountered.

A. **The Truth Cycle and The Truth Spiral** show the processes the truth of God's Word must undergo to produce results and transformation in our lives.
B. **The Indwelling: Truth Illustrated** explains the oneness of believers with Christ and the Father, using an illustration.
C. **Locating Everything** invites the reader to attend to the prepositions and other "little words" found in Scripture, as they are vital keys to unlocking meanings. It explains prepositions (because they have a huge significance in this book) and shows how they help us to locate everything—including ourselves and our glorious heritage in Christ.

A. The Truth Cycle and the Truth Spiral

"And we all, with unveiled face, **continually** seeing as in a mirror the glory of the Lord, are **progressively** being transfigured into His image from [one degree of] glory to [even more] glory, which comes from the Lord, [who is] the Spirit" (2 Corinthians 3:18 AMP).

As a young believer, I thought the primary purpose of reading the Bible was to get revelations or insights. I have since realized that the ultimate goal of Scripture is our transformation into the likeness of Christ. Thus the insights we receive from Scripture are but a part of a process that we must engage if we are to be changed from one degree of glory to another, as we look into the mirror of God's Word. This process is outlined below in the Truth Cycle and the Truth Spiral; they show how God's Word produces transformation in our lives. Understanding this process is vital to maximizing the amazing truths unveiled in this book.

The Truth Cycle

Truth remains mere information until we engage it through a deliberate process that causes it to release its inherent power:

Unengaged truth:

**Truth remains mere
information until engaged**

We engage truth through the processes of the Truth Cycle:

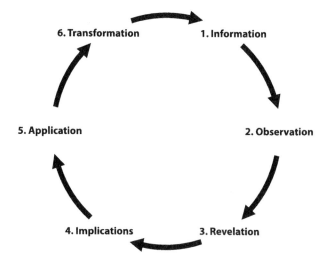

6. Transformation   **1. Information**

5. Application   **2. Observation**

4. Implications   **3. Revelation**

Engaging truth via the Truth Cycle

1. **INFORMATION**: First we receive information from God through His Word, which is truth.
2. **OBSERVATION**: Next, with the help of the Holy Spirit, our Teacher, we carefully observe the information we have received by paying attention to the details of what the Word says. We look carefully into the mirror of the perfect law of liberty, and as we meditate and study the Word we see things we could never have seen with the casual glance.
3. **REVELATION**: Revelation (insight) flows out of our careful, prayerful, and attentive observation of the written Word. Light and insight flood our hearts as the Spirit unveils the Word and brings life from its letters.
4. **IMPLICATION**: We ask, "What are the implications of the revelations arising from our observation of the information we have received from God's Word? What do these revelations imply? If these things are like this, then what?"
5. **APPLICATION**: From a clear understanding of the implications of the truths we have encountered, we apply the Word to our lives

and thereby become doers of the Word and heirs of the promises of God. Also, knowing the implications helps compel application; this in turn leads to transformation.

6. **TRANSFORMATION**: This results from applying/obeying the Word; it is at this point that we experience the Word and it becomes "flesh" in us. Its exceedingly great and precious promises manifest in our lives, and we experience its power.

Our *transformation* arising from our *application* of God's Word leads us to discover further *information* (the first component of the Truth Cycle), leading to closer *observation* and deeper *revelations* from the Word, with greater *implications* requiring *application*, resulting in further *transformation*.

This Truth Cycle continues as an upward and outward spiral (the Truth Spiral) as we journey from time to eternity. It consists of cumulative Truth Cycles repeated at ever higher levels in a continuous, unbroken fashion. Thus we are transformed from one degree of glory to another by God's Spirit working in us through His Word. [It should be noted that engaging falsehood results in a downward and inward spiral that is the very opposite of the Truth Spiral]. The Truth Spiral is illustrated below.

The Truth Spiral

The Truth Cycle, once completed (from information to transformation, i.e., numbers 1–6), never repeats at the same level. This is because transformation implies a higher level of glory than that at which truth was initially encountered. It is impossible to apply the Word of God and remain the same: it results in transformation, which moves the doer of the Word to another level. Thus, once completed, the Truth Cycle becomes a spiral: it spirals upwards to new levels of information and insight into the Word, which, if followed through to application, lead to further transformation. This is illustrated below:

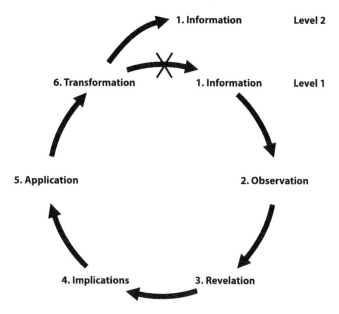

1. Information   **Level 2**

6. Transformation   **1. Information**   **Level 1**

5. Application   **2. Observation**

4. Implications   **3. Revelation**

*Transformation opens up an upward and outward
spiral as the transformed individual changes levels*

The transformed individual continues to receive further truth (information) from God's Word, thereby repeating the same process to even greater transformation (as shown below). This cumulative sacred spiral leads to changes in degrees of glory and will culminate in our ultimate transformation into the highest degree of glory possible: the very image and likeness of Christ Himself.

9

The effect of repeated truth spirals is shown below:

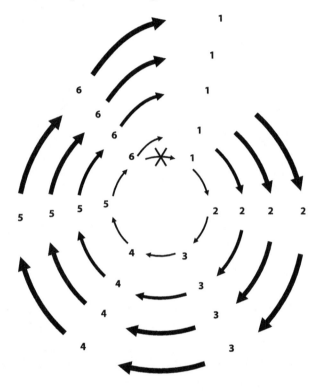

Repeated spirals occur as truth (information) is encountered at higher levels thereby creating an upward and outward spiral

The illustration below shows the side view of the Truth Spiral and how transformation leads to changing levels of glory:

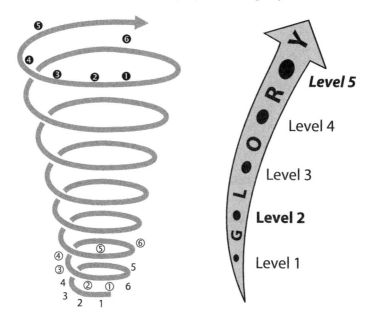

Transformation to new levels by engaging and applying truth

Changing levels of glory arising from transformation

Note:
1=Information; 2=Observation; 3=Revelation;
4=Implication; 5=Application; 6=Transformation

In light of the above, the reader is encouraged to closely *observe* the *information* (truths) presented in this book. This will birth insights and *revelations* from the Word. Next, the *implications* of the revealed truths should be kept in constant view. Take 1 John 4:4, for instance: "You, dear children, are from God and have overcome them, because the one who is in you is greater than the one who is in the world." What are the implications of our being "of God"? What are the implications of having the greater One living in us? The next process in our experience of the Truth Cycle is to consider practical *applications* of the truth encountered. For instance, should we live in fear or worry while the greater One indwells us? Is there a situation that can possibly arise that this greater One cannot handle? As the truth is applied, it produces *transformation* in our lives, changing us from one degree of glory to another.

If the reader diligently applies this process to the eternal, unchanging truths of the Indwelling, it will result in an upward spiral of nonstop transformation into the glorious image of our Lord and Savior, Jesus Christ.

B. THE INDWELLING: TRUTH ILLUSTRATED

The following Scriptures, which proclaim the Indwelling, are reflected in the diagram below:

- "You, dear children, are from God and have overcome them, because **the one who is in you** is greater than the one who is in the world" (1 John 4:4).
- "Christ **in** you, the hope of glory" (Colossians 1:27).
- "On that day you will realize that **I am in my Father, and you are in me, and I am in you**" (John 14:20).
- "My prayer is not for them alone. I pray also for those who will believe in me through their message, that all of them may be one, **Father, just as you are in me and I am in you**. I have given them the glory that you gave me, that they may be one as we are one—**I in them and you in me**" (John 17:20–23).

It is to be noted that the symbols used are for illustrative purposes only. Also, while the illustration is two-dimensional, the personalities indicated are not two-dimensional beings. The neat lines shown do not exist in reality: the Father, His Son Jesus Christ, and the Holy Spirit are, seamlessly, one. And the believer, through redemption, has become a temple indwelt by the Godhead.

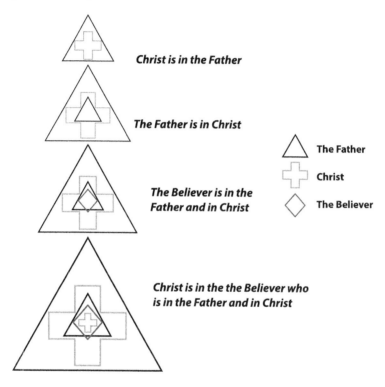

Christ is in the Father

The Father is in Christ

△ **The Father**

✚ **Christ**

◇ **The Believer**

The Believer is in the Father and in Christ

Christ is in the the Believer who is in the Father and in Christ

C. LOCATING EVERYTHING

The Power of Prepositions

Prepositions are one of the most crucial tools of the English language. As with tenses, it is practically impossible to make sense of a sentence without them. They are so vital to understanding and maximizing the astounding potentials discussed in this book.

Prepositions help us to locate things—both in space and time. According to the Cambridge Dictionary (online version), there are over 100 prepositions in English. These include single-word prepositions such as *above, after, before, beside, between, in, on, near, under, upon, and within,* as well as groups of words like *in front of, inside of, near to, together with,* and *on top of.*[1]

As basic as the foregoing is, it is fundamental to understanding the amazing truths presented in *The Indwelling.* Since prepositions abound in Scripture, without paying careful attention to them the reader will not be able to accurately locate herself, her heritage, or God's power.

Many believers find it difficult to get anything meaningful from reading their Bibles; for them, finding revelation from the Word is a continual struggle. What they may not realize is that the little words to which they pay little attention hold the key.

The prepositions in Scripture help us to pinpoint ourselves, to locate our inheritance, and to accurately locate God and His power relative to us. Without them, we could be looking for the living among the dead—like the doubting apostles who sought the risen Lord in an empty tomb. We would not even know to what covenant—old or new— we belong. The prepositions used in Scripture also help us to locate the devil—by revealing his present position—*under* the feet of Jesus Christ and the believer!

Consider the following verses of Scripture, paying particular attention to the prepositions highlighted:

"Our Father who is *in* heaven, Hallowed be Your name." Matthew 6:9 NASB

"But because of his great love for us, God, who is rich in mercy, made us alive *with* Christ even when we were dead in transgressions—it is by grace you have been saved. And God raised us up *with* Christ and seated us *with* him in the heavenly realms *in* Christ Jesus." Ephesians 2:4–6

"Christ *in* you, the hope of glory." Colossians 1:27

We see how the prepositions in these Scriptures help to communicate invaluable truth about our inheritance. For instance, we are clearly told that Christ is *in* the believer—not on or behind—and that His presence *in* us (with all its wondrous implications) is our hope of glory.

The Indwelling unveils your location in Christ, and His location in you. God knows grammar; He undoubtedly knows what He is talking about when He uses certain words where He could have used others. He says what He means and means what He says.

I now invite you to explore the uncharted dimensions of your kingdom heritage unveiled in *The Indwelling*.

PART ONE

Unveiling the Indwelling

in·dwell (ĭn-dwĕl′)
v. in·dwelt (-dwĕlt′), in·dwell·ing, in·dwells
v.intr.
1. To exist as an animating or divine inner spirit, force, or
principle.
2. To be located or implanted inside something.
v.tr.
To inhabit or reside within as such a spirit, force, or principle.[2]

The Indwelling

Someone lives *in* you.

To begin to understand this statement, picture a pregnant woman. She is *indwelt* by her baby. For nine months, the baby is literally *implanted* within the mother's womb. One day, according to the time of life, the baby will be born, but until then she lives inside her mother. Indeed, every human being who has been born into the world since Adam and Eve entered by first indwelling a mother. Even Jesus, the incarnate Word, indwelt Mary to enter the world. Thus the Indwelling is God's way of bringing us into the world, and, as we will see in this book, it's also His way of guiding us in this world and bringing us into the glorious realities of the next.

Humans are not just physical beings; we are spiritual beings as well. And as surely as a physical indwelling is possible, so is the spiritual—even more so since there are no physical boundaries and limitations in the spiritual realm.

Somewhere in the depths of your being lives another being. Deep in the recesses of your person resides another Person. And your lot in life—physically or emotionally, at home or on the streets, in business or in ministry, spiritually or financially, and for all time and eternity—is totally dependent on the identity of the being who indwells you, and your relationship with that being.

These are not wild speculations. They are true. We intend to prove them conclusively in the book you hold in your hands. You will discover how your security, authority, victory, and significance are dependent on your relationship with the One who *indwells* you.

Consider these statements:

"As for you, you were dead in your transgressions and sins, in which you used to live when you followed the ways of this world and of the ruler of the kingdom of the air, the spirit who is now at work in those who are disobedient" (Ephesians 2:1-2).

Paul says there is a spirit at work *in* the children of disobedience: that spirit is identified here as "the ruler of the kingdom of the air." A ruler ("prince" in some translations) is a personality, not a force. He is at work in people. He was at work in all of us, in fact, until we were made alive in Christ—a very different prince—the Prince of peace. This does not mean that Satan is personally present in every unsaved person. He is not omnipresent, but he indwells the unbelieving by his nature that is within them. We inherited that nature through The Fall.

The children of disobedience are the way they are because there is a spirit—a being—working *in* them. Note the preposition carefully: it's *in*, not on. What is holding children of disobedience in bondage is not on them but inside them; and it is not a thing but a person—a spirit being. Any genuine deliverance must deal with this being, and must begin inside, or they remain in the grips of the power that enslaves them.

Sin's Indwelling

The apostle Paul was once in a deep quandary; he was held captive by things he hated but couldn't eliminate. The passage that follows resonates with his powerlessness against the mighty tyrant who indwelt and controlled him:

> For what I am doing, I do not understand; for I am not practicing what I *would* like to *do*, but **I am doing the very thing I hate.** But if I do the very thing I do not want *to do*, I agree with the Law,

confessing that the Law is good. ***So now, no longer am I the one doing it, but sin which dwells in me.*** For I know that nothing good dwells in me, that is, in my flesh; for the willing is present in me, but the doing of the good *is* not. For ***the good that I want, I do not do, but I practice the very evil that I do not want.*** But if I am doing the very thing I do not want, I am no longer the one doing it, but ***sin which dwells in me.***

I find then the principle that ***evil is present in me***, the one who wants to do good. For I joyfully concur with the law of God in the inner man, but I see a different law in the members of my body, waging war against the law of my mind and making me a prisoner of the law of sin which is in my members. Wretched man that I am! Who will set me free from the body of this death?" (Romans 7:15-24 NASB).

Paul realized that the matter of sin was not simply a question of what someone did; it was a problem of an indwelling master controlling his life, contrary to his deepest desires. Sin *indwelt* him, making him do the very things he hated—as it does everyone—until Jesus Christ drove out the tyrant and set Paul free.

The Indwelling is the reason many find it difficult to be free of things they hate. They struggle in vain against sin, thinking that religious observances, New Year resolutions, strict discipline, and ascetic practices will bring deliverance, all to no avail. This is why every religion has failed in its quest to eliminate sin: they do not have what it takes to dislodge sin from the hearts of those that embrace them. This is possible only through the finished work of Jesus Christ: in Christ, the old sinful nature is crucified and the risen Lord sits enthroned in the heart of the believer. *Indwelling sin is unseated by the indwelling Christ*—resulting in permanent freedom.

We read in 2 Corinthians 4:3-4, "If our gospel be hid, it is hid to them that are lost: ***In whom*** the god of this world hath blinded the minds of them which believe not, lest the light of the glorious gospel of Christ, who is the image of God, should shine unto them" (KJV). They are lost because of something the devil has done *inside* them.

Similarly, the children of light have God working *inside* them—indwelling them—to will and to do His good pleasure. He indwells them and does His saving work from within their hearts.

How can these things be? We invite you to keep reading. You will discover why it is possible, and how it works, and how this might be the light that spells liberty and victory to you, and to many others through you.

The Divine Indwelling

You see, God made man in His own image. And God is *indwelt* too (we will return to this in a moment). So man, made in His image, was also made to be *indwelt*—to be *in*-habited—like God who made man in His own likeness.

God is indwelt?

The Bible teaches so—repeatedly.

He is indwelt by His glorious attributes. His holiness, power, majesty, wisdom, and righteousness abound in Him in their infinitude.

He is indwelt by His eternal Son.

He is indwelt by His Word.

The Son is indwelt by the Father.

The Son is indwelt by the Spirit.

God is indwelt by His people: "**In Him** we live and move and have our being" (Acts 17:28). This is not just a statement in the Bible. It is sober truth.

Keep in mind that God is not a man. This is vital in terms of our understanding and maximizing the revelation of the Indwelling. Trying to understand the Indwelling from a physical perspective (as in, how can a person live inside another person?) is like Nicodemus trying to understand the new birth in physical terms. Jesus explained,

> "Very truly I tell you, no one can see the kingdom of God unless they are born again."
> "How can someone be born when they are old?" Nicodemus asked. "Surely they cannot enter a second time into their mother's womb to be born!"

Jesus answered, "Very truly I tell you, no one can enter the kingdom of God unless they are born of water and the Spirit. Flesh gives birth to flesh, but the Spirit gives birth to spirit" (John 3:3–6).

The Indwelling is a spiritual reality and must be understood and received as such by faith. God is not a man; He is a Spirit. As a Spirit, He can indwell and be indwelt.

The apostles had a similar dilemma when Jesus told them the Father dwelt in Him. How could the Father, a person, indwell Christ, another person? Philip said, "Lord, show us the Father and that will be enough for us" (John 14:8). Jesus answered:

> "Don't you know me, Philip, even after I have been among you such a long time? Anyone who has seen me has seen the Father. How can you say, 'Show us the Father'? Don't you believe that I am in the Father, and that the Father is in me? The words I say to you I do not speak on my own authority. Rather, it is the Father, ***living in me,*** who is doing his work. Believe me when I say that ***I am in the Father and the Father is in me***" (vv. 9–11).

The Indwelling must be understood from a spiritual standpoint. Spirits can indwell and be indwelt. As a spirit, man too can indwell and be indwelt. And the consequences of that indwelling—our subject in this book—are absolutely astounding.

Our indwelling by divinity is the secret to everything. Our Christian faith, experience and fruitful service are all predicated on it.

Eternal Life

The Indwelling *is* eternal life. Eternal life is not separate from the Person of Christ. It is not a gift that He gives apart from Himself—like someone giving a watch or a car. It is the gift of Himself into a life; the life that God gives us is resident in His Son: "And this is the testimony: that God has given us eternal life, and ***this life is in His Son***. Whoever has the Son has life; whoever does not have the Son of God does not have life" (1 John 5:11–12).

Eternal life is all about a Person living inside a person—when Jesus Christ, in whom was life, and who *is* life, enters into a hitherto dead sinner.

Jesus made the following opening statements in His high priestly prayer to the Father (John 17:1–3): "Father, the hour has come. Glorify your Son, that your Son also may glorify you. For you granted him authority over all the people that he might give eternal life to all those you have given him. Now this is eternal life: that they know you, the only true God, and Jesus Christ, whom you have sent."

Eternal life, then, is to know the indwelling of the Father and the Son. It is to come alive with the very life of God residing inside you. The life of the Father and the Son becomes our life. We become partakers of divine nature, sharing in God's own life.

"We know that the Son of God has come, and has given us understanding to know the One who is real. *Our lives are indissolubly bound to the One who is real, because they are indissolubly bound to his Son Jesus Christ.* This is the real God, and this is eternal life" (1 John 5:20 BARCLAYS).

Our lives are indissolubly, i.e., inseparably, bound to His life. The union is so inseparable that Scripture declares, "The one who is united and joined to the Lord is one spirit with Him" (1 Corinthians 6:17 AMP). We are in Him who is real and true, and He is in us. It is this indwelling—this inextricable, indivisible union of the life of God with us—that imparts eternal life. We will be ablaze with His life—for all eternity.

The Victory That Overcomes

The Indwelling is the secret of the victory that has overcome the world and makes us overcomers in every situation in life.

"For everyone born of God overcomes the world. This is the victory that has overcome the world, even our faith. Who is it that overcomes the world? Only the one who believes that Jesus is the Son of God" (1 John 5:4–5).

On the surface it seems as though it is our faith by itself—our ability to conjure up enough confidence in the battles of life—that makes it possible for us to walk in victory. Faith is the victory because it makes the main thing, the Indwelling, possible. That is the reason for the telling question in verse 5: "Who is it that overcomes the world?"

Believing that Jesus is the Son of God is the key. In the previous chapter of this letter, the apostle John reveals what this does to a person: "If anyone acknowledges that Jesus is the Son of God, ***God lives in them and they in God***" (1 John 4:15). Believing that Jesus is the Son of God makes the Indwelling possible. This indwelling—the residence of the Father and the Son inside the believer—then makes the triumphant life their normal heritage.

"As for you, out of God you are, little born-ones, and you have gained a complete victory over them and are still victors, because ***greater is He who is in you than he who is in the world.***" (1 John 4:4 WUEST)

We gain the victory and remain victorious because of Someone who lives in us. Since the One in us is greater than the one in the world, it is impossible for the world to overcome us. It is remarkable that this verse definitely states that there is also a personality in the world. The believer is indwelt by God and the Prince of Peace, while the world and those governed by it are indwelt by the prince of darkness. *It turns out that everyone on earth is controlled by a prince*—either the Prince of Peace or the prince of this world—and will enjoy the benefits or suffer the consequences of their indwelling.

Life is a function of the one who indwells you. It will determine your outcomes—in time and eternity.

The Secret of Fruitfulness

The Indwelling is the secret of fruitfulness. Our fruitfulness is totally dependent on Christ's presence and life flowing in us and through us. Fruitfulness is not a result of our frantic activities or strenuous exertion, but of His indwelling. We read Jesus' words in John 15:4-8,

"Remain in me, as I also remain in you. No branch can bear fruit by itself; it must remain in the vine. Neither can you bear fruit unless you remain in me.

I am the vine; you are the branches. If you remain in me and I in you, you will bear much fruit; apart from me you can do nothing. If you do not remain in me, you are like a branch that is thrown away and withers; such branches are picked up, thrown into the fire and burned. If you remain in me and my words remain in you, ask whatever you wish, and it will be done for you. This is to my Father's glory, that you bear much fruit, showing yourselves to be my disciples."

Jesus is the Vine; we are the branches. The same life that flows in the Vine pours into the branches. The Vine and the branches are not separate entities: they are one. Only by abiding in the Vine —remaining *in* Him—can a branch receive the necessary nourishment that makes fruitfulness possible. A branch once disconnected soon withers and becomes wood for the fire. We will discuss this truth in detail in Chapter 8 ("The Indwelling Christ").

The Secret of Evangelism

The Indwelling is the key to effective evangelism. We are called to be Christ's witnesses, but, in reality, it is the indwelling Christ who must testify to Himself, in the power of the Holy Spirit, through us. Our testimonies are bereft of life-changing and life-giving power. But the testimony of the indwelling Spirit carries the very life of God.

We see this in the life and ministry of Paul. He told the Galatian church that "God, who had chosen me and set me apart before I was born, and called me through His grace, was pleased **to reveal His Son in me so that I might preach Him** among the Gentiles [as the good news—the way of salvation]" (Galatians 1:15–16 AMP).

God called Paul from his mother's womb; He sovereignly ordained him to be an apostle to the Gentiles, to do great exploits for the gospel, and to write about half the books of the New Testament. All of these were in God's plan for Paul, but none of them could come to pass until something else had happened: God revealed, unveiled, and disclosed His Son *within* Paul! The preposition here is crucial: it was not a revelation of Jesus Christ *to* Paul that made him an effective witness in preaching Christ among the Gentiles. It was the revelation of Christ *in* Paul—the Indwelling—that was the springboard for the fulfillment of the great ministry of the renowned apostle. The Christ whom Paul met on the road to Damascus took up residence inside him—indwelt him—and worked in Paul both to will and to do His good pleasure.

Paul's speech and preaching "were not with wise and persuasive words, but with a demonstration of the Spirit's power" (1 Corinthians 2:4). It was the power of the indwelling Spirit that gave him great boldness, convicted his hearers of their sins, and enabled him to cast out devils and to perform other mighty miracles that confirmed the gospel he preached.

On the day of Pentecost, the apostles were *filled* with the Holy Spirit (Acts 2). This was the Indwelling at work: the Spirit who came on them in the upper room as tongues of fire took up residence inside them, and set their tongues on fire! Suddenly, timid Peter became a fiery witness—and three thousand souls were added to the Church in one day! And it was that indwelling Spirit who worked the works of wonder that confirmed the gospel they preached. His power backed up the Word, breaking hardened hearts and setting souls on fire.

Without the revelation of the Indwelling, our witness to the gospel would be weak and puny. We would lack a compelling sense and vision of the vital reality of what we are talking about. But a partaker of the Indwelling is not testifying to theories: he speaks of a Christ he knows, one who lives within him. And then that indwelling Christ who promised to "draw all people" unto Himself (see John 12:32) confirms His Word by the power of the indwelling Holy Spirit.

Now, as it pleased the Father to reveal His Son *within* Paul, it has also pleased Him to reveal Christ *in* you so that you might proclaim Him.

The Key to the Effective Prayer Life

The Indwelling holds the key to effective prayer. You see, prayer is much more than an activity. It is Spirit-driven communion with God. There is a spirit of prayer, and without the active participation of this spirit, our prayers are fruitless and pointless.

"And I will pour out on the house of David and the inhabitants of Jerusalem *a spirit of grace and supplication.* They will look on me, the one they have pierced, and they will mourn for him as one mourns for an only child, and grieve bitterly for him as one grieves for a firstborn son" (Zechariah 12:10).

From this prophetic statement, we see the result of the outpouring of the Spirit of grace and supplication on God's people: with the help of this Spirit, they will look on the One they have pierced and mourn for Him. Their hearts will cry out to God for the Savior and the salvation that the nation once rejected. And God will hear from heaven.

In the New Testament, we see that it is the indwelling Holy Spirit who enables believers to pray effectively: the Spirit of adoption (sonship) helps us to approach God as Father, something foundational in prayer: "The Spirit you received does not make you slaves, so that you live in fear again; rather, the Spirit you received brought about your adoption to sonship. *And by him we cry, 'Abba, Father'*" (Romans 8:15).

The indwelling Holy Spirit helps our infirmities and makes intercession for us:

> So too the [Holy] Spirit comes to our aid and bears us up in our weakness; for we do not know what prayer to offer nor how to offer it worthily as we ought, but *the Spirit Himself goes to meet our supplication and pleads in our behalf* with unspeakable yearnings and groanings too deep for utterance. And He Who searches the hearts of men knows what is in the mind of the [Holy] Spirit [what His intent is], because *the Spirit intercedes and pleads [before God] in behalf of the saints according to and in harmony with God's will* (Romans 8:26–27 AMPC).

Prayer would be a joy if it were no longer us struggling in our own strength to commune with the Father—if the resident Intercessor, the indwelling Holy Spirit Himself, were making intercession for us.

The Power Is in the Indwelling

The power you need for life and godliness lies in the Indwelling. This is discussed in detail in this book. The Holy Spirit, who empowers believers to be Christ's witnesses, indwells them. There is mighty power at work in us, by which God is able to do exceedingly abundantly above all we ask or think (see Ephesians 3:19-20).

What will put you over in life is not outside. It's going to operate from within you.

Guarantee of the Glory

The reality of the Indwelling is the guarantee of present and eternal glory for the child of God. "To them God has chosen to make known among the Gentiles the glorious riches of this mystery, which is ***Christ in you, the hope of glory***" (Colossians 1:27). God has also chosen to make the glorious riches of this mystery known to you. And that revelation will change your life forever.

Ultimately, when time gives way to eternity, the Indwelling is our "gate pass" into heaven. It is the only proof that we belong to Him. Christ in us is our hope of glory. When we arrive at those pearly gates, what will identify us as bona fide citizens of heaven will be the seal of the Spirit within us. It is by Him that we have been sealed for the day of final redemption:

"And do not grieve the Holy Spirit of God [but seek to please Him], ***by whom you were sealed and marked [branded as God's own] for the day of redemption*** [the final deliverance from the consequences of sin]. "Don't give God's Holy Spirit any reason to be upset with you. ***He has put his seal on you*** for the day you will be set free from the world of sin" (Ephesians 4:30 AMP; GW).

The Purpose of the Indwelling

Why would God do this? Why would the eternal, omnipotent Creator of heaven and earth take up residence within us and make our bodies His temples? Why would He put His own Spirit within us? This will become clearer during the course of this book, but the following are appropriate at this point:

He did it so we can have life. Only by the Indwelling could we come to share His life—to become partakers of His divine nature. The divine attributes, which are exclusively His, become operational in us. We experience increasing dimensions of His peace, wisdom, and power. His love is poured out into our hearts by the Holy Spirit whom He has given us (see Romans 5:5).

By virtue of the Indwelling, we partake of His holiness. We can live victoriously over sin because He lives within us. We no longer struggle against sin in our own strength; His indwelling Spirit energizes us in the path of righteousness.

He did this to guarantee our full redemption and freedom. Our deliverance is permanent because the One who set us free now lives within us. We are not cleansed by the blood of the Lamb and then left unoccupied. That would expose us to worse danger than we were in before He came to save us. As in the case of the outcast demon that went and brought seven demons more wicked than itself to live in the empty heart from which it was cast out, the devil that Christ defeated would fortify itself and inhabit our vacant hearts (see Luke 11:15–26). But the Indwelling makes that impossible. The Christ who saves us indwells us, thereby making our deliverance irreversible.

The Indwelling identifies us. It proves that we belong to Christ. It's His stamp of ownership within us. The indwelling of the Holy Spirit seals us for the day of redemption (see Romans 8:9; Ephesians 4:30).

The Indwelling guarantees our participation in the inheritance of the saints in the light. We become joint-heirs with Jesus Christ and fellow-heirs with the saints through the Indwelling.

The Father indwells us to show His supreme love for us. He so loved us that He gave Himself up for us and then made our hearts His home!

The Indwelling is God's way of providing an operational base on earth for living His life and continuing His work. This is why He purchased our bodies: so they could become His temples. We become mobile carriers of the Almighty, and from within us He reaches out to love the unlovable; to save, heal, feed, and minister in a host of other ways to a lost and hurting world. Just as He used the apostles, He takes up residence in us to continue all He began to do and teach through the Lord Jesus Christ (see Acts 1:1). The only way to continue the ministry of reconciliation through the Church is to have the same Spirit that lived in Christ indwell us.

And as has been mentioned above, the Indwelling will guarantee our final transformation—the redemption of our bodies—from mortality to immortality. Death will then be swallowed up in absolute victory.

Are these things true? Are they fact or fiction? Are they reality or speculation?

There is no other way to find out than to carefully examine the testimony of the Word of God, which cannot lie. I invite you to do that with me as we discover the amazing possibilities wrapped in a life with the Almighty living on the inside.

2

Inside and Outside

The internal powers the external.

This statement is one of the most fundamental facts of the current technological and digital revolution impacting the world. It begins with what is on the inside.

Intel Inside

In today's high-tech world, automobiles, computers, tablets, phones, airplanes, weaponry, and all other wonders of the digital age are all driven by something inside.

In the world of computing, one of the foremost companies leading the inside revolution is Intel Corporation. Intel was founded by Gordon Moore and Robert Noyce and is a huge player in the global microprocessor market.[3, 4] Along with other chipmakers like Samsung, Intel supplies the chips most computer and phone users never see, but that power their devices. Interestingly, Intel does not dabble into many other aspects of the computer business. The company focuses on the hidden chips inside.

The Intel logo is sublime in its simplicity, but perfect for what the company represents:

"Intel Inside and the Intel Inside logo are trademarks of Intel Corporation or its subsidiaries in the U.S. and/or other countries."

Genius Is on the Inside

The world has seen geniuses; they dot the horizon in every generation, and out of the depths of their persons they bring forth ideas and inventions that literally change the way we live. They leave their marks on the world, and long after they are gone earth bears the imprint of their sojourn.

A closer look shows that it all came from inside. Albert Einstein's equations came from inside. The works of great painters like Leonardo da Vinci, Vincent van Gogh, Paul Cezanne, Michelangelo, and a host of others came from inside. The music of great composers came from inside. Something external might have sparked their inspirations, but ultimately it was their innate and trained genius that brought forth their works.

Isaac Watts didn't look like a genius, but he was. Nothing about him looked attractive on the outside. He was rejected by several ladies to whom he proposed marriage. He ministered for only a few years as a pastor. As his health failed, he eventually moved in and lived with a kind family for 36 years—for the rest of his life, till his death at age 75. There Isaac Watts lived,

> the prisoner of ill-health and feebleness, but breathing forth, like a nightingale in the shade, those undying melodies, which will sing on while the world lasts. . . . His great desire was to be of help to the worshipper in drawing near to God. He tried to express the

breathings and aspirations of the Christian soul; its love, its fears, its hopes, its faith, its wonder, its sorrow, and its joy, and to lead it to sing the praises of God with understanding.[5]

Isaac Watts never married. But out of this life, which many would label a failure by worldly standards, came theological works, poems, and hundreds of hymns that have been sung around the world for nearly 270 years. And they will be sung until Christ returns. His works include "Oh God Our Help In Ages Past," "When I Survey the Wondrous Cross," and "Jesus shall Reign." He is credited with being the father of modern hymns.

The technological and digital revolution, of which the founders of Intel were frontrunners, came from inside. The innovation and design that have catapulted corporations like Microsoft, Apple, and Samsung to the forefront have come from *inside* visionary leaders and pioneers like Bill Gates and Steve Jobs, who were willing to go out on a limb to try out their ideas that preceded their times.

Wealth Is Inside

Wealth is inside, not primarily outside. Once upon a time, natural resources were the principal source of the wealth of individuals and nations. But even then, many of these resources were not on the surface but came from *inside*—they had to be mined from deep within the earth. This is still the case with gold, oil, precious stones, and minerals. And the people who tap such wealth have to develop strategies and equipment—from *inside,* through inventions and innovative ideas—to get them out, refine them, and make them profitable.

In his book *Change Your Thinking Change Your Life,* Brian Tracy quoted Claude M. Bristol, who made the following statement: "Thought is the original source of all wealth, all success, all material gain, all great discoveries and inventions, and of all achievement."

Tracy went on to say, "We have passed from a world based on material limitations into a world that is determined by mental concepts. We have moved from the age of *things* into the 'Psychozoic Age,' the age of the mind. Wealth and opportunities are contained more in the person you are and the way you think than in the assets you have acquired in life so far."[6]

The information and technological revolutions mentioned above have created far more wealth than have natural resources. That is why several companies in Silicon Valley are wealthier than whole nations. Trillion dollar companies like Apple or Amazon make far more money each year than many countries—e.g., Nigeria, with about 200 million people.[7, 8] The wealth of these companies does not come from material natural resources, like crude oil or minerals, but from immaterial resources of inventive, innovative genius from inside their people. It is not a mistake that the richest persons in the world today do not make their money primarily from natural resources but from their minds—from inside.

Some have distorted the truth of the power within into humanist cults and movements that leave God out of the equation. Through transcendental meditation and other practices, they seek to release the hidden forces of the human spirit. But the center of such lives cannot hold without God, for in Him all things hold together (see Colossians 1:17).

How the Outside Took Over in the Garden

Long before the computer and tech revolution, somewhere in the annals of eternity, God determined that He would do His work *from inside*. And when He made man, He made man in His image and likeness, not primarily physically but on the *inside*.

God made man to function from within. He was to exercise dominion over the earth from inside; his spirit was in direct fellowship with God, and out of this inner core he superintended God's earth—until sin came in through the back door and overturned the order.

The Fall in the garden was Satan's craftily concocted coup from the outside against the inside. In the garden, Satan overturned God's order for earth and instituted his perverted rule, which still controls the world order to this day—the tyranny of the outward over the inward, of the flesh over the spirit. There are stark indicators pointing to the imposition of the external on what Adam and Eve knew to be right in their hearts:

"When ***the woman saw*** that the fruit of the tree was good for food and ***pleasing to the eye,*** and *also **desirable*** for gaining wisdom, ***she took some and ate it***. She also gave some to her husband, who was with her, and he ate it. Then the eyes of both of them were opened, and they realized they were naked; so they sewed fig leaves together and made coverings for themselves" (Genesis 3:6-7).

The evil trilogy described by the apostle John in 1 John 2:15-17—the lust of the flesh, the lust of the eyes, and the pride of life, are manifest in this record of The Fall. And since then, humans continue to fall through the pursuit of the external—the pleasures of life, the deceitfulness of riches, and the glitzy glamor of the flesh, to the detriment of their souls.

Satan uses the external to hijack the internal—and collect the eternal. He uses what is outside to corrupt what is inside, and thereafter control the inside. He uses the visible to obscure the invisible. It's important to keep this principle in mind constantly. It will help us to guard our hearts with all diligence and continually resist the invasion of our inner life by the chaos and pressures raging outside.

Salvation restores the divine order—the rule of the inside over the outside. The saved individual speaks, lives, and functions *out of the abundance of the heart*. She keeps her heart with all diligence, knowing that the issues of life flow from there. She is concerned about the state of her heart before God, not simply about the outward beauty that ornaments, hair arrangements, and fine clothes can bestow.

Jesus and the Inside

Jesus' ministry concentrated on the inside. One doesn't have to look far to see this. He rebuked the religious elite for their hypocrisy:

"Woe to you, teachers of the law and Pharisees, you hypocrites! You clean the ***outside*** of the cup and dish, but ***inside*** they are full of greed and self-indulgence. Blind Pharisee! ***First clean*** *the inside* of the cup and dish, and then the outside also will be clean.

Woe to you, teachers of the law and Pharisees, you hypocrites! You are like whitewashed tombs, which look beautiful *on the outside* but on the *inside* are full of the bones of the dead and everything unclean. In the same way, on the *outside* you appear to people as righteous but on the *inside* you are full of hypocrisy and wickedness" (Matthew 23:25-28).

The interplay between *outside* and *inside* in this discourse is instructive of Jesus' focus. The Pharisees were like whitewashed tombs looking beautiful outside but full of rottenness inside. If they would first cleanse the inside, then the outside would be clean too.

We see Jesus' own modus operandi in this instruction. He practiced what He preached: to transform us, He first paid the steep price that made a new heart possible, thereby cleansing us within. Then He works from within to transform our external behavior. He began His saving work inside—from our hearts!

When religious leaders, who were possessed with a rabid zeal for externals, challenged Him about hand washing, He said, "Listen and understand: What goes into someone's mouth does not defile them, but what comes out of their mouth, that is what defiles them. . . . But the things that come out of a person's mouth come from the heart, and these defile them. For *out of the heart* come evil thoughts—murder, adultery, sexual immorality, theft, false testimony, slander" (Matthew 15:10-11, 18-19). Jesus was concerned about goings-on in the heart, the inner core from which everything else proceeds.

We will all be defined by what comes from inside us—what proceeds from the deepest chambers of our hearts. If we are defeated inside, we are defeated indeed. The great thing is that it is not only the evil mentioned in the preceding passage that can proceed out of the heart. What proceeds from inside is dependent on what we have stored inside. As we store truth, insight, knowledge, and wisdom within, they will also proceed out of our hearts to glorify God and bless many.

How the Kingdom Works

The kingdom of God, like the King of that kingdom, operates from inside.

"Some Pharisees asked Jesus when the Kingdom of God would come. His answer was, "The Kingdom of God does not come in such a way as to be seen. No one will say, 'Look, here it is!' or, 'There it is!'; **because the Kingdom of God is within you**. (Luke 17:20-21 GNT).

"He told them another parable. 'The kingdom of heaven is like leaven that a woman took and *hid* in three measures of flour, till it was all leavened'" (Matthew 13:33 ESV).

In these passages, we find that the kingdom of God works from within to produce external, observable results. If one looked at the dough, the yeast would be invisible; ultimately, however, its effect would be noticeable as it leavens the dough from within.

God Looks at the Heart

The Lord taught Samuel an unforgettable lesson at Jesse's house, where Samuel had gone on the Lord's instruction to anoint a king:

> When they arrived, Samuel saw Eliab and thought, "Surely the LORD's anointed stands here before the LORD."
> But the LORD said to Samuel, "Do not consider his appearance or his height, for I have rejected him. The LORD does not look at the things people look at. *People look at the outward appearance, but the LORD looks at the heart*" (1 Samuel 16:6-7).

He spoke through His prophet Jeremiah: "The heart is deceitful above all things and is extremely sick; who can understand it fully *and* know its secret motives? *I, the LORD, search and examine the mind, I test the heart*, to give to each man according to his ways, according to the results of his deeds" (Jeremiah 17:9-10 AMP).

If we will enjoy the amazing benefits of the Indwelling, we must attend to our hearts. Refuse to toe the line of this hypocritical, Pharisaic generation—"actors on the stage of life, playing the role of that which they are not" (Matthew 23:27-28 WUEST). Refuse to make your walk with God an external, theatrical performance to please people. Be real.

While it is true that the Lord looks at the heart and sees the deceitful and desperately wicked hearts of all, He has also made provision to give us another heart—one in which He can dwell.

"I'll pour pure water over you and scrub you clean. *I'll give you a new heart, put a new spirit in you.* I'll remove the stone heart from your body and replace it with a heart that's God-willed, not self-willed. *I'll put my Spirit in you* and make it possible for you to do what I tell you and live by my commands" (Ezekiel 36:25-27 MSG).

The process of this promised transformation is noteworthy: first is the cleansing; then the removal of the heart of stone and its replacement with a new heart of obedience. Then comes the Indwelling: He puts His Spirit inside us. Once His Spirit resides within, He *causes us*—makes it possible for us—to do what God says.

You might wish to pause at this moment and ask the Lord for a new heart. He gives freely to everyone without finding fault. Ask Him to wash away every sin, guilt, and condemnation and fulfill this glorious promise in your life.

Apostles, Patriarchs, and the Inside

Christ's apostles followed His example in prioritizing the inside over the outside. Not that they were legalists or ascetics who neglected their bodies, but they knew what mattered most. Old Testament men of God understood this principle too.

Peter: "Your beauty should not come from outward adornment, such as elaborate hairstyles and the wearing of gold jewelry or fine clothes. Rather, it should be that of *your inner self*, the unfading beauty of a gentle and quiet spirit, which is of great worth in God's sight" (1 Peter 3:3-4).

Paul: "Therefore we do not lose heart. Though **outwardly** we are wasting away, yet **inwardly** we are being renewed day by day" (2 Corinthians 4:16).

David: "Behold, You desire truth ***in the innermost being***, and ***in the hidden part [of my heart]*** You will make me know wisdom" (Psalm 51:6 AMP).

Solomon: "Watch over your heart with all diligence, for from *it* flow the springs of life" (Proverbs 4:23 AMP).

Inside is so vital; it is the place of the Indwelling—the place God planned to be His operational base in the lives of all those who would yield their lives to His saving work.

3

There's a Whole Lot Going On Inside You!

Human nature and the human heart are a mystery!
Psalm 64:6b God's Word

There is a whole lot going on *inside* you! There are internal organs, thoughts, ideas, plans, joy, peace, prayers, anxieties, secrets, strategies, etc., but there is yet a whole lot more going on inside. The whole medical field of psychology attempts to unearth the goings-on in the depths of our personalities to try to bring relief to the raging turmoil within.

In the relentless crush of external pressures, we often neglect to attend to what is going on inside us.

"Bless the LORD, O my soul, and ***all that is within me,*** bless his holy name! Bless the LORD, O my soul, and forget not all his benefits," (Psalm 103:1–2 ESV).

David acknowledges in this Scripture that there is plenty within him, and that his whole being must bless the Lord and keep His many benefits in view.

The human spirit was made in the image of God and has capacity that is way beyond our imagination. You see, from the outset man was designed as a dwelling place for God. The Indwelling is not an emergency arrangement. God knew from the eternal past that He would indwell humanity; He knew He would put His Spirit inside people, and therefore made provision for His Spirit to reside. So He made the man in His own image, and, like God, the heart of man is deep—very deep indeed. It is this God-designed space that people try to fill with all kinds of other things—but the hole remains in their hearts. They were designed to be filled by God and God alone.

The Man with a Legion Inside

To gain further understanding of the capacity of the heart, we note that more than 2,000 pigs could not contain, for one minute, what one man had carried for years. This unfortunate, demon-possessed man lived in the tombs—alone with the dead. No chains could bind him—he had broken every chain used to restrain him. I invite you to read the story of the deliverance of this demoniac by Jesus, which reveals a great mystery about the uncharted dimensions of the human spirit:

> When Jesus was still some distance away, the man saw him, ran to meet him, and bowed low before him. With a shriek, he screamed, "Why are you interfering with me, Jesus, Son of the Most High God? In the name of God, I beg you, don't torture me!" For Jesus had already said to the spirit, "Come out of the man, you evil spirit."
>
> Then Jesus demanded, "What is your name?"
>
> And he replied, *"My name is Legion, because there are many of us inside this man*." Then the evil spirits begged him again and again not to send them to some distant place.
>
> There happened to be a large herd of pigs feeding on the hillside nearby. "Send us into those pigs," the spirits begged. "Let us enter them."
>
> So Jesus gave them permission. *The evil spirits came out of the man and entered the pigs*, and the entire herd of about 2,000 pigs plunged down the steep hillside into the lake and drowned in the water.
>
> The herdsmen fled to the nearby town and the surrounding countryside, spreading the news as they ran. People rushed out

to see what had happened. A crowd soon gathered around Jesus, and they saw the man who had been possessed by the legion of demons. He was sitting there fully clothed and perfectly sane, and they were all afraid. Then those who had seen what happened told the others about the demon-possessed man and the pigs. And the crowd began pleading with Jesus to go away and leave them alone (Mark 5:6–17 NLT).

This encounter is very revealing. A whole legion of demons had entered and taken possession of one individual. They lived *inside* him; he was their home—one they had no intention of moving out of—until they were driven out by the Lord.

The *Jamieson-Fausset-Brown Commentary on the Whole Bible* provides the following insight on this verse of Scripture: "And he answered, saying, My name is Legion: for we are many—or, as in Luke (Lu 8:30) 'because many devils [demons] were entered into him.' *A legion, in the Roman army, amounted, at its full complement, to six thousand;* but here the word is used, as such words with us, and even this one, for *an indefinitely large number*—large enough however to rush, as soon as permission was given, into two thousand swine and destroy them."9

Whatever the exact figures, a whole battalion of *beings*—demons in this case—found a home in one man! No wonder no one could bind or restrain the demoniac: the combined force of thousands of demons inside him gave him superhuman strength to break any shackle! Behold both the wickedness of the devil and the capacity of the interior of man!

When Jesus eventually gave the demons leave to enter the pigs, the legion of demons *came out* of the man and *entered them:* they possessed the pigs as they had possessed the man from whom they had just been ejected. The pigs, lacking human capacity, could not contain for a second what a human being had carried for a long time. They rushed over the precipice into the lake and drowned.

Praise God for His mercies that have kept us from experiencing such a wicked oppression by the enemy. But this story provides insight into the depths of human personality.

They Shall Cast Out Demons

Just as Jesus cast the legion of demons out of the Gadarene demoniac, He has given authority to all believers to cast out demons. He told His disciples, "These miraculous signs will accompany those who believe: They will cast out demons in my name, and they will speak in new languages. They will be able to handle snakes with safety, and if they drink anything poisonous, it won't hurt them. They will be able to place their hands on the sick, and they will be healed." (Mark 16:17–18 NLT).

This authority to cast out demons must not be taken lightly. Incidentally, it is the first of all the signs the Lord said will follow the believing ones—an indication of how seriously Jesus took the activity of demons—yet some deny their existence today. To cast demons *out* of people means that the demons *indwelt* those from whom they are cast out. We see then that Jesus acknowledged the fact that demons live *inside* people; as the Deliverer, He delegated authority to His followers to set the captives free.

The casting out of demons was a prominent feature of Jesus' ministry. From studying such instances, we see that the demonic indwelling brought all kinds of bondage, diseases, and oppression to people. Indwelling demons made people mad, deaf and dumb, and paralyzed.

Mark 9:14–27 tells of an instance that occurred when Jesus came down from the Mount of Transfiguration with Peter, James, and John. Certain facts emerge from the narrative (quotes and paraphrases below are from the Amplified Bible translation):

- The demon entered the boy when he was a child (v. 21).
- "Whenever it seizes him [intending to do harm], it throws him down, and he foams [at the mouth], and grinds his teeth and becomes stiff" (v. 18).
- When the spirit saw Him (Jesus), at once it completely convulsed the boy, and he fell to the ground and kept rolling about, foaming [at the mouth] (v. 20).
- The demon spirit had often thrown him into fire and water, intending to kill him (v. 22).
- Jesus rebuked the unclean spirit, saying to it, "You deaf and mute

46

spirit, I command you, come out of him and never enter him again" (v. 25). This implies that the evil spirit *indwelt* the boy and would go out of him and return at will.

• After giving a [hoarse, clamoring, fear-stricken] shriek of anguish and convulsing him terribly, it came out (v. 26).

When the demon spirit came out of the boy, all the manifestations of its evil indwelling disappeared: the convulsions, foaming at the mouth, grinding of the teeth, falling into fire, etc., all ceased. The boy became perfectly healthy. It was a being living inside him that had made him convulsive and suicidal.

We see, then, that many (but not all) of the inexplicable diseases and suicides occurring today may be due to the activity of demons. Until God's power is manifested to set such captives free, and the greater One indwells the inner chambers of the heart, freedom will remain elusive.

The Empty, Clean House

"When the unclean spirit comes out of a person, it roams through waterless places in search [of a place] of rest; and not finding any, it says, *'I will go back to my house (person) from which I came.'* And when it comes, it finds the place swept and put in order. Then it goes and brings seven other spirits more evil than itself, and *they go in [the person] and live there*; and the last state of that person becomes worse than the first" (Luke 11:24–26 AMP).

This is remarkable: a demon looking for rest, refreshment, and ease! He had found it in a human being—by possessing the person—but now he was out in the cold. This tells a lot about demons and their desperate need for human vessels in which to rest and from which to operate. The demon even referred to his previous captive as his house: *"I will go back to my house (person) from which I came."*

How wicked Satan and his cohorts are. The very heart of man that was designed to be the house of God—the dwelling place of the Almighty—became the haunt of demons, with Satan and his minions sitting in the place that rightfully belonged to God. No wonder Jesus said to cast out devils; they occupy stolen thrones in the heart-houses of people.

In this case that Jesus spoke about, the numbers are smaller, but note that the demons are not necessarily smaller. The demon that was ejected was content to be subservient to other demons more wicked than itself—if that would have secured that individual to be under its influence—a lesson Christians can learn in reverse on the issue of submitting selfish interests to a larger kingdom objective.

Where there was once one demon, seven other spirits, more wicked than the original loner, have taken over. And don't miss this: all of this is going on *inside a person.*

Now behold the wisdom of God manifest in the Indwelling: Jesus Christ will not make the fatal mistake He warned against—the mistake of cleaning out a soul and leaving it empty. He will not drive out the devil from a life and wash the heart with His precious blood *without occupying that heart-house with His presence.* He would otherwise have left that life worse off than when He had met the possessed individual: the demon He cast out could have gone, gotten seven other demons more wicked than itself, and occupied the house that Christ had cleansed! Impossible!

So what does Jesus Christ do? First, He breaks the oppression of the devil over a life. Then He washes the heart-house thoroughly with His blood. Next comes the Indwelling: He fills this clean, precious heart-house *with the Father, Himself, and the Holy Spirit,* thereby accomplishing His original design for man. This indwelling of the triune God in the heart-house makes it impossible for it to revert back to the devil. When the demons that were cast out return to check out their former house, they find it occupied by the stronger man, the Almighty Lion of the Tribe of Judah. They know they have lost that territory—permanently.

A Satanic Triad of Evil

The truth of the Indwelling is clearly seen in an event that was revealed to the apostle John on the island of Patmos. Detailed eschatology is beyond the scope of this book, but some crucial insights on the operations of the Indwelling can be noted from this event. Following the outpouring of the sixth bowl of God's wrath on earth, John saw a strange and shocking display of the indwelling by a satanic trinity:

"Then I saw three impure spirits that looked like frogs; ***they came out of the mouth of the dragon, out of the mouth of the beast and out of the mouth of the false prophet***. They are demonic spirits that perform signs, and they go out to the kings of the whole world, to gather them for the battle on the great day of God Almighty" (Revelation 16:13-14).

John saw unclean spirits that looked like frogs—beings, personalities—"leap" and "crawl" (NLT, MSG) out of the mouths of the dragon, the beast, and the false prophet! In other words, these filthy spirits had *indwelt* Satan himself, the Antichrist, and the false prophet! These were demon spirits performing miraculous signs and wonders to deceive the world, and they lived *inside* Satan and his principal instruments. Their release was perfectly timed to accomplish an important satanic objective!

From the foregoing, we see that Satan himself is *indwelt* by his demons! He is capable of hosting lesser spirits in the depths of his twisted personality and of releasing them to actualize his agenda. If someone were to see the Antichrist or the false prophet, they would look thoroughly human—like anyone else on the streets. Scripture does not teach that these agents of Satan are marked by any special physical characteristics; they have supernatural powers, but they themselves look human. What an observer cannot see is the legions of demons *indwelling* them and giving them the power to do the lying wonders by which they delude the world. The unclean spirits that John saw were the ones that came out of their mouths. Who knows the myriads of evil spirits still lurking in the dark dungeons of the inner chambers of these cohorts of Satan?

The assignment of these evil spirits is remarkable: "They go out to the kings of the entire inhabited earth, to gather them together for the war of the great day of God, the Almighty" (Revelation 16:14b AMP). These evil spirits will be responsible for persuading world leaders to pursue a foolhardy course: to fight against God and His Christ! These demon spirits will convince and mobilize mortals to fight against the Immortal—to fight against God Almighty!

People often wonder why leaders and rulers make the reckless decisions they do—and why they could be so blinded to choose the courses that have plunged their families, corporations, nations, and the world into chaos and unbelievable bloodshed. How could Adolf Hitler have even contemplated the idea of world domination, and then have gone about to accomplish it in such an unprecedented and brutal orgy of mindless bloodletting? How could Osama bin Laden and the organization he founded, Al Qaeda, have done the horrific things they did (and still do)? How could celebrities and societal icons champion the legalization of abominable lifestyles? How could African leaders rape and pillage their countries and then gloat as they rule over their impoverished and malnourished nations? How can pot-bellied presidents preside with glee over people in penury?

It is our firm conviction that many such inexplicable and unwise choices and actions of rulers are the result of satanic manipulation through the activity of demons. They are led by spirits—just as believers in Christ are led by a very different Spirit! It's the Indwelling at work. Demons from the pit of hell indwell and influence rulers and persons in authority; they instill grandiose ideas and delusions of grandeur into their minds. They then make and execute choices that help advance the satanic agenda in their areas of influence.

This insight underscores why it is so important to pray for leaders, persons of influence, and everyone at all levels of authority. Fathers and mothers, presidents and prime ministers, CEOs, ministers of the gospel, university presidents, union leaders, music and movie stars, etc., are all targets of Satan and his demons. Satan schemes to influence the influencers—to infiltrate the minds and hearts of those whom multitudes follow. Without the fervent prayers of the saints, such persons are wide open to satanic manipulation and demonic control—with dire consequences for those over whom they superintend or exert influence.

Believers in Christ may look ordinary on the outside, but they are indwelt—a Spirit resides inside every child of God! And He is the greater One, our guarantee of glory and of victory over the world and the one who lives in it.

The Depths of the Heart

It is a poor commentary on our spirituality that we are fixated on the external. We know so little about the uncharted waters of the spiritual life—and the incredible depths to which they go.

David pleaded with God to preserve his life from fear of the enemy, and from the secret plots of the wicked. He said to God, "They devise injustices, saying, "We are ready with a well-conceived plot"; ***For the inward thought and the heart of a man are deep.***" (Psalm 64:6 NASB).

Let's read the second clause of this rather unfamiliar verse of Scripture from several translations and see what insights we can obtain:

- "For the inward thought and the heart of a man are deep (mysterious, unsearchable)" (AMP).
- "The human heart and mind are a mystery" (GNT).
- "Human nature and the human heart are a mystery!" (GW).

Man's heart is deep and unsearchable by other humans. Man is a deep mystery. It is no small thing to be made in the image of God and then have that image marred and commandeered by the prince of darkness. Only the redemptive work of Christ has capacity to recreate the heart of man to fulfill the original purpose of his creation: to be a dwelling place for God.

We find further light on the depths of the heart from David's inspired statement in Psalm 5:9: "For there is nothing trustworthy or reliable or truthful in what they say; ***their heart is destruction [just a treacherous chasm, a yawning gulf of lies].*** Their throat is an open grave; They [glibly] flatter with their [silken] tongue" (AMP). How deep the heart is—a chasm filled with destruction, a yawning gulf.

Do you begin to get the picture? Eugene Petersen in the Message paraphrase says that only the great Detective, God, can detect "the mystery in the dark of the cellar heart" (Psalm 64:6). The heart of man is like a dark, dank cellar, and it is capable of containing in its chambers far, far more than we can imagine.

The Heart of a Fallen Apostle

One begins to get an idea of what happened to Judas. His heart was deep. The Lord Jesus knew what He was talking about when He said to the apostles, "Have I not chosen you, the Twelve? **Yet one of you is a devil!**" (He meant Judas, the son of Simon Iscariot, who, though one of the Twelve, was later to betray him)" (John 6:70-71).

As treasurer, Judas kept the funds and was stealing from them, but the other disciples did not know this. He found a way to cover it all up. He was in the mix with the Master and the other apostles, but none of them knew what was going on in the dark cellars of his heart. Even though he had with him on a daily basis the Great Physician who pardoned the worst of sinners, he never brought up the mortal combat he was having with covetousness, seeking the Master's merciful intervention.

Judas was a member of two distinct fellowships. He could fellowship with the light and with darkness at the same time. He listened to Jesus' many teachings and probably shouted "Amen" at the right moments, but he also attended secret meetings with the Sanhedrin. He could eat with the Master *at the same time he was plotting to betray Him to death* for money! The heart is deep indeed.

The stage was now set for the final act that would push him beyond the precipice into perdition: the Last Supper. Here, Judas sat with Jesus and the other eleven apostles. He heard Jesus say one of them was going to betray Him. And even though he was now in the process of executing that betrayal and had already collected the money from his collaborators, he still had the heart to ask Jesus, "Master, is it I?" (Matt 26:25 KJV)

When eventually Jesus gave him a piece of bread He had dipped, Judas received it—from someone he was actively plotting to kill! "As soon as Judas took the bread, **Satan entered him**. So Jesus told him, 'What you are about to do, do quickly'" (John 13:27).

We run the risk of assuming that the Bible sometimes doesn't mean exactly what it says. Or maybe we have never really paid attention to the details of Scripture. Here we have an explicit statement of what happened to Judas. Satan, a person, entered into Judas, another person. This is an indwelling—of the satanic variety.

Satan had been manipulating and influencing Judas for a long time. It is possible that other lesser devils and elemental spirits were in charge of the operation up until this time. But this was the hour of darkness, and the prince of darkness didn't want to take any chances. He desperately wanted to seize his opportunity against the Son of Man, so he took total control of the vessel he had prepared for the assignment. Satan entered into and took possession of Judas. From this moment on, Judas's fate was sealed.

How deep was the heart of Judas that it had room enough for the devil? This mystery is great indeed.

Observe that as soon as Satan indwelt Judas, it was easy for Judas to do his bidding; he had taken control of him. The devil was no longer speaking to Judas from outside, whispering treachery into his itching ears. He was now at the center of his heart, from which the issues of his life flowed. The kiss of betrayal and Judas's subsequent suicide were the works of a person *inside* him. Of course, when Judas died, Satan didn't die with him; he moved out of the "house" that had served him so effectively to seek other "houses" from which to operate.

This is the satanic perversion of a divine strategy. The indwelling of the Holy Spirit is the key to the life that pleases God, for it will no longer be the individual striving in his own strength to please God, but God Himself working from within to glorify Himself. Realizing that God had ordained to put His Spirit inside man, thereby making it possible for man to do His will, Satan is exploiting the same strategy of possessing people on the inside to accomplish his evil agenda! He is the prince of the power of the air, but he doesn't do his pernicious work from the air: he operates from *inside* people. He is the spirit that now works *inside* the children of disobedience (see Ephesians 2:2).

From the foregoing, we see why we must never trust our hearts. We must continually ask the Lord to shine the light of His Word and search us by His Spirit, to ensure that there is nothing contrary to His nature lurking anywhere in us. "He who trusts in his own heart is a fool, but whoever walks wisely will be delivered" (Proverbs 28:26).

Don't ever assume that you know anybody. You really don't. We don't even know ourselves well enough. This is why David again prayed to God, "Search me [thoroughly], O God, and know my heart; test me and know my anxious thoughts; and see if there is any wicked *or* hurtful way in me. And lead me in the way everlasting" (Psalm 139:23–24 AMP).

As surely as Satan *entered* into Judas, if you are a child of God, Jesus Christ has *entered* into you. If Satan can enter a person, then Jesus can too. You see, at the same table of the Lord's Supper where Satan entered into Judas, Jesus entered the other apostles. At that covenant table, they partook of His body and blood; they put their faith in Him, opened their hearts in love, and became one with Him. Likewise, at salvation, we received the holy sop from heaven—the bread of life (God's Word) "dipped" in the atoning blood of the Lamb. We *received* Him, and when we did, Jesus entered into us and His Spirit took possession of us. Christ is in you—not figuratively or metaphorically but in reality—and He is your hope of glory.

If one were to have seen Judas after Satan entered into him, he would still have looked quite ordinary. There would have been no horns or hooves sticking out of his body! One could have passed by him and not have noticed anything—never have had an inkling of what or whom Judas carried inside him. Meanwhile, Satan would have been sitting inside Judas, looking out through the windows of his soul as he plotted his doomed moves against the Son of Man. Anyone passing Judas would not have known they had just passed Satan incarnate!

Similarly, and yet conversely, we look ordinary outside, but we carry treasure in our earthen vessels. As you will discover in *The Indwelling*, a believer is far from ordinary: he is indwelt by the triune God. The challenge is that, just as Judas didn't know the one who indwelt him, most believers have never realized that the greater One lives within them; they have never given thought or attention to the mighty One who indwells them.

The Heart as a Storehouse

The heart is a storehouse—a place where diverse things can be stored. This further indicates that the human heart has capacity to contain *beings* or *things*—or both.

Consider Luke 6:45: "A good man brings good things out of **the**

good stored up in his heart, and an evil man brings evil things out of **the evil stored up in his heart**. For the mouth speaks what the heart is full of."

Observe, then, that good or evil can be *stored up* in the heart. There is no indication of the quantities that can be stored up inside the heart, implying that an astounding amount of good, such as the Word of God, truth, light, wisdom, understanding, knowledge, etc., can be stored up *inside a person*. It is out of this store that the individual operates. What is stored up in the heart overflows into the life of the person. Take note that you cannot call forth more than you have stored in your inner treasury.

The New Living Translation speaks about *a treasury* within the heart: "A good person produces good things from **the treasury of a good heart**, and an evil person produces evil things from **the treasury of an evil heart**. What you say flows from what is in your heart" (Luke 6:45).

Thus both the good heart and the evil heart are *treasuries*. A treasury is a place where money or other things of value are stored. And you bring what you treasure out of your treasury to meet the need of each hour.

Marvel no more at why the devil is so desperate to have evil stored up in the hearts of people. He uses every means possible: the media, the internet, culture, celebrities, politicians—whatever and whoever is available—to saturate even the atmosphere with evil. He is streaming trash over the internet, and then he has people *downloading* it into their spirits. He knows that once he has created a treasury of evil—of pride, greed, lust, covetousness, anger, and bitterness *inside* the heart—he can call forth evil therefrom. This is how iniquity abounds on the earth in these end times: it abounds in society because it abounds in the heart.

You can also understand why God commands us to deliberately store up the most valuable things in life in our hearts.

He counsels us to store up His Word in our hearts: "My son, keep my words and store up my commands within you" (Proverbs 7:1).

"Let the message of Christ dwell among you richly as you teach and admonish one another with all wisdom through psalms, hymns, and songs from the Spirit, singing to God with gratitude in your hearts" (Colossians 3:16).

Since a treasury is never accidental, those who do not deliberately develop *a treasury* of good in their hearts have nothing to bring forth. Such hearts will grow weeds and will eventually be overtaken by evil. And they proceed to fill the great depths of the heart of man.

The Lord Searches the Heart

We see that it is only the Lord Himself who has the ability to search out the heart of man—to fathom the depths of the heart. He alone can see into the dark cellars of the heart—chambers of the inner life that are capable of hiding the darkest evils from the cleverest eyes—and flood them with His light.

"I, the LORD, search and examine the mind, I test the heart, to give to each man according to his ways, according to the results of his deeds" (Jeremiah 17:10 AMP). Notice from this Scripture that God searches the hearts and minds of people to reward them according to their ways and their doings. He looks beyond doings and actions to the depths of the heart from which they have emanated.

The nature and mystery of the heart and the inward parts of humans together constitute a major reason we must never presume to question God's justice and some of the things He allows that confound our limited understanding. He knows what we don't know. He sees what we can't see. His wisdom and absolute righteousness guarantee that He will always do what is right and fair. We must trust Him—even as He deals with our own hearts and lives.

Made for God

The amazing depths of the heart were made for God. As there can be no vacuum in nature, these depths must be filled with something or someone. They will either be filled with the Word, God's Spirit and presence, or by something else—and less.

Indeed, the Indwelling is the greatest manifestation of the love of God. God so loved the world that He gave His only begotten Son for our salvation—so that whoever believes in Him will not perish but have eternal life (see John 3:16). But, as we will see, Jesus does not save a person from outside: He saves from inside the heart. Thus, the finished work of Jesus on the Cross made the Indwelling possible. His saving work is only complete in a life when He, the Father, and the Holy Spirit are enthroned in the heart.

Our hearts were custom made for the Indwelling. In the sections that follow, we will discover that the Indwelling has been the divine objective with humanity. From God being *for* us, He came to be *with* us, so that He could be *in* us. His purpose was so that He could do exceedingly abundantly above all we ask or think—according to His power that works *in* us. What love!

4

The Three Dimensions of God's Presence

"My Presence will go with you, and I will give you rest."

Exodus 33:14

The presence of God is a subject that has drawn the attention of students of experiential Christianity who desire to know God indeed, not just in theory.

God is omnipresent; He is everywhere. But besides omnipresence, the Bible gives many indications of other aspects of His presence. While God is everywhere, we read repeatedly that God was in certain places, or that He was with certain persons. The Bible even speaks of God *coming* and *going* from certain places (Psalm 68:7–8; Isaiah 64:1–3; Habakkuk 3:3). How could God be "coming" or "going" from one place to another when He is already everywhere by virtue of His omnipresence? This is indicative of the fact that there are different dimensions of God's presence. As we will see, Moses specifically requested God's presence with him and the Israelites as they journeyed to the Promised Land. Many have referred to this as His manifest presence. Moses was not asking for omnipresence, but for the clearly discernible presence of God, to be with His people.

Apart from being in the direct presence of God—i.e., right before His throne in heaven—the Bible indicates at least three other dimensions of God's presence. The Lord Jesus Christ walked in all three dimensions, and they are the believer's inheritance as well. God never intended for His children to relate with Him on the basis of His omnipresence. He desires that we enjoy His manifest presence.

AN AMAZING PROGRESSION

A study of the believer's heritage and relationship with God shows an amazing progression of the divine presence. They indicate increasing levels of His presence and of the believer's intimacy with Him.

God *for* Us

The Bible speaks about God being *for* us.

David declared, "Then my enemies will turn back when I call for help. By this I will know that God is for me" (Psalm 56:9).

And Paul concurred by the Holy Spirit, "If God is for us, who can be against us?" (Romans 8:31).

This would be enough if it were all we had going for us.

God *with* Us

But the Word provides further revelation of what belongs to us because we belong to Him: God is *with* us!

"The LORD Almighty is with us; the God of Jacob is our fortress" (Psalm 46:7).

You see, God can be for us from afar. He could champion our matters and undertake to provide solutions to the issues of our lives, but do so from a distance. But He does much more than that for us. He is *with* us. This connotes presence, not mere provision or action on our behalf. His being *with* us is far more precious than His being *for* us.

Moses understood the power of His presence. As he interceded to reverse God's displeasure over an idolatrous nation, Moses pleaded with God,

"You have been telling me, 'Lead these people,' but you have not let me know whom you will send me with. You have said, 'I know you by name and you have found favor with me.' If you are pleased with me, teach me your ways so I may know you and continue to find favor with you. Remember that this nation is your people."

The LORD replied, "My Presence will go with you, and I will give you rest."

Then Moses said to him, "If your Presence does not go with us, do not send us from here. How will anyone know that you are pleased with me and with your people unless you go with us? *What else will distinguish me and your people from all the other people on the face of the earth?*"

And the LORD said to Moses, "I will do the very thing you have asked, because I am pleased with you and know you by name" (Exodus 33:12–17).

When God refused to travel further with Israel and proposed to send an angel who would still bring them into the Promised Land, Moses would not have it. He wanted the divine presence. Moses knew that God's presence with a person or a nation is the distinguishing factor. That presence would set such a person or people apart as unique and unassailable. Who or what could successfully challenge people who didn't just have God *for* them but had God *with* them?

Indeed, God's presence distinguished Israel from every other nation. All through their journeys in the wilderness, the pillars of cloud and of fire, signs of God's manifest presence, never departed from them.

"By day the LORD went ahead of them in a pillar of cloud to guide them on their way and by night in a pillar of fire to give them light, so that they could travel by day or night. Neither the pillar of cloud by day nor the pillar of fire by night left its place in front of the people" (Exodus 13:21–22). God's presence enables us to go "by day and night"—to make progress towards our destiny and His purpose for us, no matter what.

He was present and divided the Red Sea for them. He personally supervised their crossing the sea—on dry land. As the armies of Pharaoh pursued them into the midst of the sea (without permission, on a highway built by another!),

> The LORD looked down from the pillar of fire and cloud at the Egyptian army and threw it into confusion. He jammed the wheels of their chariots so that they had difficulty driving. And the Egyptians said, "Let's get away from the Israelites! The LORD is fighting for them against Egypt."
>
> Then the LORD said to Moses, "Stretch out your hand over the sea so that the waters may flow back over the Egyptians and their chariots and horsemen." Moses stretched out his hand over the sea, and at daybreak the sea went back to its place. The Egyptians were fleeing toward it, and the LORD swept them into the sea. The water flowed back and covered the chariots and horsemen—the entire army of Pharaoh that had followed the Israelites into the sea. Not one of them survived (Exodus 14:24-28).

Observe that God was not fighting this battle for Israel from afar. He was present. He was *with* them.

He was with them as they traversed the wilderness, and He did astonishing miracles for them: water from the rock, manna from heaven for 40 years, healings through the serpent on the pole, etc.

Eventually, when they arrived in the Promised Land, God was with them as they settled in. He was with them in the temple services: His tabernacle was there among them. He was with them on the battlefield at the many battles they fought with their perennial enemies, the Philistines, and other hostile nations. He was with them in their crises—something the heathen nations acknowledged as true—though heretofore unheard of.

God was with Israel to frustrate the boasts of the descendants of Uncle Esau—the inhabitants of Mount Seir, who harbored a perpetual hatred against them. Ezekiel 35:10 records their plan to annihilate Israel and annex their territory; however, the last part of the verse is very instructive: "Because you have said, 'These two nations and countries will be ours and we will take possession of them,' ***even though I knew the LORD was there . . .***" The people of Mount Seir wanted to dispossess a people (Israel and Judah) who enjoyed Yahweh's presence—an absolute impossibility. Satan still purports to do the same to the people of the Indwelling—to terrorize and harass God's dear children—*whereas the Lord Himself resides in their hearts!* But he will perpetually be disappointed; his everlasting confusion shall never be forgotten.

Apart from Israel's experience, Scripture tells of the amazing impact of God's presence with several individuals.

He was with Joseph and made all he did to prosper—pre-prison, in prison, and post-prison! God's presence with him was manifest—something Potiphar, the keeper of the prison, and Pharaoh himself all testified to (see Genesis 39:3, 23).

The Lord was with David. This was the secret of his victories in mortal combat with vicious enemies.

The Lord was with Hezekiah and other godly kings of Israel. His presence was manifest in the blessings He poured on His people during their reign.

But He had something infinitely bigger in mind for the beneficiaries of the finished work of Christ.

The Ultimate: God *in* Us

Despite all the unquantifiable benefits of God being for and with people, God was not yet done. He planned something greater for us. Beyond being *for* us and being *with* us, He had an ultimate aim in view: to be *in* us, and we *in* Him.

How was God going to execute this awesome purpose? How could desperately wicked human hearts be prepared to become the dwelling place of a holy God? Man had to be prepared for the Indwelling.

Enter Emmanuel—God *with* us. *God for us sent God with us (Emmanuel, the Incarnate Son, Jesus Christ) to make our hearts ready so that God could be in us.* Jesus lived, suffered, died and was raised from the dead to make the Indwelling possible. The Cross was not an end in itself, but a means to an end: God used it to deal with the old sinful nature, to make possible new hearts in which He could dwell. Now, because of Christ's finished work that gave birth to the new creation, all three dimensions of the divine presence belong to us. They are our heritage in Christ. The most holy God can now make His home in human hearts and use them as His holy headquarters on earth to advance His kingdom.

The believer in Christ has God *for* him or her. God is for you; He is not against you, and He is not neutral towards you. He is not for you just occasionally, or depending on the circumstances; He is for you perpetually. He will be for you for all eternity. Because of what Jesus did for you and your faith in Jesus, God is not counting your sins against you, or standing aloof watching to see when you slip or sin so that He can descend on you with judgment. Discard that idea of God. Indeed, if it were not for the Lord who has been on your side, you would not be here now. The enemy who is against you would have destroyed you. But the God who is on your side said *No*. Meditate on this until it comes alive in your spirit. The eternal, omnipotent Creator of heaven and earth is *for* you. And if God be for us, who can be against us?

So, what do you think? With God on our side like this, how can we lose? If God didn't hesitate to put everything on the line ***for us***, embracing our condition and exposing himself to the worst by sending his own Son, is there anything else he wouldn't gladly and freely do ***for us***? And who would dare tangle with God by messing with one of God's chosen? Who would dare even to point a finger? The One who died ***for us***—who was raised to life ***for us***!—is in the presence of God at this very moment sticking up ***for us***. Do you think anyone is going to be able to drive a wedge between us and Christ's love ***for us***? There is no way! Not trouble, not hard times, not hatred, not hunger, not homelessness, not bullying threats, not backstabbing . . .

They kill us in cold blood because they hate you.

We're sitting ducks; they pick us off one by one.

None of this fazes us because Jesus loves us. I'm absolutely convinced that nothing—nothing living or dead, angelic or demonic, today or tomorrow, high or low, thinkable or unthinkable—absolutely nothing can get between us and God's love because of the way that Jesus our Master has embraced us (Romans 8:31–39 MSG).

Notice all the repetitions of "for us" in this amazing passage. Because God is for us, no matter the situation, we are more than conquerors through Him who has loved us—the One who fought the titanic battle that freed us forever from Satan's dominion.

But it gets better. This almighty God who is on our side is also by our side! He is *with* us! We are guaranteed His presence 24/7, every second in time and for all eternity.

I invite you to carefully read the following words from Scripture. They speak of God's eternal and irrevocable commitment never to leave or forsake you. The words you are about to read are not exaggerated. They are nothing but the truth and are spoken by a God who cannot lie, One whose Word can never fail or pass away. I encourage you to check them out for yourself from your own Bible and from as many translations as you can find, and you will find that they are accurate. As you read, keep in mind that Scripture cannot be broken.

Here it is:

> Let your character [your moral essence, your inner nature] be free from the love of money [shun greed—be financially ethical], being content with what you have; for **He has said, "I will never [under any circumstances] desert you [nor give you up nor leave you without support, nor will I in any degree leave you helpless], nor will I forsake or let you down or relax My hold on you [assuredly not]!** So we take comfort and are encouraged and confidently say,
> "The LORD is my helper [in time of need], I will not be afraid. What will man do to me?" (Hebrews 13:5-6 AMP).

God is with us. Emmanuel is still Emmanuel—God *with* us, and He will be so for all time and eternity. As He triumphantly returned to heaven following His masterful execution of our redemption, He promised us His presence: "Lo, I am with you always [remaining with you perpetually—regardless of circumstance, and on every occasion], even to the end of the age" (Matthew 28:20 AMP).

But it gets even better. True to His gracious character, God has done exceedingly abundantly above all we could ever ask or imagine—infinitely beyond our highest prayers, hopes, and dreams (see Ephesians 3:20 AMP). He surpasses our wildest imaginations with the next thing He does for the new creation.

He now dwells *in* us. He has taken up residence *inside* us. This is what we call the Indwelling. In the Old Covenant, God inhabited the praises of His people (Psalm 22:3). Under the New Covenant however, He does much more—He inhabits His people. He is on our side, by our side, and inside us.

The Indwelling is the highest level of the divine presence: God cannot be more with you than He is in you. His being with you is guaranteed if He is in you. Your heart will always be *with* you, because it is *in* you! Now He lives in your heart.

The same God whose presence Moses craved—the One who said "My presence will go with you, and I will give you rest" (Exodus 33:14)— that same Yahweh whose presence distinguished Israel now resides in you! He is the Lord who does not change. He indwells us. And His indwelling distinguishes us!

The cycle is now complete: He made us, He is for us, He redeemed us, and He is with us. Now He is in us.

These are not unfounded claims; they are the solid and irrevocable declarations of Scripture.

I believe that this is the greatest wonder of redemption. It is heaven itself to our souls—the King of heaven taking up residence in our hearts. Wonder of wonders!

Integrated into the revelation of the Indwelling is the fact that not only does God now indwell us but we also indwell Him. *In Him* we live and move and have our being (see Acts 17:28).

The Manifest Presence of God

An Important Question

For those who are genuinely hungry for God and desire experiential Christianity, the preceding discussion of the dimensions of God's presence throws up some important questions—similar to the ones Gideon asked when the angel of the Lord appeared to him.

Due to Israel's rebellion, the Lord gave the nation into the hands of the Midianites, one of their worst enemies. These oppressors ravaged and impoverished Israel over a seven-year period. When the burdened and broken nation cried to the Lord, He sent a prophet to bring her to repentance, and then an angel to announce deliverance. God was going to use Gideon to rout the Midianite hordes and set Israel free.

> When the angel of the LORD appeared to Gideon, he said, "The LORD is with you, mighty warrior."
>
> "Pardon me, my lord," Gideon replied, "but *if the LORD is with us, why has all this happened to us? Where are all his wonders that our ancestors told us about* when they said, 'Did not the LORD bring us up out of Egypt?' But now the LORD has abandoned us and given us into the hand of Midian" (Judges 6:12–13).

Here was Gideon threshing "wheat in the winepress to keep it from the Midianites" (v. 11), and the angel came along telling him the Lord was with him and calling him a mighty man of valor! Some shallow soul would have been overawed by the angel's words and possibly hurried to the registrar of companies to incorporate Mighty Man of Valor Ministries International, but not Gideon. Reality check: If indeed the Lord is with us, *why. . .* and *where . . . ?* Why has all this happened to us? Why are we like this? Is this what the people of His presence should look like? And where are all His miracles and wonders that we have heard and read about? Where are His footprints and fingerprints on our lives, families, affairs, and nation?

These were questions of manifest presence. Gideon was in effect not satisfied with a theoretical presence that didn't have concrete manifestations. He was after the tangible results of the divine presence. Through a series of miraculous interventions, the Lord did use Gideon to bring deliverance to a troubled nation. Gideon's focus on tangible reality is a lesson for all genuine seekers, especially leaders. God cannot use us significantly if we are satisfied with empty platitudes, even as modern "Midianites" manifest their oppressive might, unhindered. We must touch reality.

Experiencing the Manifest Presence

As mentioned at the beginning of this chapter, God never intended that His people relate with Him on the basis of omnipresence. In both the new and old covenants, His manifest presence was designed to be the distinguishing factor that demarcated His people from the world.

So how do we experience the manifest presence of God? How can we enjoy concrete and ceaseless manifestations of the divine presence? The answer to these questions will continue to unfold as you read *The Indwelling*, especially chapter 18, "Embracing the Indwelling." In reality, the manifest presence is actually the tangible revelation, with definite manifestations, of the three dimensions of the divine presence discussed in this chapter. It is what God does for people He is for, with, and/or within. It is revealed in all the supernatural works and gifts of the Holy Spirit and the signs and wonders that happen when God is present. It could be the presence of the *Shekinah* glory of God—the visible, shining cloud that showed up in both the Old and New Testaments and in revivals like the Pentecostal outpouring on Azusa Street. Or it could be the still, small voice of the Holy Spirit speaking deep in the hearts of believers to guide them in the will and purposes of God.

We will see more manifestations of God's presence when we wholeheartedly embrace the dimensions of His presence for us, with us, and in us, and then dredge the channels for the river of His Spirit to flow freely by removing everything contrary to His character. As we walk in faith and obedience, the One who is for us, with us, and within us reveals Himself by undeniable works of wonder.

We will be discovering the infinite possibilities of the Indwelling as we journey through this book. This is not a mere academic exercise in barren philosophy or wishful thinking, but the unveiling of solid truth that must be experienced—in ever-increasing measure.

5

Temples of the Living God

"Do you not know that you are the temple of God and that the Spirit of God dwells in you?"

1 Corinthians 3:16 NKJV

The Taj Mahal in Agra, Uttar Pradesh, India, and Table Mountain in Cape Town, South Africa, are among the most unforgettable places I have visited. The unbelievable wealth and intricate detail of the Taj Mahal, a mausoleum built by the Mughal emperor Shah Jahan for his favorite wife on the south bank of the Yamuna River, indeed qualify it to be one of the original Seven Wonders of the World. The natural marvel of Table Mountain, an imposing flat-topped mountain overlooking the city of Cape Town, is also something to behold.

However, temples have been among the most intriguing monuments I've seen in my ministry-related travel. From the Mahabodhi Temple Complex (the most revered of all Buddhist sacred sites) in Bodh Gaya in the northeastern Indian state of Bihar to the temple of Hanuman, the monkey god, in New Delhi to the massive Hare Krishna temple in Durban, South Africa, I have often wondered at the colossal edifices humans have created in their worship of diverse deities.

Temples are replete in religion: they are the sacred places of worship designed to contain or house the deity with whom the worshippers come to connect. Judaism, Hinduism, Islam, African traditional religions, and a multitude of other religions all have their temples and shrines.

Tents and Temples

We see diverse temples in Scripture—the temples of the various gods and idols of the heathen, as well as the temples built by King Solomon and others after him to the Lord God Almighty.

Prior to the temple King Solomon built, the equivalent of the temple for the Israelites had been the tabernacle in the wilderness, which Moses built. It was strictly built according to a heavenly pattern that God revealed to Moses. That tabernacle (or tent of meeting, as it was also called) had three major sections: the outer court, the holy place, and the holy of holies (often translated, as in the NIV, "Most Holy Place")—the innermost sanctuary of the sacred tent. It was at this tabernacle that Moses often met with God. The Israelites carried it in their journeys through the wilderness until they arrived in the Promised Land.

King David had it in mind to build a proper temple (instead of a tent) for the Lord, but the Lord told him it would be his son, Solomon, who would build the temple. The temple that Solomon eventually built was a masterpiece, the like of which had never been built in human history. It took him seven years and the equivalent of billions, in today's currency, in gold and other precious materials to complete.

At the dedication of the temple, Solomon poured out his heart in prayer. The full prayer is found in 1 Kings 8 and 2 Chronicles 6 and remains a model to date for the dedication of sacred buildings.

Solomon's prayer is filled with revelations about the personality and character of God. Even as he dedicated the temple, he wondered, "But will God indeed dwell on the earth? Behold, heaven and the heaven of heavens cannot contain You. How much less this temple which I have built!" "Can it be that God will actually move into our neighborhood? Why, the cosmos itself isn't large enough to give you breathing room, let alone this Temple I've built" (1 Kings 8:27 NKJV; MSG).

The idea of the God of the universe dwelling *on earth* with humans—moving into the neighborhood—was too huge for Solomon to understand. Since the heavens cannot contain God, then how much less could a house on a tiny planet in one corner of the universe do so! The best King Solomon could ask was that the temple honor God's name, that His eyes would watch over it, and that His ears would be open to the prayers offered there.

In his prayer Solomon kept referring to heaven as "God's dwelling place" (1 Kings 8:30, 39, 43, 49). He asked that when people prayed at the temple (or towards it if they were not physically there), God would hear in heaven, His dwelling place, and answer.

After Solomon dedicated the temple, "the LORD said to him: 'I have heard the prayer and plea you have made before me; I have consecrated this temple, which you have built, by putting my Name there forever. My eyes and my heart will always be there'" (1 Kings 9:3). However, the Lord warned that there would be dire consequences if the nation abandoned Him to serve other gods. Then He would turn His eyes away from the temple, and it would become a byword. This did happen—to the extent that the temple was totally destroyed by the Babylonians and all its treasures carried into captivity.

As we will see in this chapter, the believer's case is different. God did not just put His name inside us: He indwells us! The God of the universe now lives in human temples! The same God who cannot be contained by the heavens now dwells within us and desires that we be filled with all the fullness of Himself (Ephesians 3:19). This is the miracle of the Indwelling.

Paul at Athens

Paul's spirit was deeply grieved and roused to anger when he saw the city of Athens full of idols. The city was a junkyard of idols! They even had an altar with the inscription "to the God nobody knows" (Acts 17:22–23 MSG).

As he stood with a burdened and burning heart on Mars Hill, Paul told his listeners, "The God who made the world and everything in it, this Master of sky and land, ***doesn't live in custom-made shrines*** or need the human race to run errands for him, as if he couldn't take care of them himself. He makes the creatures; the creatures don't make him" (Acts 17:24-25 MSG). He proceeded to introduce them to the One they were worshipping ignorantly—to the one true God.

It is the gods of the heathen that are enshrined in their temples—a clear indication of their limitations! They are not omnipresent; their worshippers must come to their temples to seek or encounter them.

But how different Yahweh is! "In Him we live and move and have our being" (Acts 17:28). He lives in living temples—in the hearts of His redeemed sons and daughters. And the redeemed in turn live and move in Him. He indwells them and they indwell Him.

This is a great mystery, but it describes the heritage of believers. They are in Christ and Christ is in them. They are in the Father and the Father is in them. The Spirit is in them and they walk in the Spirit. Divinity resides in them, and they are resident in divinity. They have entered into a glorious oneness with the Eternal—for all time and eternity.

Temples of the Living God

Christians are repeatedly described as temples of the living God. The language is clear and compelling.

- They are reminded that they are the temple of God—with the Holy Spirit residing in them:

Do you not know that **you are God's temple and that God's Spirit dwells in you**? (1 Corinthians 3:16 ESV)

This fact is something they are supposed to know; hence the charge begins with "Do you not know . . . ?"

- They are expressly told that *their bodies* are the temples of God, housing the Holy Spirit who dwells in their recreated spirits. For this reason, they must flee sexual immorality, which defiles the body:

"Do you not know that *your body is the temple (the very sanctuary) of the Holy Spirit Who lives within you,* Whom you have received [as a Gift] from God? You are not your own, you were bought with a price [purchased with a preciousness and paid for, made His own]. So then, honor God and bring glory to Him in your body" (1Cor.6:19-20 AMPC)

- They are commanded to live consecrated and clean lives, befitting the temple of the Almighty God:

"What agreement [can there be between] a temple of God and idols? For ***we are the temple of the living God; even as God said, I will dwell in and with and among them and will walk in and with and among them,*** and I will be their God, and they shall be My people. So, come out from among [unbelievers], and separate (sever) yourselves from them, says the Lord, and touch not [any] unclean thing; then I will receive you kindly and treat you with favor, and I will be a Father to you, and you shall be My sons and daughters, says the Lord Almighty" (2Corinthians 6:16-18 AMPC).

Notice the clear and categorical statements in this passage: *believers are the temple of the living God.* God dwells *in and with and among them and walks in and with and among them.* This is stupendous. The Church has not majored on the amazing truth of the Indwelling and its inexpressible possibilities.

- As God's temples, believers are warned against defiling and destroying God's temple, i.e., their bodies in which God resides:

"If anyone defiles the temple of God, God will destroy him. ***For the temple of God is holy, which temple you are.***" (1Corinthians 3:17 NKJV)

The language in these verses is totally unequivocal: the facts being stated are not in doubt. And they are not parables or mere figurative speech. There is no guesswork here. These verses do not ask believers to pray so they can become temples of God. They speak of a present reality—the fact that they *are* temples of the living God. Their bodies and spirits are the very sanctuary of the Holy Spirit, who lives within them. This is the reality of the Indwelling: God Himself lives in believers. They are His temple in which He resides.

The Holy of Holies

In the New Testament, different words are used for "temple" in different places. This is due to the fact that the temple had divisions—the outer court, the holy place, and the holy of holies (or, as rendered in the NIV, the Most Holy Place). These divisions can be collectively or individually referred to as the "temple." One will have to look more closely to know which division is spoken of, or whether the entire temple complex is being discussed. The definitions provided below are from the Strong's Hebrew and Greek Dictionaries, E-Sword version.[10]

First is the word

1. **Hieron**: a sacred place, that is, the entire precinct; the temple area.
   - This word is used of Jesus teaching in the temple (*hieron*), and chasing moneychangers out of the area (see Mark 11:15–16).
   - It is also used of Peter and John going to the temple (*hieron*), where they healed the crippled man at the temple gate called Beautiful at the hour of prayer (Acts 3:1–10). It is the general word for the temple in Scripture, except when the inner sanctuary is being discussed.
   - This word is not used in Scripture to refer to believers when speaking of their heritage as temples of the living God.

The other word used for "temple" is

2. **Naos**: from the primary word *naio*, meaning "to dwell"; "shrine" or "temple."
   - This is the word used of Zechariah (the father of John the Baptist) ministering and burning incense in the temple (*naos*), when the angel Gabriel appeared to him (Luke 1:9, 21–22). The reference is not to the temple area but to the inner sanctuary of the temple—the holy of holies.
   - Jesus used "temple" (*naos*) to refer to Himself when He spoke of raising the temple back up in three days (John 2:19–22). He was speaking of the temple (*naos*) of His body. We see from this reference that *Jesus Himself was also the temple* (naos, in-

ner sanctuary, holy of holies) of the living God. He was indwelt by the Father and the Holy Spirit in His earthly walk. Later, in John 2:23-25, we see that Jesus would not commit Himself to people who had believed in Him "for He Himself knew what was *in* man." (v. 25, NASB). This refers to His knowledge of the evil that indwelt them and therefore made them unworthy of His trust. They were temples of something or someone else, and He, the Temple of the living God, had no agreement with them. The Indwelling was the primary determinant of how Jesus assessed people—by what or who was in them, not by human testimony.

- *Naos* is also used to describe the veil of the temple (*naos*) that was torn from top to bottom when Jesus died, showing that the way into the very presence of God had now been opened (Luke 23:45).
- Amazingly, this is the same word that is used of believers as temples (*naos*) of the living God. This can be seen from Kenneth Wuest's translation of the passages we have discussed above.

"Do you not know that ***all of you are God's inner sanctuary and that the Spirit of God is making His home in you?*** If, as is the case, anyone morally corrupts ***the inner sanctuary of God***, this person God will bring to the place of ruin, for ***the inner sanctuary of God is holy***, of which holy character you are" (1 Corinthians 3:16-17 WUEST).

"Or do you not know that ***your body is an inner sanctuary of the Holy Spirit,*** whom you have from God, and that you are not your own?" (1 Corinthians 6:19 WUEST)

"And what agreement does ***the inner sanctuary of God*** have with idols? For, as for us, ***we are an inner sanctuary of the living God***, even as God said, ***I will dwell in them in fellowship with them as in a home and I will live my life in and through them***. And I will be their God and they themselves will be my people" (2 Corinthians 6:16 WUEST).

- *Thus, as Jesus was the* naos *of the living God, believers are also the* naos *of the living God. We are as much God's temple as Jesus was His temple.* He has given us, as members of His body, the exclusive privilege of the Indwelling that He enjoyed from all eternity. Hallelujah!

We are the *naos* of the living God—the shrine, the holy of holies, and the inner sanctuary of God Almighty. He lives in you as His home. *He is living His life in and through you!* Let your spirit soak in this truth: you are God's holy of holies! The same Father who indwelt Jesus now indwells you. The same Spirit who was in Him is now resident in you. See yourself like that, for that is who you are. The Almighty lives in you. You are His temple.

A clear understanding of these truths will settle several issues with finality. Take, for instance, the matter of God's will about healing for His children. Could it be the will of God for His temple, our bodies, to be dilapidated and weakened by disease, ravaged by sickness? Does it glorify God for His *naos,* His holy of holies, to be demeaned and destroyed by all kinds of diseases? This cannot possibly be God's will.

Throughout the history of Israel, God commended kings who repaired His temple and judged those who defiled and desecrated it. Jesus made a whip and drove strangers and moneychangers out of the temple of God. Interestingly, immediately after He did this, Scripture records that the blind and lame came to Him in the temple and He healed them.

Once you have definitely surrendered your body to the Lord as His temple, ensure that nothing immoral defiles your body. Then take the whip of God's Word and drive out every stranger who is "buying and selling" in your body. They have no right to be in that body. They are trespassing on holy ground.

God wants His temple kept holy—set apart from sin and sickness and all corrupting addictions—so that He can fill it with Himself. This way, every whit of His temple will show forth His glory: "The voice of the LORD makes the deer to calve and strips the forests bare; and *in His temple everything says, 'Glory!'*" (Psalm 29:9 NASB).

Nothing like this has ever before been heard or seen, or has even entered into the imagination of anyone—that creatures would be indwelt by their Creator! The prophets who prophesied about these things could not themselves understand them. They wondered who would be the recipients of this astounding design. Now, through the finished work of Jesus Christ, we are the heirs of something that was but a mystifying prophecy in their days. Glory be to God!

Jesus and the Indwelling

Jesus was indwelt by the Father and the Holy Spirit. As seen above, He was (and is) the temple of the Living God. As Son of Man, He was the temple of the Holy Spirit. God had prepared a body for Him when He came into the world, and the Holy Spirit used that body as His holy headquarters. From this operational base and with the total cooperation of the man Jesus, the Spirit worked to the fullest to execute the Father's purpose in Christ.

The Spirit who came on Jesus at His baptism didn't merely sit on His head; the Holy Spirit filled Him and thereafter took possession of Him. Immediately following His baptism at the River Jordan, the Spirit led him into the wilderness, where He was tempted by the devil (see Luke 4:1). Following His triumph at His temptation, He returned in the power of the indwelling Spirit (see Luke 4:14).

Even demons recognized that Jesus was indwelt. Consider this incident in the ministry of Jesus:

> In the synagogue there was a man possessed by a demon, an impure spirit. He cried out at the top of his voice, "Go away! ***What do you want with us, Jesus of Nazareth? Have you come to destroy us? I know who you are—the Holy One of God!***"
> "Be quiet!" Jesus said sternly. "Come out of him!" Then the demon threw the man down before them all and came out without out injuring him (Luke 4:33-35).

Notice that the demon first called the Lord "Jesus of Nazareth" but then proceeded to say, "I know who you are—the Holy One of God!" What the evil spirit said in effect was this: "On the outside you are a man, Jesus of Nazareth, but you are much more than that. There is Someone living inside this 'regular' Jesus of Nazareth! I can see through you! Don't confuse me with this body. I know who you are: God in human flesh!" The demon could quite plainly see what the Pharisees and Sadducees couldn't—and was terrified.

This happened several times in Jesus' ministry: the demons would first call Him Jesus and then proclaim His concealed identity: Son of the Most High God (see Matthew 8:29; Mark 5:7; Luke 8:28).

"Demons left in droves, screaming, 'Son of God! You're the Son of God!' But he shut them up, refusing to let them *speak because they knew too much, knew him to be the Messiah*." "He cured their sick bodies and tormented spirits. *Because the demons knew his true identity, he didn't let them say a word*" (Luke 4:41; Mark 1:34 MSG).

It is our firm conviction that, just as they knew Jesus, demon spirits also know believers. They know who you are. Free from the limitations of a body, they can see what you cannot see. An evil spirit actually said to the seven sons of Sceva, who were attempting to cast out demons, purportedly in Jesus' name, "I know Jesus and I've heard of Paul, but who are you?" (Acts 19:15)

Believer, you look ordinary outside, but they can see the same Jesus who disarmed and crushed them, living inside you! They can see the same Holy Spirit who anointed Jesus indwelling you. They know you—and tremble—when they see you coming, carrying the Man of Calvary in your heart. The problem is that most believers don't know the reality of the Indwelling, something even demons can so clearly see. We walk in that reality by faith in the revealed Word of God—even though we may not see it or feel like it.

We see, then, that every time Jesus confronted the demon-possessed, it was indwelling versus indwelling—the indwelling Holy Spirit in Christ versus the indwelling demons in the oppressed. They were mobile human temples carrying demons, but Jesus was also a mobile temple carrying the Father God within. The greater One in Him routed the demons in the oppressed, bringing deliverance. The Indwelling prevailed every time.

Jesus' entire ministry was the manifestation of the operation of the Indwelling to the fullest measure. Everything He did was the work of the One who indwelt Him. This must be our own pattern for ministry if we are to be effective.

God, Our Temple

Fast forward with me to the final scenes of earth's future. The old earth has passed away, and God has created new heavens and a new earth. Now He allows His apostle John to see the end of the story. In describing what he saw in God's glorious celestial city, the eternal home of all the redeemed, John noted something very significant: *"I saw no temple in [the city], for the Lord God Almighty [the Omnipotent, the Ruler of all] and the Lamb are its temple.* And the city has no need of the sun nor of the moon to give light to it, for the glory (splendor, radiance) of God has illumined it, and the Lamb is its lamp and lights" (Revelation 21:22–23 AMP).

God Himself becomes the literal and eternal temple of His true worshippers! They will worship Him for all eternity, but they will not do so from outside, but from *within Himself.* He indwells His people, and now they indwell Him, their temple! No wonder worship will be eternal and boundless in heaven: the worshippers reside inside the awesome One they worship, and He resides inside them!

Now the words of the Lord Jesus to the Samaritan woman have come to their fullest fulfillment: "Woman," Jesus replied, "believe me, a time is coming when you will worship the Father neither on this mountain nor in Jerusalem. . . . Yet a time is coming and has now come when the true worshipers will worship the Father in the Spirit and in truth, for they are the kind of worshipers the Father seeks. God is spirit, and his worshipers must worship in spirit and in truth" (John 4:21, 23–24).

She was fixated on worship based on external locations—on Mount Gerizim or in Jerusalem. However, Jesus lifted the veil to tell her what was coming: true worshippers who would worship the Father in spirit and truth. This is what every believer does today—worship the Father with the help of the Holy Spirit, out of their recreated spirits, in the truth of His Word. Ultimately, to worship in spirit is to worship *in* the eternal Spirit, Yahweh, who has become the temple of His redeemed.

Wonder of wonders! You and I are partakers of this astonishing inheritance.

When God Relocates His Headquarters

Eventually, God is going to relocate His headquarters from heaven to the new earth. This final move will usher in the everlasting dimensions of the Indwelling. *The eternal Yahweh now literally relocates to earth to dwell with people whom He indwells.* These realities are more than the heart can contain, but they are real. These words are faithful and true. Here is the witness of Scripture to this truth:

"Then I saw 'a new heaven and a new earth,' for the first heaven and the first earth had passed away, and there was no longer any sea. I saw the Holy City, the new Jerusalem, coming down out of heaven from God, prepared as a bride beautifully dressed for her husband. And I heard a loud voice from the throne saying, '**Look! God's dwelling place is now among the people, and he will dwell with them. They will be his people, and God himself will be with them and be their God.** 'He will wipe every tear from their eyes. There will be no more death or mourning or crying or pain, for the old order of things has passed away'" (Revelation 21:1-4).

Try to fathom what is going on here. The almighty, boundless God of the universe is moving His holy city, New Jerusalem, from the heavens to the new earth—to dwell with redeemed mankind. "God himself will be with them and be their God"; the emphasis is that it is *God Himself*—in the unending fullness of all He is—moving to the new earth to live with His people. Of all the places in the universe where God could choose to stay, in His infinite love and oneness with the redeemed, He decides to dwell with His people—literally. We now see why there will be no more death or sorrow or crying or pain: these things cannot survive the literal, manifest presence of the holy, omnipotent Creator of heaven and earth: death or pain cannot survive the presence of His blazing life; sorrow will be eternally overwhelmed by the bliss of His presence, and crying by indescribable joy.

Notice the wonder with which this event is described: "I heard a voice thunder from the Throne: '**Look! Look! God has moved into the neighborhood**, making his home with men and women! They're his people, he's their God'" (Revelation 21:3 MSG).

Following this defining moment of the universe, the One seated on the throne spoke; the words He said are proof that His goal of indwelling and dwelling with humanity was now accomplished: "Then he said, '*It's happened*. I'm A to Z. I'm the Beginning, I'm the Conclusion. From Water-of-Life Well I give freely to the thirsty. Conquerors inherit all this. I'll be God to them, they'll be sons and daughters to me'" (Revelation 21:6–7 MSG).

This is the eternal weight of glory to which God has called us in Christ. Everything else pales into absolute insignificance in the light of this amazing heritage. Treasure it. Hold fast to it. Live in the light of this moment by keeping His temple, your body, holy. You will find yourself proven wise at the end of time.

The Lord Is in His Holy Temple

As we draw this chapter to a close, my mind runs to a very interesting verse in Habakkuk: "But the Lord is in His holy temple; let all the earth hush and keep silence before Him" (Habakkuk 2:20 AMPC).

We have seen several temples so far. I believe this Scripture is applicable to all true temples of the Lord, in which He resides. So we can say, "The Lord is in His holy temple in heaven; let all the earth hush and be silent before Him."

But in my meditation, I see the temple here as the child of God in whom the Father dwells. He is a member of a holy nation; therefore he is a holy temple. Picture the Lord seated in His majesty *in this holy, human temple*. He sits enthroned and rules over all; nothing can uproot Him from His throne in the heart of His redeemed child. There is nothing He cannot handle in the life of this believing one. Let all the earth hush and be silent before Him.

What peace and glory when the Lord sits enthroned in the temple of our hearts. From His throne in our hearts, He can quell and quench every uprising and impose His peace that passes all understanding on the storms of our lives. He makes us more than conquerors. And this is not some future possibility; it is our present heritage in Christ. Arise and possess your possessions.

6

The Power That Works in Us

> *"Glory belongs to God, whose power is at work in us. By this power he can do infinitely more than we can ask or imagine. Glory belongs to God in the church and in Christ Jesus for all time and eternity! Amen."*
>
> Ephesians 3:20-21 God's Word

God never designed us to operate from externalities. He made humans in His own image—including the ability to function from within, irrespective of what might be going on outside. It's the way God is. He functions from within His person. Once upon a time there was nothing—only God. Before there were ever externals, He was there. So His personality and purpose cannot be defined by, nor be thwarted by externals. Rather, something comes out of Him to establish and *impose* His will on all external realities. He accomplishes this by His power with which He is able to subdue everything and everyone under His person (see Philippians 3:21).

Christianity was not designed to work from outside. You were designed to operate from within—for your spirit, ruled by God's Spirit and infused with His power, to be in control of your body, and of your response to the external.

In this chapter we will explore the amazing and multidimensional power of God that is presently at work inside every believer.

God at Work in Christ

"It was God [personally present] in Christ, reconciling and restoring the world to favor with Himself, not counting up and holding against [men] their trespasses [but cancelling them], and committing to us the message of reconciliation (of the restoration to favor)" (2 Corinthians 5:19 AMPC).

Observe the plain statement of this Scripture: God didn't just send Christ from heaven to earth and then sit back to watch Him accomplish redemption. No. He was *personally present in Christ* to reconcile the world to Himself. This is the Indwelling—the Father working in the Son to accomplish His eternal purpose. And this is a pattern for all works of the Father, and for all sons and daughters.

God was at work in Christ working all the mighty miracles that accompanied His ministry. When Philip asked Jesus to "show us the Father," Jesus replied,

> "Don't you know me, Philip, even after I have been among you such a long time? Anyone who has seen me has seen the Father. How can you say, 'Show us the Father'? Don't you believe that I am in the Father, and that the Father is in me? *The words I say to you I do not speak on my own authority. Rather, it is the Father, living in me, who is doing his work.* Believe me when I say that *I am in the Father and the Father is in me*; or at least believe on the evidence of the works themselves. Very truly I tell you, whoever believes in me will do the works I have been doing, and they will do even greater things than these, because I am going to the Father" (John 14:9-12).

This is remarkable. The miracles Jesus did were the works of Someone—the Father—living inside Him! Even the words He spoke were the words of the indwelling Father. And those words, spoken on the Father's authority, produced the works of wonder that made people marvel.

In this revelation of the Indwelling, we see how and why Jesus could make the astounding promise of John 14:12—that the one who believes in Him will not only do the works He did, but do even greater, because He was returning to the Father. The Indwelling is the secret of "greater works": the same Father who worked the works in Christ would be the One working the same works, and more, in the believing ones. This would be made possible by Christ returning to the Father following His atoning sacrifice, resurrection, and exaltation. His continual intercession for His own from His seat at the Father's side would then guarantee that whatever they asked in His name would be done for them, thereby ensuring the greater works He promised.

God was at work in Christ to raise Him from the dead and to exalt Christ to the place of highest honor at His right hand: this truth is found in Paul's prayer for the Ephesian believers, where he asked God to open their eyes to see "the exceeding greatness of His power toward us who believe, according to the working of His mighty power **which He worked in Christ** when He raised Him from the dead and seated Him at His right hand in the heavenly places, far above all principality and power and might and dominion, and every name that is named, not only in this age but also in that which is to come" (Ephesians 1:18-21 NKJV).

This same resurrection power that God worked in Christ to raise Him from the dead is exactly "the exceeding greatness of His power toward us who believe." And one day—Oh, the glory of this priceless promise!—that same power will change our lowly bodies to conform to the glorious body of our Head. Death will then have been swallowed up in victory.

This is astounding. The amazing thing is that, just as the Father was at work in Christ, He is now at work in us, individually and collectively, working with the same power with which He worked in Christ.

God at Work in You

"So then, my beloved, just as you have always obeyed, not as in my presence only, but now much more in my absence, work out your salvation with fear and trembling; for **it is God who is at work in you**, both to will and to work for His good pleasure" (Philippians 2:12-13 NASB).

Paul urges believers to work out their salvation with fear and trembling. They are not to work for, or work in, their salvation but to work it out. Jesus worked for it, and the Holy Spirit worked it into their hearts. Now they are to work it out—to allow it to flow out of their hearts and manifest in loving and godly living in every aspect of their lives. But even the outworking of the salvation that God worked in us is made possible only because God Himself is at work in us. "For it is [not your strength, but it is] God who is effectively at work in you, both to will and to work [that is, strengthening, energizing, and creating in you the longing and the ability to fulfill your purpose] for His good pleasure" (Philippians 2:13 AMP).

The truth of God being at work *in* (not just *through*) believers is an undisputed fact, clearly taught all through the New Testament. It is the masterstroke of the new creation: instead of commandments engraved on tablets of stone, God now writes His law on the hearts of His regenerated children. He puts His Spirit within them. They are not compelled by laws and threats of punishment to do His will. They are driven from within—by God's Spirit and His truth carved into their hearts.

Nothing less than God Himself working in you will have any capacity to fulfill His highest purposes in your life and to bring entire satisfaction to His heart. It takes God to do something acceptable to God!

God at Work in Peter and Paul

It was God at work in the greatest apostles performing the mighty signs and wonders that marked their lives and ministries. We read in Galatians 2:8 that "God, who was at work in Peter as an apostle to the circumcised, was also at work in me as an apostle to the Gentiles." In other words, it was God at work in both Peter and Paul to fulfill their commissions to the Jews and Gentiles alike.

It was God working in Peter on the day of Pentecost. It wasn't Peter who convicted thousands of his hearers of their sins and brought them to humble surrender to Christ. It wasn't Peter who healed the crippled man by the gate called Beautiful. It was the Holy Spirit working in Peter to discern and deal with the deception of Ananias and his wife, Sapphira. It wasn't Peter who orchestrated the extraordinary miracles that attended his ministry, such as healing terminal illnesses, raising the dead, and even having his shadow heal those it overshadowed. It was God at work in Peter. It was actually the shadow of the Almighty who indwelt Peter, not Peter's shadow, which was responsible for these amazing miracles. Peter was the willing vessel; God was the worker.

Paul declared the same to be true of himself: the same Person who worked in Peter was at work in Paul. He labored more than all the other apostles, yet it was not Paul but the grace of God working in him. In fact, it was Christ speaking *in* Paul. Just as the Father spoke in and through Christ (see John 14:10), it was Christ speaking *in* and through Paul (2 Corinthians 13:3). When we look at the incredible legacy of his ministry, we wonder how one person could have accomplished so much. But it was God at work, not Paul at work. And God was at work *in* Paul. Divinity made humanity His headquarters of operation, and the results were astounding.

Paul described the great mystery of God that had been hidden for ages, and his ministry in making that mystery a reality among the Gentiles: "To them God has chosen to make known among the Gentiles the glorious riches of this mystery, which is Christ in you, the hope of glory" (Colossians 1:27). This is the mystery of the Indwelling: Christ *in* you, the hope of glory. It is a *glorious* mystery—a mystery loaded with an eternal weight of glory, and astounding, multidimensional riches to those who receive it and walk in the fullness of its reality.

Paul then explained his commitment to preaching Christ and Christ alone: "Him we preach and proclaim, warning and admonishing everyone and instructing everyone in all wisdom (comprehensive insight into the ways and purposes of God), that we may present every person mature (full-grown, fully initiated, complete, and perfect) in Christ (the Anointed One). For this I labor [unto weariness], ***striving with all the superhuman energy which He so mightily enkindles and works within me***" (Colossians 1:28–29 AMPC).

The emphasized portion of Colossians 1:29 above gives insight into how Paul was able to do all he did. Let's explore this statement further by reading it from other translations: they refer to it variously as

- The energy that he stirs up in me so mightily (CJB).
- The mighty strength which Christ supplies and which is at work in me (GNT).
- His power, which mightily works within me (NASB).
- His energy, which Christ so powerfully works in me (NIV).

The import of these facts is mindboggling. The energy of God working mightily in a human being! The power of God exerting its superhuman ability *inside a person!* Superhuman enablement for a superhuman assignment!

This is the triumphant life, and God never meant it for Paul alone. It is the heritage of all the redeemed. We may not all realize and maximize it, but it belongs to us. When the Church begins to major on the reality of the Indwelling and its awesome implications, the world will see a new breed of believers. They will turn the world upside down. It will be the manifestation of the sons of God—something creation has been waiting for on tiptoe.

God at Work in Men and Women of God

If we understood the mystery of the Indwelling, we will not be overawed by great apostles or prominent men or women of God. Everything they have is available to every member of the Body. The only difference is that they have tapped into it and are walking in the reality of it. We will honor such persons as our brothers and sisters in Christ in whom our Father is working. We will receive their ministry as blessings of grace from the Father. If they themselves are smart, they will acknowledge God and remain humble, knowing that the power or grace manifesting through them is not of themselves. They will not portray themselves as possessors of an exclusive "anointing"—something only they could have. And they will encourage the rest of the brethren not to be dependent on them but to reach out for the highest and best God has in store.

You see, there are no exclusive blessings in the New Covenant. What Jesus did for every man of God, He did for every child of God. After declaring the great mystery of the Indwelling, Paul stated his commitment to teaching and admonishing *everyone* in all wisdom, "so that we may present ***every person*** complete in Christ [mature, full trained, and perfect in Him—the Anointed]" (Colossians 1:28 AMP). The fullest measure of all redemption benefits is available to *everyone* who is in Christ. The Father has provided for every member of His family to reach their fullest potential in Christ.

God's work within is still the open secret of the victorious Christian life, and of triumphant, impactful kingdom service. The key is to be the willing and yielded vessel through whom the indwelling One can live His life and work His work without hindrance, and to trust Him with ever-increasing faith for His mighty works through us.

We are encouraged to believe God for great things—such as those He did through the lives of apostles and other fathers in the faith. If God could work in them to do the amazing things we see in their lives, then He can work in us too. "Remember your leaders, who spoke the word of God to you. Consider the outcome of their way of life and ***imitate their faith***. Jesus Christ is the same yesterday and today and forever" (Hebrews 13:7–8).

We can imitate their faith because the Christ who worked in them is the same yesterday, today, and forever. He can work in us as mightily as He worked in them—if we will trust Him as they did and step out based on His exceedingly great and precious promises.

The Indwelling automatically and permanently lays to rest the lie that the age of miracles is past. There was never an age of miracles. It was always God at work in His servants, performing miracles. And as long as the same God lives and still indwells people, then miracles will remain the norm, not the exception. God can do it all again.

God is at work in you—as He has ever been in humans. The same God who worked in Christ, in Peter, in Paul, and in other heroes and heroines of faith now works in you. He longs to do exceedingly abundantly above all you can ever ask or think or imagine. Let nothing limit Him in you.

God's Word at Work in You

God's Word is at work in you, and it is far more than ink on paper. It is God-indwelt, because God and His Word are one. He has given us the written Word so that we might thereby come to encounter and know the Living Word. That Word so full of God's life and power is at work in you.

Paul confirmed this in his letter to the Thessalonians: "And we also [especially] thank God continually for this, that when you received the message of God [which you heard] from us, you welcomed it not as the word of [mere] men, but as it truly is, *the Word of God, which is effectually at work in you who believe* [exercising its superhuman power in those who adhere to and trust in and rely on it]" (1 Thessalonians 2:13 AMPC).

Remarkable! The Word of God is superhuman. The wonder of wonders is that it has the capacity to exercise its superhuman power *inside* humans who believe it. This is why it is impossible to put the Word first and come up last. Its superhuman ability works effectually in those who find it, to cause them to triumph in life.

God's Word is alive with His life. Every word that God speaks "is living and active and full of power [making it operative, energizing, and effective]' (Hebrews 4:12 AMP). The same life that God breathed into Adam at the beginning is present in His Word. That life was so strong that even after The Fall, it sustained man for almost a millennium: people lived as long as 930 years (Adam), 912 years (Seth), 962 years (Jared), 969 years (Methuselah), and 950 years (Noah). This longevity was the residual effect of the very life of God in human bodies. When Enoch was translated at 365 years of age, he must have seemed a young man by comparison! As sin and evil multiplied on earth, that life kept dwindling until the expected human lifespan came to 120 years, then further down to 70 (see Genesis 6:3; Psalm 90:10). To understand this truth, picture a fan that is suddenly disconnected from power. It keeps revolving, initially faster, then more and more slowly until it eventually grinds to a halt. Man was cut off from the life of God, but the effect of that life lingered for some time, imparting vitality and longevity to him. Imagine how different things would have been if humans had never been disconnected from that life!

Now, that Word that bears the very life of God is at work in you. Think what the powerful Word, so full of God's life, will do in you if you keep it in the midst of your heart. "My son, pay attention to what I say; turn your heart to my words. Do not let them out of your sight, ***keep them within your heart***; for they are life to those who find them and health to one's whole body" (Proverbs 4:20–22).

God's Word working in us:
- **Caused us to be born again:** "For you have been born again, not of perishable seed, but of imperishable, through the living and enduring word of God" (1 Peter 1:23).
- **Helps us grow:** "Like newborn babes, crave pure spiritual milk, so that by it you may grow up in your salvation" (1 Peter 2:2).
- **Makes us clean:** "You are already clean because of the word I have spoken to you" (John 15:3).
- **Sanctifies us:** "Sanctify them by the truth; your word is truth" (John 17:17).
- **Heals us:** "He sent out his word and healed them; he rescued them from the grave" (Psalm 107:20).

It is noteworthy, however, that the Word does not accomplish any of the foregoing from outside, but from *inside* us. It is as it works effectually *in* us with its superhuman power that it brings about these wonderful results. The Word of God is light, but it cannot be light to a life until it enters: "The *entrance* of Your words gives light; It gives understanding to the simple" (Psalm 119:130 NKJV).

That is how the Word does its work: from inside. It is sharper than any double-edged sword; it enters into your spirit, stirring faith in your heart. Your faith in that Word causes it to explode in triumph against all the issues of your life, thereby making you an overcomer. It is the Word at work in you, working effectually to implement the wonders of redemption.

This is why believers are urged to ***"keep them in the midst of your heart"***—to store up those words in their hearts, to have God's Word dwell in them richly, not scantily. "Let the Word of Christ dwell in you richly...abundantly...plenteously...copiously" (various translations of Colossians 3:16). The more that superhuman Word abides in you, the more of its power you will experience in your life and ministry.

Since God is at work in us, and He is all He is in us, it follows that all divine attributes are at work in us. His wisdom, creativity, holiness, knowledge, and power are all working in us. His peace that surpasses understanding stands guard over our hearts. His love that has been shed abroad in our hearts by His Spirit floods our hearts with His compassion.

The Power That Works in Us

Many times believers eagerly expect something spectacular from outside to happen to solve their problems and resolve their dilemmas. It's like a magical big bang miracle that will manifest God's power in their situations. All the while they neglect the power that is at work *in them.*

"Now to Him who is able to [carry out His purpose and] do superabundantly more than all that we are ask or think [infinitely beyond our greatest prayers, hopes, or dreams], *according to His power that is at work within us*, to Him be the glory in the church and in Christ Jesus through all generations forever and ever. Amen" Ephesians 3:20-21 AMP).

We know that God is able to do exceedingly abundantly above all we ask or think, but we fail to note *how* He does it. Thus, when we pray we expect some external supernatural manifestation that will attend to our need. We are fixated on the external—for the fire to fall and consume what is troubling us, or for an earthquake to shake the foundations of our "prisons," etc.

How does God do infinitely beyond our highest prayers, desires, thoughts, hopes, or dreams? The Message's paraphrase of the passage clarifies: "God can do anything, you know—far more than you could ever imagine or guess or request in your wildest dreams! *He does it not by pushing us around but by working within us,* his Spirit deeply and gently within us" (Ephesians 3:20).

Can you see it? God doesn't work by pushing us around; He works *within* us by His mighty Holy Spirit. His power is at work in you. And that superhuman power can do superabundantly, far over and above all that we dare to ask or think. It's the indwelling power that guarantees the exceeding, abundant life.

The Exceeding Greatness of His Power

In Ephesians 1, we read that Paul prayed earnestly for the Ephesian believers. After he heard of their faith in the Lord Jesus and the love they had for all the saints, there was something he knew they needed if they were to walk in the full possibilities of the faith they had just embraced. They needed their eyes opened to *see* something. He prayed for them, asking

> "That the God of our Lord Jesus Christ, the Father of glory, may give to you the spirit of wisdom and revelation in the knowledge of Him, the eyes of your understanding being enlightened; that you may know what is the hope of His calling, what are the riches of the glory of His inheritance in the saints, and what is **the exceeding greatness of His power toward us who believe,** according to the working of His mighty power which He worked in Christ when He raised Him from the dead and seated Him at His right hand in the heavenly places, far above all principality and power and might and dominion, and every name that is named, not only in this age but also in that which is to come." (Ephesians 1:17–21 NKJV).

Only by revelation, made possible by the Holy Spirit, could the Ephesian believers come to fully know the hope contained in the call they had answered. Otherwise, they would have been in the faith but not able to enjoy the glory of the inheritance God has for all saints. And they would never have come to experience *his incomparably great power for us who believe*—the same power God worked in Christ when He raised Him from the dead.

Here again, we see that this power is at work in believers, as it was in Christ. It is "the immeasurable and unlimited and surpassing greatness of His power *in and for us* who believe, as demonstrated in the working of His mighty strength, which He exerted in Christ..." (Ephesians 1:19-20 AMPC).

God is able to do exceedingly abundantly above all we ask or think. He does this by the exceeding greatness of His power, by which He raised Jesus Christ from the dead. By virtue of the Indwelling, that power is at work in every believer.

There is power at work in you. It is no ordinary power; it is the unquantifiable and totally unlimited power of God—the same resurrection power with which He raised Christ from the dead. The immeasurable, unlimited, and surpassingly great power of God is at work in *you*!

"I ask—ask the God of our Master, Jesus Christ, the God of glory—to make you intelligent and discerning in knowing him personally, your eyes focused and clear, so that you can see exactly what it is he is calling you to do, grasp the immensity of this glorious way of life he has for his followers, oh, the utter extravagance of his work in us who trust him—endless energy, boundless strength!" (Ephesians 1:17-19 MSG).

Keep praying this prayer for yourself as you read *The Indwelling* and as you study God's Word. And don't forget the Truth Spiral we encountered in the introduction to this book: information—observation—revelation—implication—application—transformation. What could be the implications of these amazing revelations of our heritage in Christ? Something will happen to us that will astound the world when our eyes are opened to see the immensity of our inheritance and the unlimited life that is guaranteed by the Indwelling.

PART TWO

The triune God indwells the believer individually and His Body, the Church, collectively. In the chapters that follow, we will attend separately to our indwelling by the Father, the Son, and the Holy Spirit. The reader is reminded, however, that these three Persons are One. There are no neat boundaries in the Godhead. The trinity is seamlessly interwoven from all eternity. To be indwelt by one is to be indwelt by all. To be indwelt by the Father is to be indwelt by Christ, and vice versa. To be indwelt by the Holy Spirit is to be indwelt by the Father and the Son.

"By this we know and understand and have the proof that He [really] abides in us, by the Spirit whom He has given us [as a gift]."
1 John 3:24b AMP

7

The Father's Indwelling

*"And what agreement does the inner sanctuary of God have with idols? **For, as for us, we are an inner sanctuary of the living God, even as God said, I will dwell in them in fellowship with them as in a home and I will live my life in and through them.** And I will be their God and they themselves will be my people."*
2 Corinthians 6:16 WUEST

One of the most amazing revelations of Scripture is that the Father God lives *inside* the believer. This is astounding. The only reason one can even contemplate it and accept its truthfulness is that it was stated by Jesus Christ Himself.

What might be the possibilities of a life indwelt by the omnipotent Creator of heaven and earth—the Father of our Lord Jesus Christ, the Father of lights, and the Father of glory?

Partakers of the Divine Nature—by Birth!

In Scripture, God the Father is called the Father of spirits: "We have all had human fathers who disciplined us and we respected them for it. How much more should we submit to **the Father of spirits** and live?" (Hebrews 12:9).

He is also the Father of lights: "Every good gift and every perfect gift is from above, and comes down from **the Father of lights,** with whom there is no variation or shadow of turning. Of His own will He brought us forth by the word of truth, that we might be a kind of first-fruits of His creatures." (Jas. 1:17-18 NKJV)

Of His own free will, the Father begot us—brought us forth—by His Spirit. We are born of God: He is the Father of our recreated spirits. We are begotten of Him, and as such we possess His very nature. We cannot be begotten by the Father of lights and not be light: the children of Light are light! Now, the Father of lights has made us the lights of the world!

"No one born (begotten) of God [deliberately, knowingly, and habitually] practices sin, for **God's nature abides in him [His principle of life, the divine sperm, remains permanently within him];** and he cannot practice sinning because he is born (begotten) of God. (1 John.3:9 AMPC)

Observe here that one who is born of God cannot deliberately and habitually practice sin; the reason is given: God's principle of life—His very nature, the divine sperm—abides in Him permanently. Thus it is impossible for such a person to live contrary to the indwelling nature.

We are partakers of the divine nature—by birth. The apostle Peter confirms what John the beloved stated above: "His divine power has given to us all things that pertain to life and godliness, through the knowledge of Him who called us by glory and virtue, by which have been given to us exceedingly great and precious promises, that through these you may be **partakers of the divine nature**, having escaped the corruption that is in the world through lust." (2 Peter 1:3-4 NKJV).

The Father indwells us by His very nature within us. Within His nature lie all His glorious attributes, and they are in us because He indwells us. Thus we are holy and righteous, not because of anything we have or could do, but by His very nature within us. We have His power and wisdom within us. We do not have these attributes to the fullest but can grow in them as we increase in the knowledge of Him who has called us out of darkness into His marvelous light.

An Amazing Promise

"On that day [when that time comes] you will know for yourselves that
I am in My Father, and you are in Me, and I am in you" (John 14:20
AMP). Or, as rendered in the NIV, "On that day *you will realize* that I
am in my Father, and you are in me, and I am in you."

The day of which Jesus spoke has arrived. It came after His finished
work—after He paid the full price for our redemption and took His place
at the right hand of the Father and then poured out the Holy Spirit. Now
we know that He is in the Father. But He is not alone inside the Father:
we are in Him and He is in us. There will be an explosion of His life and
power in us when we *realize* this truth.

The multidimensional interpenetration revealed in this verse is incredible, but true. Jesus is in the Father. The Father is in Jesus. Therefore Jesus and the Father are one. We are in Jesus and Jesus is in us.
Therefore we are one with Christ. Since the Father is in Jesus and Jesus
is in us, therefore the Father is in us. Since we are in Jesus, who is in the
Father, we too are in the Father—with Jesus in us! It is impossible to
disentangle this intricate knotting of our very beings with divinity. This
is who we are in Christ. We are one with Christ and the Father.

Jesus proceeded to clarify what He meant to His bewildered disciples who heard these words for the first time: "The person who has
My commands and keeps them is the one who [really] loves Me; and
whoever [really] loves Me will be loved by My Father, and I will love
him and reveal Myself to him [I will make Myself real to him]" (John
14:21 AMP).

He says that because we love Him, we keep His commandments—
and they are not burdensome. For loving Him, we will be loved by the
Father. This is not the general love of God for the world, but a special
love that is conditional on loving Jesus. Many know and eulogize the
general, unconditional love of God, but they know nothing of this conditional and special love that God has for those who have opened their
hearts in love to His beloved Son.

God loves the world. But as the Father, He loves His children infinitely more. Let this sink into your spirit. God does not love you just
as He loves every other person on the streets. He loves you as He loves

Jesus (see John 17:23 for this amazing truth stated by Jesus Himself). The Father's love for you is greater by far than His love for others who are yet to receive and welcome the Son of His love, Jesus Christ. This is why it is so important that the believer walks in and abides in the love of God.

"No man has at any time [yet] seen God. But *if we love one another, God abides (lives and remains) in us* and His love (that love which is essentially His) is brought to completion (to its full maturity, runs its full course, is perfected) in us!" (1 John 4:12 AMPC).

Notice the plain statement of this Scripture. No one has seen God at any time, but if we love one another, the very same God whom no one has ever seen *lives in us!* That is the Indwelling. The love of God has been shed abroad in your heart, and as you continue to walk in that love, *God dwells in you.*

A few verses later we read these words—words that are forever settled in heaven, words that can never be broken or pass away: "If anyone acknowledges that Jesus is the Son of God, *God lives in them and they in God.* And so we know and rely on the love God has for us. God is love. *Whoever lives in love lives in God, and God in him*" (1 John 4:15-16). There is no ambiguity whatsoever in these verses. Do you acknowledge that Jesus Christ is the Son of God? I believe you do; therefore, God lives in you. Think deeply about what you are reading. It's no light matter to claim that God lives *in* a person and the person *in* God.

Let's read these verses from another translation for further clarity: "Anyone who confesses (acknowledges, owns) that Jesus is the Son of God, *God abides (lives, makes His home) in him and he [abides, lives, makes his home] in God.* And we know (understand, recognize, are conscious of, by observation and by experience) and believe (adhere to and put faith in and rely on) the love God cherishes for us. *God is love, and he who dwells and continues in love dwells and continues in God, and God dwells and continues in him.*" (1 John 4:15-16 AMPC)

Notice that John says "anyone" at the beginning of verse 15. This is not the exclusive preserve of some great men or women of God. If *anyone* acknowledges and confesses that Jesus is the Son of God, God lives in that person, and the person lives in God. This is the Indwelling—the eternal, omnipotent God of the universe making His home in a human.

The believer in Christ is indwelt by the Father God and indwells the Father, who is love. And He loves His children infinitely more that any can comprehend.

The Bible never teaches that God loves every human being equally. That notion is a myth or sentiment at best. A father cannot love the crowd in the city square as he loves his family. He may care about all others deeply and strive to improve their welfare, but there will always be something special about his family. Likewise, God loves His family specially; they are dear to Him, His prized and purchased possession, His peculiar treasure.

First, the Father loves Jesus supremely. Then He loves those who have received Him as much as He loves Jesus. They are His children—as Jesus is His Son—and they are indwelt by Jesus, so He cannot love Jesus more than He loves the one in whom Jesus lives and reigns.

Next, the Father loves the world of sinners and desires them to come to know Jesus Christ, His only begotten Son, whom He sent for their salvation. The Father's attitude towards them, then, depends on what they do with His indescribable gift, His Son Jesus, when they hear of what He did for them.

In fact, Scripture teaches that there are things and even people God hates. But your case is different if you are His child. The Father loves you and desires to manifest Himself to you.

What Jesus said to the apostles was so revolutionary that "Judas (not Judas Iscariot) said, 'But, Lord, why do you intend to show yourself to us and not to the world?'" (John 14:22). Jesus had guaranteed that He would manifest, reveal, disclose, and make Himself real to the one who loves Him. He was not going to be a story to the believing one. He would be real to such a person—as real as someone standing next to them.

Many believers don't know this manifestation of Christ—the certainty of His being *real* and present in their everyday lives. This is why it is easier for them to borrow or seek help from others who seem more tangible and near, rather than look to Christ to supply their needs. They believe in a historical Jesus who died and rose, is somewhere in heaven, and will someday come back to take them there. But they know nothing of the blessed reality of His everyday, personal presence. When they pray, it's a long shot in the dark—in the hope that someone out there will hear and intervene in their situations.

This is not how the New Covenant was designed to function. It is built on reality—from start to finish—not theory or imagination. Jesus Christ is not a story; He is a person. He is real, and He lives in you. The Father is not a figment of imagination. He makes His abode in you. The Holy Spirit's life and power flow within you. The very Spirit of the One who raised Jesus Christ from the dead indwells you and is quickening your mortal body even as you read this.

The apostles and early disciples could not have faced the incredible might of Rome or brutal suppression by established religion with just stories. They touched reality. They experienced Jesus Christ. They knew He was real, and they knew the reality of His presence and indwelling. The Bible is not a mere collection of stories. It is God's Word—the Father speaking to us.

Jesus didn't relent or recant. He explained to Judas and the other apostles, "If anyone [really] loves Me, he will keep My word (teaching); and My Father will love him, and **We will come to him and make Our dwelling place with him**" (John 14:23 AMP).

In this amazing Scripture, Jesus states that He and the Father make their home, their abode and special dwelling place, in and with the person who loves Him and keeps His Word. Now imagine the endless possibilities of having the Father God and the Lord Jesus Christ making their home in you.

This is the heritage of the new creation. We are indwelt by the trinity. We are not empty vessels. The Father lives in you. The Son lives in you. And the Holy Spirit lives in you.

God Shines in Our Hearts!

The Father God Himself now shines in our hearts. We have become His home—His abode—the abode of the Father of lights, the One who is light and in whom there is no darkness at all: "For God, who said, 'Let light shine out of darkness,' made his light shine in our hearts to give us the light of the knowledge of God's glory, displayed in the face of Christ" (2 Corinthians 4:6). Or, as rendered in the CEV, "God commanded light to shine in the dark. Now ***God is shining in our hearts*** to let you know that his glory is seen in Jesus Christ".

Don't miss the truth in this Scripture. God, who commanded the light to shine out of darkness, is not somewhere in heaven commanding light to shine in our hearts. That was what He did in the first creation. In the New Covenant He does something extraordinary. He decided to *indwell* His own—to work from within. Now *He Himself* is shining in our hearts to give the light of the knowledge of the glory of God in the face of Jesus Christ.

There is a huge difference between God standing without, speaking light into our hearts, and God Himself shinning *within* our hearts. This is treasure of the infinite variety—the unquantifiable heritage of the believer in Christ.

In the Old Covenant, God came down in fire on Mount Sinai; the whole mountain was ablaze, and smoke billowed from it as from a furnace. It was a terrifying scene. Even Moses was quaking with fear! God gave his people commandments written on tablets of stone. But in the New Covenant, God decided to do something radically different. He would come down from heaven in the Person of His Son Jesus Christ, pay the price for our redemption and make our hearts fit for His abode. He would then come and *dwell in us*—shinning in our hearts—speaking and leading us from within!

"But this precious treasure—this light and power that now shine within us—is held in a perishable container, that is, in our weak bodies. Everyone can see that the glorious power within must be from God and is not our own" (2 Corinthians 4:7 TLB). We look ordinary on the outside—like clay pots or earthen vessels—but God Himself is shining in our hearts. The almighty Creator of heaven and earth lives in jars of clay! He shines in the fullness of His light and power from within us.

It was because of this indwelling treasure that Paul could declare, "We are hard pressed on every side, but not crushed; perplexed, but not in despair; persecuted, but not abandoned; struck down, but not destroyed. We always carry around in our body the death of Jesus, so that the life of Jesus may also be revealed in our body" (2 Corinthians 4:8-10). No external pressure can crush the One who indwells us. We will be persecuted, but we cannot be abandoned—the Lord Himself lives in us! The Indwelling was the secret to Paul's uncrushable and indefatigable life and ministry. He kept bouncing back—even after being stoned and left for dead—because the life of the indwelling Christ was continually made manifest in his mortal body. Nothing and no one could take him out until his race was run and his task completed.

Carrying Divinity Within Humanity

I believe it is the paradox of the treasure in the clay pot that makes it so difficult for believers to walk in the fullness of the revelation of the Indwelling. You look so ordinary—like every other person. Therefore your experience and expectation must be the same. Not at all! There is treasure within you. God is the treasure of the new creation. He is the treasured heritage of His people. And theirs is not a treasure hidden away in a chest in some cave or island; they carry their treasure in their hearts! He sits enthroned in their hearts and from there wields His awesome power in and through them, for His glory.

Believers, then, must learn to resist the distraction of what is going on outside so they can focus on what is happening inside—in their inward man. "Though outwardly we are wasting away, yet inwardly we are being renewed day by day. For our light and momentary troubles are achieving for us an eternal glory that far outweighs them all. So we fix our eyes not on what is seen, but on what is unseen, since what is seen is temporary, but what is unseen is eternal" (2 Corinthians 4:16–18).

We must fix our eyes on things unseen—on invisible realities. The weaknesses and issues of the outward man—the pain and death and external pressures—all conspire to seize our focus, but we must resist that temptation. By focusing on and cultivating the continuous renewing of the inward man and the invisible reality of the Indwelling, we will walk in unbroken victory. The boundless resources of the indwelling treasure will rise to triumph over all external pressures and issues. In "all these things" we will be more than conquerors through Him who has loved us, and now indwells us.

I Will Walk in Them

Do not be unequally yoked together with unbelievers. For what fellowship has righteousness with lawlessness? And what communion has light with darkness? And what accord has Christ with Belial? Or what part has a believer with an unbeliever? And what agreement has the temple of God with idols? *For you are the temple of the living God. As God has said: "I will dwell in them and walk among them. I will be their God, and they shall be My people."* Therefore "Come out from among them and be separate, says the Lord. Do not touch what is unclean, and I will receive you." "I will be a Father to you, and you shall be My sons and daughters", Says the Lord Almighty (2 Corinthians 6:14-18 NKJV).

Paul urged the Corinthians to be separate—to live the life to which God had called them and not to be yoked with unbelievers. He compares the believer to the unbeliever: he calls the believer righteousness and the unbeliever lawlessness. He refers to the believer as the temple of God—and the unbeliever as a temple too: of idols. Then he declares that we are temples of the living God—as God had promised we would be—His dwelling place.

"For we are the temple of the living God; even as God said, *I will dwell in and with and among them and will walk in and with and among them*, and I will be their God, and they shall be My people" (2 Corinthians 6:16 AMPC). This is the Indwelling—God dwelling and walking in, with, and among His people. Now He is their God—not like the gods of the heathen, whom they have to carry about on mules, but the One who indwells His people and works in them, with them, and for them.

Here's the same verse from Kenneth Wuest's translation: "And what agreement does *the inner sanctuary of God* have with idols? For, as for us, *we are an inner sanctuary of the living God*, even as God said, *I will dwell in them in fellowship with them as in a home and I will live my life in and through them*. And I will be their God and they themselves will be my people."

The Father sits enthroned in heaven, but He indwells His children at the same time. They are His inner sanctuary, His holy of holies. He fills all in all. He is everywhere in His omnipresence but dwells in and with His people in His manifest presence. He is not a God who is far away; He is as near as a whisper. Just as He promised, *He dwells in them in fellowship with them as in a home and lives His life in and through them.* He lives in His people, and they too live, move, and have their being in Him. "For in him we live and move and have our being . . . . 'We are his offspring'" (Acts 17:28).

What are the implications of these great realities? Who can fathom the possibilities of almighty God living His life in and through a person?

The Father of the Lord Jesus Christ lives in you. This bears repetition. It's not just some nice promise in the Bible. It is your present reality. He dwells in you, speaks in you, and loves in you. He is living His life in you. You have become His home, and He, yours. His abode in you is not temporary: you are His home for all time and eternity. Meditate on this until it saturates your soul—and thrills your spirit with unending wonder and worship.

Entering the Divine Oneness

The Indwelling means that the believer has entered into the oneness of the Father, the Son and the Holy Spirit. Jesus prayed

> "that they may all be one; *just as You, Father, are in Me and I in You*, that they also may be one in Us, so that the world may believe [without any doubt] that You sent Me.
> "I have given to them the glory and honor which You have given Me, that they may be one, just as We are one; *I in them and You in Me, that they may be perfected and completed into one*, so that the world may know [without any doubt] that You sent Me, and [that You] have loved them, just as You have loved Me" (John 17:21-23 AMP).

This prayer for oneness is not for believers to be one amongst themselves. It is not a prayer for Christian unity. This has been our understanding of unity, but that is not what Jesus prayed for here. *Jesus was praying that believers enter an existing oneness—that they become integrated into the eternal oneness that exists between the Father, Son, and Holy Spirit.*

As we have already seen, Jesus and the Father are one. The Father is in Him, and He is in the Father. They are inseparable. This is why Jesus could say, "Anyone who has seen me has seen the Father" (John 14:9). Now Jesus is in us, and we are in Him. But don't forget that He is in the Father. So *He is in the Father—with us in Him.* Therefore, we are now in the Father. And since the Father is in Jesus, and Jesus is in us, then the Father is in us too. The Holy Spirit is of the Father and the Son, and now that same Spirit indwells us—we are filled with the Spirit of God! We are one.

This astounding revelation is illustrated in the diagram below.

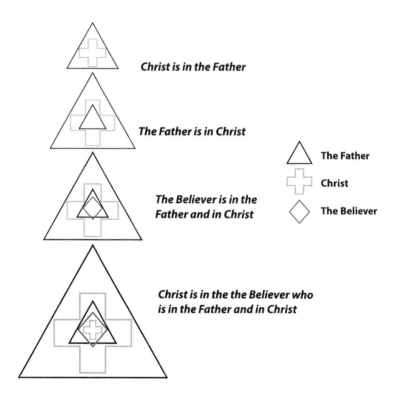

Christ is in the Father

The Father is in Christ

The Believer is in the Father and in Christ

Christ is in the the Believer who is in the Father and in Christ

△ **The Father**

✛ **Christ**

◇ **The Believer**

Notice how intricate this gets. It seems confusing, but it is not. It is a revelation of a unity so total that it is impossible to know where one ends and another begins. The neat lines separating each entity in the illustration do not exist in reality. The Indwelling personalities are in a spiritual union unimpeded by the limiting boundaries of the physical realm. The Father, Son, and Holy Spirit have always been one, and now, through redemption, humans have entered into this eternal oneness. We are not God, but we have become partakers of His divine nature because of what Christ has done for us. It is only by entering this existing oneness that we can have eternal life or be one among ourselves. This is why unity has eluded Christians over the millennia—we have sought to be one among ourselves, without seeing the true unity Jesus prayed about.

In this oneness made possible by the Indwelling, all our differences disappear. There is neither Jew nor Greek, slave nor free, male nor female. We are one. We have been subsumed into the boundless ocean of divinity. We are not God, but God dwells in us, and we in God.

Never before had anything like this entered the mind of man. Eye had not seen, ear had not heard, nor had it entered into the imagination of humans or angels that the eternal, omnipotent Creator of all things would dwell in people, and they in Him.

No other religion dares suggest such a thing. Their idols and deities are totally incapacitated in this regard. The idols of the heathen cannot dwell in them, or they in their gods. The elemental spirits and demons behind the idols could possess and indwell their worshippers, but those spirits could not be indwelt by them. But the believer's case is radically different. He is the temple of the living God, not a home for a deaf, dumb, and dead idol. In God he lives, and moves, and has his being. He is one with divinity.

Jesus declared in His petition to the Father, "I have given them the glory that you gave me, that they may be one as we are one" (John 17:22). What is this glory that the Father gave Jesus that He graciously gave to His Body? It is the glory of the Indwelling. The greatest glory Jesus had with the Father from all eternity—and the basis of all His glorious attributes—is His oneness with the Father—that the Father dwells in Him, and He in the Father. Here Jesus gives this glory to His Body, the Church, that we might be one, with Him and the Father dwelling in us, and we in them. Now, the Father who indwells the Head also indwells the Body!

It is this oneness—the oneness of the indwelling Father, Son, and Holy Spirit with the believer and its explosive implications that will cause the world to know and believe that God sent Jesus. When believers begin to walk in the revelation of their oneness with the Father, the world will see a new breed of humans—humans who are indwelt by deity—with all the powers and attributes of the divine walking in them, talking in them, working in them, and working through them—living His life through them. The fullest dimension of this will be equivalent to the manifestation of the sons of God—something that has been the earnest expectation of all creation (see Romans 8:19).

That day is here. And you are an heir of this incalculable treasure—the glorious treasure of the Indwelling by the Father, the Son, and the Holy Spirit.

Hidden in Christ in God

Colossians 3:3-4 is a revelation of the Indwelling: "For you died, and *your life is now hidden with Christ in God.* When Christ, who is your life, appears, then *you also* will appear with him in glory". It is clearly stated that you died—your old life is dead; old things have passed away, and you are now a new creature in Christ. You are no longer who you used to be. Your life is now *hidden* with Christ in God.

Hidden? How? Where?

The hiding is in the Indwelling: you are hidden because you are *in* Christ. You indwell Christ; you have been baptized *into* Christ and have put on Christ (see Galatians 3:27). You are no longer where you used to be—outside of God and His covenants: you are now an integral member of Christ's Body. Christ is *in* you and you are *in* Christ.

Notice the next phase of the hiding process: your life is hidden with Christ *in God*. Because you are in Christ, and Christ is in the Father God, you are now in the Father God. Since the Father also indwells Christ, then the Father is also in you. You are inside Christ and Christ is inside the Father. The hiding is now complete. Nothing can access you where you are located in Christ in God. Nothing and no one can pluck you out of His hands.

Using the same symbols as in the preceding illustration, this is what your new status looks like:

You are in Christ:

"Therefore if any person is *[ingrafted] in Christ* (the Messiah) he is a new creation (a new creature altogether)..." 2Cor.5:17 AMP

Next, Christ is in God the Father, with you inside Him:

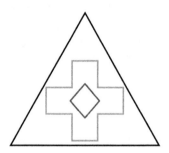

Your life is now *hidden with Christ in God.*

What is being illustrated here is not a theorem that we are attempting to prove: it is the truth of God's Word that cannot lie. We are using simple diagrams to convey deeper eternal truth: your life is now hidden in Christ, and in God. Who can find something that God has hidden?

In the light of this revelation, the fears harassing God's children are shown to be totally unfounded: What can assail you while you are abiding in Christ? What can uproot you from your secure location in Christ in God? You can see now why *abiding in Christ* is the most important task of the believer. It secures everything else—our security, health, victory, fruitfulness, and eternity in His presence.

We find that God's covenant nation, Israel, was also *hidden*. This fact is found in Psalm 83; it reveals the futility of Satan's plans against a hidden nation: "Do not keep silent, O God; do not hold Your peace or be still, O God. For behold, Your enemies are in tumult, and those who hate You have raised their heads [in hatred of You]. They concoct crafty schemes against Your people, and conspire together against **Your hidden and precious ones**" (Psalm 83:1-3 AMP).

Think of what the enemy purports to do here: crafty schemes and consultations against *hidden ones?* How successful can these schemes and consultations against God's cherished, sheltered, treasured, and protected ones be (NIV, NKJV, NASB, RSV)?

The psalmist asked God to arise to the defense of His hidden ones from the conspiracy and attack of these wicked nations—the Edomites, Moabites, Ammonites, Ishmaelites, etc.

Then in verse 12 we read what these nations were thinking as they mobilized against Israel: they said, "Let us take to ourselves **the houses of God** in possession" (NKJV). They were conspiring to collect God's houses—His holy land, His dwelling place, His temple—for themselves! Where would Yahweh be when they came to drive Him out and take possession?

Believer, if you knew your true heritage, you would laugh long and strong against every conspiracy of the devil. He thinks to accomplish the impossible: to yank you out of Yahweh! The prince of darkness purports to walk into the Light and pluck you out of the depths of the Most High! He is consulting against a hidden one—one whom the Lord Himself indwells and shelters under the shadow of His wings. He is consulting against someone who is "hidden in Christ in God"!

You are a hidden and a precious one. You are God's house—His dwelling place. Never forget that. Remind yourself that you are not exposed to the whims and caprices of the enemy. You were outside before—a sheep without a shepherd, wide open to every wolf and woe. But now you have a Shepherd—the only Shepherd who hides His sheep, not in a pen or sheepfold but *inside Himself!* The devil has to cut through God, and then through Christ, before he can reach you. Fortify yourself in this identity: the more you believe it, the more real it becomes to you. It is the indescribable wonder of the Indwelling: Christ and the Father indwelling you by the Holy Spirit, and you indwelling the Godhead.

What are the implications of these undeniable facts? What would happen if every believer were to walk in the reality of these truths, conscious of the fact that they carry divinity within their humanity?

Our fears would melt away. What could happen to us, except what He permits to happen? Since even the birds of the air cannot fall to the ground without His knowledge and permission, how could one hair from our heads, numbered as they are, fall to the ground without His knowledge? What could happen to us that the One in whom we are hidden would be unable to handle?

We will lose every sense of condemnation. If we are so accepted that we aren't simply welcome into His presence but granted space *inside His person,* then we can be sure that there is no condemnation to us in Christ Jesus. He Himself has become our righteousness.

The concept of lack would be deleted from our mentality. See how unthinkable it is? What could we lack while we abide inside the endless, boundless Yahweh, Author of all things and lawful Owner of the universe? What could a branch lack as long as it abides in the Vine?

We will know beyond doubt that our security is guaranteed. All we have to do is abide in Christ. Christ will eternally abide in the Father, so as long as we abide in Christ we will be safe. We will know for certain that no weapon formed against us shall prosper. We will go through the waters and fires of life, but they will not be able to overflow or consume us.

"Whoever dwells in the shelter of the Most High will rest in the shadow of the Almighty" (Psalm 91:1). We are the heirs of all the amazing blessings of Psalm 91 and so many more. We do not merely dwell in the secret place of the Most High: we dwell in the Most High Himself! He Himself is our secret place. His Name is our strong tower: we've run *into* Him and we are safe. We are not separate entities abiding under the shadow of the Almighty: the Almighty Himself indwells us, and we indwell Him. Oh the wonders of redemption! Oh, the glories of the New Covenant!

We will manifest the power of the One who indwells us, in whom we live and move and have our being. The shadow of the Almighty overshadows us as we go about life. What can be impossible under that omnipotent Shadow?

We will love as He loves. We will not be striving in our own power to forgive or love people: it will be His compassion flowing through us to enfold and uplift many.

Our prayer points will change. Instead of praying desperately, as though we could use our prayers to protect ourselves from the devil and his agents, our confidence will rest in our divine location—our placement in the all-conquering Christ and in all He has accomplished for us.

Our perspectives will change too—we will see everything from our location, through the eyes of Christ and the Father God. We will see beyond time into eternity and live in view of what will endure.

"When Christ, who is your life, appears, then *you also* will appear with him in glory." (Colossians 3:4). This glory is not in any way inferior to the glory of Christ Himself. Remember that He gave us the glory that the Father gave Him. We also will appear with Him in glory. He was the only Son in glory, but He paid the price to bring *many* sons to glory (see Hebrews 2:10). This is our heritage. It is guaranteed by the Indwelling.

We will now proceed to unlock the mysteries of our indwelling by the Lord Jesus Christ Himself.

8

The Indwelling Christ

Christ in you, the hope of glory —Colossians 1:27

I Can See Jesus in Your Eyes!

In a post on his Facebook page, the evangelist Reinhard Bonnke told the story of an encounter that brought the truth of the Indwelling to him with clarity:

> During the years of our tent-crusades in Africa, my music-minister Adam Mtsweni and I were looking for a new platform-organ and went from shop to shop in the city of Johannesburg. It was noon, and there was one more shop we were heading for. On arrival I saw a salesman hanging around during the lunch-break, and I thought he had hardly noticed it. My colleague and I went from instrument to instrument, but suddenly that lone salesman stood in front of me. His eyes were wide open and his face as white as a sheet. "Sir", he stammered, "I can see Jesus in your eyes." I was dumbfounded. "How can this be?" I thought, "a total stranger says he can see Jesus in my eyes?" We had something like a revival in the music-shop, and when I left walking to the

car I said, "Lord, I will never understand how something like this is possible." Then the Holy Spirit spoke to me. "No problem! Jesus lives in your heart, and sometimes he likes to look out of the windows!" What a wonderful truth. In John 14:23 *"Jesus answered and said unto him, If a man love me, he will keep my words: and my Father will love him, and we will come unto him, and make our abode with him."*[11]

People may not get to see Jesus in your eyes as the salesman did in the eyes of the famous evangelist, but He indwells you. The Indwelling is the heritage of all the redeemed. Jesus lives *in* your heart.

Christianity is the only faith in which the deity worshiped indwells the worshipper, and vice versa. No other religious system of worship promises this to the worshipper. But it is the heritage of the blood-begotten children of God. He lives in them, and they live in Him.

The revelation of the Indwelling Christ is the cornerstone of the New Covenant. As we have seen, the Old Covenant was based on externals, but in the New, God indwells His people and works from within them to glorify Himself. In this chapter, we focus on the reality of the indwelling Christ. The reader is reminded that since the Father and the Son are one, the residence of Christ automatically implies the residence of the Father and the Holy Spirit. The triune God—Father, Son, and Holy Spirit—indwells the believer!

Jesus on the Inside

There is a song that old-time saints love to sing. It goes like this:

> Jesus on the inside
> Working on the outside
> Oh what a change in my life
> Oh what a change in my life
>
> Holy Ghost on the inside
> Working on the outside

Oh what a change in my life
Oh what a change in my life.

This is the reality of the New Covenant. The Christ who saved believers now lives inside them, and from the throne of their hearts, He works His wondrous change in and through their lives.

Jesus on the inside, resisting temptation and saying *No* to sin.

Jesus on the inside, pardoning "unpardonable" injuries, wounds, and hurts.

Jesus on the inside, loving the unlovable.

Jesus on the inside, infusing us with strength through the darkest nights of the soul.

Jesus on the inside, blessing the poor and lifting the needy.

Jesus on the inside, healing the sick and liberating the oppressed.

Jesus on the inside, imparting grace to prevail despite great persecutions.

The father of a dear Christian sister locked her up and was beating her mercilessly—for following Jesus. He rained blows and lashes on her. After a while, through her tears, she asked her father to pause and listen to something she wanted to tell him. She said, "Father, this Jesus you are trying to beat out of me is not on the surface. He is inside. He has entered into me; therefore you will not be able to get Him out by beating me." Her father stopped beating her, concluding that she was beyond reclamation.

It's really all about Jesus living His life in us, transforming us and working through us.

This is why the old, unregenerate life had to die. Our old self died so that Christ could live and reign in its stead. "We know that our old (unrenewed) self was nailed to the cross with Him in order that [our] body [which is the instrument] of sin might be made ineffective and inactive for evil, that we might no longer be the slaves of sin" (Romans 6:6 AMPC).

Paul was very emphatic about this in his epistles: the old life has been crucified with Christ and has passed away. All things have become new—with Christ in charge inside the believer.

"I have been crucified with Christ [that is, in Him I have shared

His crucifixion]; *it is no longer I who live, but Christ lives in me.* The life I now live in the body I live by faith [by adhering to, relying on, and completely trusting] in the Son of God, who loved me and gave Himself up for me" (Galatians 2:20 AMP).

What Paul says here is true for every believer: Christ the Messiah, the Anointed One, lives in you—with all of His anointing—in the fullness of all He is and has ever been. We died with Christ; now, made alive by the saving grace of God, we live with His life on the inside of us. It is no longer we who live; it is Christ who lives in us. And as we walk in the light of His Word, He makes His permanent home in us and manifests His love and power through us.

Paul's entire ministry was to "implant" and entrench Christ in the hearts of all by the preaching of the gospel. He said to the Galatians, "My little children, for whom I am again in [the pains of] labor *until Christ is completely and permanently formed within you . . .*" (Galatians 4:19 AMP). They had received Christ, but Paul's travail was not complete until Jesus Christ was completely formed within them, i.e., until they experienced His indwelling to the fullest measure. He asked the Corinthians (on whom he had bestowed so much labor), *"Do you not recognize . . . [by an ongoing experience] that Jesus Christ is in you*—unless indeed you fail the test and are rejected as counterfeit?" (2 Corinthians 13:5 AMP). He traversed land and sea, arguing with Jews and reasoning with Greeks, challenging the enlightened and confronting barbarians—to introduce them to the mystery of the indwelling Christ.

God's Great Mystery: Christ in You, the Hope of Glory

"I now rejoice in my sufferings for you, and fill up in my flesh what is lacking in the afflictions of Christ, for the sake of His body, which is the church, of which I became a minister according to the stewardship from God which was given to me for you, to fulfill the word of God, *the mystery which has been hidden from ages and from generations, but now has been revealed to His saints.*

To them God willed to make known what are ***the riches of the glory of this mystery among the Gentiles: which is Christ in you, the hope of glory.*** Him we preach, warning every man and teaching every man in all wisdom, that we may present every man perfect in Christ Jesus." (Colossians 1:24-28 NKJV)

Here Paul speaks of a mystery hidden from ages and generations but that has now been revealed to the saints. A mystery is a great secret that God had kept to Himself but then revealed to His people so they could understand His purpose and benefit from it. So God decided to make known the riches of this mystery—the great possibilities it unfolds for those that embrace it

"This mystery has been kept in the dark for a long time, but now it's out in the open. God wanted everyone, not just Jews, to know this rich and glorious secret inside and out, regardless of their background, regardless of their religious standing. ***The mystery in a nutshell is just this: Christ is in you, so therefore you can look forward to sharing in God's glory***. It's that simple. That is the substance of our Message" (Colossians 1:26-27 MSG).

The indwelling Christ is God's secret. This is the mystery of all mysteries—that God will actually live inside people. That is why it is impossible to comprehend and receive the Indwelling unless the Spirit of God opens one's eyes to it.

You see, Jesus Christ is glorious. Following His finished work on the Cross, "God raised him from death and set him on a throne in deep heaven, in charge of running the universe, everything from galaxies to governments, no name and no power exempt from his rule. And not just for the time being, but forever. He is in charge of it all, has the final word on everything" (Ephesians 1:20–22 MSG).

But this glorified Christ at the right hand of God does not become *your* hope of glory until He indwells you: "*Christ IN you, the Hope of realizing the glory*" (Colossians 1:27 AMPC). It is until a person is IN Christ, and Christ is IN him or her, that a life of present and eternal glory is guaranteed.

Christ *in* you, the hope of glory! Christ in you, the hope of deliverance from sin, the hope of healing, the hope of power, of provision, and of every conceivable blessing from God. Christ in us is our hope and guarantee of present and ultimate glory. He is our hope and guarantee of glory in both time and eternity. Some would want to consign the glory to the afterlife, but the text suggests no such thing. Others might be tempted to spiritualize the glory, but we must not spiritualize what God has generalized. Christ in us is our hope of all dimensions of glory—spiritual glory, the glory of answered prayer, financial glory, academic glory, and eternal glory. He is our hope of a glorious ministry such as we see with the apostles in the book of Acts. We have no other hope of glory or of anything else apart from the indwelling Christ. But ours is a hope that never disappoints.

Since Paul realized that the indwelling Christ was God's secret, he had no other message to preach. He "made the decision to know nothing [that is, to forego philosophical or theological discussions regarding inconsequential things and opinions while] among you *except Jesus Christ, and Him crucified*" (1 Corinthians 2:2 AMP). He preached Christ, "warning every man and teaching every man in all wisdom, that we may present every man perfect in Christ Jesus" (Colossians 1:28 NKJV).

In the very next verse we read how Paul was able to communicate the mystery of the gospel so effectively: "For this I labor [unto weariness], *striving with all the superhuman energy which He so mightily enkindles and works within me*" (Colossians 1:29 AMPC). It was the superhuman energy of the indwelling Christ *within* him, propagating the mystery of the Indwelling. It was the Indwelling calling for the indwelling, as deep calls to deep: the indwelling Christ in Paul was inviting all peoples, through the gospel, to embrace the mystery of the Indwelling—to open their hearts to their only hope of glory.

The Unsearchable Riches of Christ

In Ephesians 3:1–11, Paul gave further insight into this mystery that had been "hidden in God" (see Ephesians 3:9) for generations—the mystery of Christ. Paul was appointed and enabled, through the working of God's power in him, to proclaim this mystery with its unsearchable riches to the Gentiles: "To me, though I am the very least of all the saints (God's consecrated people), this grace (favor, privilege) was granted and graciously entrusted: *to proclaim to the Gentiles the unending (boundless, fathomless, incalculable, and exhaustless) riches of Christ [wealth which no human being could have searched out]*" (Ephesians 3:8 AMPC).

The Indwelling is the key to your entrance into the unsearchable, inexhaustible, and incalculable riches of Christ. Paul was called to proclaim these riches to the Gentiles, but how were they going to get them? They had to receive Him—to have Him *inside* them—indwelling them. Then He would become their hope of glory.

The Christ who created and owns all things now lives in you; therefore, all things are yours (see 1 Corinthians 3:21–23). The riches of Christ encompass everything—the spiritual and the physical, the visible and invisible, time and eternity. As earlier stated, we must not spiritualize what God has generalized by restricting the riches of Christ only to the "spiritual." They include everything; He made it all; He owns it all. And now He lives in you with all His boundless, fathomless, and incalculable riches.

The believer becomes a joint-heir of the indwelling Christ. *You are a co-heir with Christ because Christ, the Heir of all things, dwells in you.* You cannot have Him in you and not be an heir: the Heir Himself lives in you, thereby guaranteeing your inheritance. As a matter of fact, the believer cannot be disinherited as long as the Heir dwells *inside* him. He is an eternal partaker of an eternal inheritance, assured by the indwelling Christ.

This is God's great mystery: that the Christ by whom and through whom He made all things will dwell in those who receive Him, and thereby bring them to share in the glory of God.

God's mystery is His secret of everything—of glory, of blessing, of healing, and of final translation into His presence from time to eternity. To ignore it is to ignore the great secret to all that God is and possesses, and wants to do for us. While the Jews seek a sign and the Gentiles pursue knowledge, God offers Christ—the wisdom and power of God—to all.

The Manifold Wisdom of God

Paul, by the Holy Spirit, reveals another purpose of God's great mystery—the mystery of the indwelling Christ: "[The purpose is] that **through the church** the complicated, many-sided wisdom of God in all its infinite variety and innumerable aspects might now be made known to the angelic rulers and authorities (principalities and powers) in the heavenly sphere. This is in accordance with the terms of the eternal and timeless purpose which He has realized and carried into effect in [the person of] Christ Jesus our Lord, In Whom, because of our faith in Him, we dare to have the boldness (courage and confidence) of free access (an unreserved approach to God with freedom and without fear)" (Ephesians 3:10–12 AMPC).

It is through the Church, comprised of partakers of the Indwelling, that God intends to reveal His wisdom to principalities and powers—to shock them with His complicated, many-sided wisdom—wisdom that could use the foolishness of the Cross to accomplish His great purpose. Principalities and powers stand speechless and helpless before the mystery of the Indwelling: they cannot fathom how the Christ who defeated them could now live in multitudes of believers at the same time.

Only believers who walk in a continual consciousness of the Indwelling can be used by God to teach the devil and his demons some important lessons. Such believers are masters over the adversary; the authority of the Christ who lives in them over the devil is indisputable, total, and absolute. And they now exercise that authority on their Master's behalf. In Christ, they have direct access to the Father: they enjoy a bold and unreserved approach to God and His throne of grace, from which they can receive everything they need for life and godliness. They are fearless in the face of the adversary.

On Calvary, the devil and his human instruments made a terrible mistake—one comparable to, or worse than, the devil's ill-advised coup against God in heaven: they crucified the Lord of glory. They thought that was the end of the story, but it was only the beginning. *Jesus' death on the Cross made the Indwelling possible.* Now the risen Lord of glory could share the glory He had with the Father—the glory of the Indwelling—with the ones for whom He died. Now He could legally possess all who would receive Him because He made them and died for them, i.e., by creation and by redemption. Now Jesus can live in billions of people at the same time—the same Christ, with the same authority and power, doing the same works and even greater! Now the devil has to contend with not one Christ, but with millions of people indwelled by the same Christ who crushed his head!

You can now understand 1 Corinthians 2:7-10:

> We declare God's wisdom, a mystery that has been hidden and that God destined for our glory before time began. None of the rulers of this age understood it, *for if they had, they would not have crucified the Lord of glory*. However, as it is written: "What no eye has seen, what no ear has heard, and what no human mind has conceived"—the things God has prepared for those who love him—these are the things God has revealed to us by his Spirit. The Spirit searches all things, even the deep things of God.

Satan never understood what God was doing through Christ, with His hidden wisdom, to accomplish His great mystery. If Satan had, he never would have crucified the Lord of glory; it would have been far better to leave Christ alone than to kill Him, only to have Him multiply Himself inside millions of people. As a mere man, Jesus could never indwell anyone, but through His death, burial, and resurrection something the devil never envisaged happened: the last Adam became a life-giving Spirit (see 1 Corinthians 15:45). Unlike the first Adam, who was simply a living being with no capacity to impart life to another, Jesus *gives* His life to those who receive Him. He indwells them!

Indeed, "No one's ever seen or heard anything like this, never so much as imagined anything quite like it—what God has arranged for those who love him" (1 Corinthians 2:9 MSG).

Eye Has Not Seen...

What is this thing that "eye has not seen, nor ear heard," which no one could ever have imagined, which God has prepared for those who love Him? We may assume that the answer is that we will end up in heaven when life on earth is over. But what guarantees heaven to us? If we focus on our promised immortality as the ultimate gift God has for those who love Him, the question remains: What will guarantee our change to immortality when the trumpet sounds?

Scripture tells us what God has prepared for those who love Him. —

'But as it is written: "Eye has not seen, nor ear heard, Nor have entered into the heart of man The things which God has prepared for those who love Him." But *God has revealed them to us through His Spirit... Now we have received, not the spirit of the world, but the Spirit who is from God, that we might know the things that have been freely given to us by God* ... For "who has known the mind of the Lord that he may instruct Him?" *But we have the mind of Christ.*' (1 Corinthians 2:9–10, 12, 16 NKJV).

We see, then, that the Indwelling holds the key: we have received the Spirit of God Himself. He indwells us and reveals God's great inheritance to us. We have the mind of Christ—the indwelling Christ.

Jesus said in John 14:23, "*Anyone who loves me* will obey my teaching. My Father will love them, and *we will come to them and make our home with them*". The ultimate glory that God has prepared for those who love Him is the glory of the Indwelling! It is the guarantee of everything. *We will go to His abode in heaven when we leave earth, because we were His abode here on earth.* Only those in whom He dwells—beneficiaries of the Indwelling—will dwell with Him eternally in heaven and in the new earth.

Notice the interplay of God's love and the Indwelling in the following passage (1 John 4:9–16):

> This is how God showed his love among us: He sent his one and only Son into the world that we might live through him. This is love: not that we loved God, but that he loved us and sent his Son as an atoning sacrifice for our sins. Dear friends, since God

so loves us, we also ought to love one another. No one has ever seen God; but if we love one another, *God lives in us* and his love is made complete in us.

This is how we know that we live in him and he in us: He has given us of his Spirit. And we have seen and testify that the Father has sent his Son to be the Savior of the world. If anyone acknowledges that Jesus is the Son of God, *God lives in them and they in God.* And so we know and rely on the love God has for us.

God is love. Whoever lives in love lives in God, and God in them.

Love and the Indwelling are inseparable. True love can never be satisfied with things; its highest treasure is the beloved, not gifts. The deepest longing of the lover and the beloved is to be one. A loving husband and his beloved wife become one flesh: they give each other the gift of themselves! The sharing of their lives is the highest bounty each can bestow. No wonder we read that he who is joined to the Lord becomes one spirit with Him (see 1 Corinthians 6:17). Love cannot be kept away from the beloved. We see it manifest even in the trinity: the Father and the Spirit indwell the Son, and the Son's supreme prize is His oneness with the Father. The ultimate manifestation of love is the Indwelling: our loving heavenly Father possesses His beloved in the fullest sense of the word—by *indwelling them!* He gives them the greatest gift of all: Himself!

God arranged that He will *indwell* all who love Him, who reciprocate His love by esteeming and receiving His Son Jesus Christ, His greatest love gift. They would become His inner sanctuary, His temple, His home, His resting place. Everything else God prepared for His beloved emanates from the Indwelling. His indwelling is eternal life to us. It is heaven to our souls—the King of heaven Himself living in us! His power, with which He is able to subdue everything, and which works in us, will one day change our lowly bodies to be conformed to the likeness of His glorious body, and we will spend eternity with Him in glory. Our translation from mortality to immortality and from time to eternity will be the definitive explosion of His life from within us—as was foreshadowed in Christ when what was in Him burst through His body at the

Transfiguration! God's Spirit indwells us and seals us, marking us out as His own for the day when He comes to take us home. And in heaven, the indwelling Lord will be our temple.

Eye has not seen anything like this—the immortal, boundless Yahweh living inside each and all of His people *in all His fullness*. Ear has not heard it. It has never entered into the hearts of men; who could have imagined such a thing? But God prepared it to be the present and eternal heritage of all who would open their hearts to Him in love.

The Resident Christ

So then, it is the resident Christ—the Savior who has taken up residence in you and dwells in you, that is your hope of glory. "Christ lives in you. This gives you assurance of sharing his glory" (Colossians 1:27b NLT).

Jesus Christ is the Savior, but He has never, will never, and can never save a soul from outside: He saves from within. Until His life dwells within the heart, the individual remains dead in trespasses and sins. Until His light comes streaming into the soul, the individual walks on in darkness.

This is why we're told that to all those who received Him He gave the power to become the children of God: "He was in the world, and though the world was made through him, the world did not recognize him. He came to that which was his own, but his own did not receive him. Yet *to all who did receive him, to those who believed in his name, he gave the right to become children of God*—children born not of natural descent, nor of human decision or a husband's will, but born of God" (John 1:10–13).

To believe in Christ as the Son of God is what makes the Indwelling possible: the Father and the Son enter into and dwell in you. To be born of God is to be indwelt by Him, to have His "genes" inside you.

For this reason, Christ can stand at the door and knock—until the individual opens the door of his heart and lets Him in. It is the resident Christ who is your hope of glory.

When Christ resides in a life, He is everything He is in that life. It is not 75% of Christ who resides within the believer, but Christ in all His glorious attributes. The Christ in you is not different from the Christ who indwelt Peter, John, Paul, or other great leaders and ministers of Christian history. You are complete in Him and He is complete in you. It is the Wonderful One, the Counselor, the Mighty God, the Everlasting Father, and the Prince of Peace who dwells in you. The Great Physician lives inside you; the Healer Himself dwells in you.

Who can accurately quantify the possibilities consequent upon the indwelling of the resident Christ?

Branches of the Vine

Jesus painted a beautiful picture of the Indwelling—the indivisible union of the believer with Himself:

> "I am the true vine, and my Father is the gardener. He cuts off every branch in me that bears no fruit, while every branch that does bear fruit he prunes so that it will be even more fruitful. You are already clean because of the word I have spoken to you. ***Remain in me, as I also remain in you.*** No branch can bear fruit by itself; it must remain in the vine. Neither can you bear fruit unless you remain in me.
>
> "***I am the vine; you are the branches. If you remain in me and I in you, you will bear much fruit;*** apart from me you can do nothing. If you do not remain in me, you are like a branch that is thrown away and withers; such branches are picked up, thrown into the fire and burned. ***If you remain in me and my words remain in you, ask whatever you wish, and it will be done for you.*** This is to my Father's glory, that you bear much fruit, showing yourselves to be my disciples" (John 15:1–8).

Jesus is the Vine—the true Vine—and we are the branches—His branches. You see, Jesus Himself is also a branch—*the* Branch. But He is not our branch; we are His branches. He is the Branch of the Father God, and we are branches of the Branch of Almighty God!

"Behold, the days are coming,' says the Lord, 'that I will perform that good thing which I have promised to the house of Israel and to the house of Judah: In those days and at that time I will cause to grow up to David *A Branch of righteousness*; He shall execute judgment and righteousness in the earth. In those days Judah will be saved, And Jerusalem will dwell safely. And this is the name by which she will be called: THE LORD OUR RIGHTEOUSNESS" (Jeremiah 33:14–16 NKJV).

To illustrate, picture a tree growing upside down—with the roots in heaven (the Father). Then picture a single Branch issuing out therefrom and extending to earth (Christ). Then picture many branches branching out of the single Branch and filling the earth (believers). Then picture fruits on the branches of the Branch. There you have a picture of the design of the Almighty to fill the earth with His life and glory. This is what God's kingdom tree looks like:

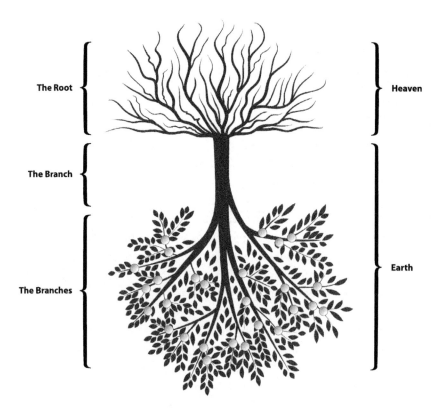

So Jesus Christ is the sole and exclusive Branch of the Father, and we are His branches. As the Father is contiguous with, and inseparable from His own Branch, so is Christ inseparable from His own branches—as long as they abide in Him, nothing can pluck them out of His hand and keeping. Observe too that the Branch connects heaven and earth: the branches of the Branch are firmly connected to the Father in heaven, even while they live on earth.

The vine and the branches are one. It is impossible to tell where one starts and the other stops. The union of the vine with a branch is not merely superficial; it runs deep—to the core of the vine. The very life of the vine flows into the branch. The nourishing sap ascends from the roots, then fills the main plant, and then spreads out to every branch. The same life that is in the vine is also in the branch. And the whole tree is collectively called the vine—the branch has no separate identity but assumes the identity of the vine.

Using the olive tree for an analogy, Paul makes the following inspired statements: "If the root is holy, so are the branches. If some of the branches have been broken off, and you, though a wild olive shoot, have been grafted in among the others and **now share in the nourishing sap from the olive root**, do not consider yourself to be superior to those other branches. If you do, consider this: You do not support the root, but the root supports you" (Romans 11:16-18).

The branches derive their holiness and everything else from the root: if the root is holy, so are the branches. If the root is pure, so are the branches. If the root is healthy, righteous, wise, powerful, anointed, blessed, peaceful, and glorious, *so are the branches*. The branch has nothing of itself, but it inherits everything from the root. Therefore, the branch has nothing to boast about.

Note too that as long as the branch is on the tree, it shares in the nourishing sap from the olive root—it partakes in "the rich nourishment from the root of God's special olive tree" (v. 17 NLT). The root sends rich nourishment into the stem and upward into the branches. Everything that is in the Root flows into the Branch and into the branches.

As a consequence of the nourishing sap pouring into the branch, it bears fruit. The branch does not struggle to be fruitful. Fruitfulness is a direct consequence of its abiding on the vine. As long as it stays in vital union with the vine, it will bring forth fruit in its season.

The astonishing thing is that this is not some empty academic analogy but a revelation of the priceless heritage of the child of God. You are a branch of the true Vine. *You are a branch of the Branch of the Almighty!* You are a branch of Jesus Christ! You are in Him and He is in you. You are one with Him. As the branch has no life of itself (it will wither if it does not abide on the vine), so you have no life of your own. As the branch inherits everything from the root, so we inherit everything that is in Christ. Since our Root, Christ, is holy, so are we—a holy nation. Since our Root, the Root of David, is righteous, so are we. He is our life, our wisdom, our righteousness, our justification, our healing, our victory, our glory, and our all in all.

The believer, then, is not just a poor, lost sinner saved by grace. That was what we were, but now we are redeemed and integrated into the boundless life of Almighty God. You are a branch of Jesus Christ. As you abide in Him, your access to His throne of grace is secured. The answers to your prayers are guaranteed: you will ask and it will be done for you—because you are an integral part of Himself, as precious to the Father as Jesus Himself.

Members of His Body

Our union with the Lord Jesus Christ is not a figment of imagination, and it is not stated in figurative speech—unless the Word doesn't mean what it says. Consider the following irrefutable statement of Scripture:

"The one who is united and joined to the Lord is *one spirit with Him*" (1 Corinthians 6:17 AMP). Or as in the Weymouth's New Testament, "He who is in union with the Master is *one with Him in spirit*".

When we read the above verse in its proper context, we realize the veracity of the unequivocal declaration of the Holy Spirit through Paul that believers are members of the body of Jesus Christ: "Do you not know that *your bodies are members of Christ himself?* Shall I then take the members of Christ and unite them with a prostitute? Never! Do you not know that he who unites himself with a prostitute is one with her in body? For it is said, 'The two will become one flesh.' But whoever is united with the Lord is one with him in spirit" (1 Corinthians 6:15-17).

Our bodies are *members of Christ Himself.* It couldn't be clearer than that. It's amazing what we find when we pay attention to the details of Scripture. Apart from being one *spirit* with the Lord, we are clearly told that our *bodies* are parts of Christ. You can now understand why we are commanded to present our bodies to God as living sacrifices, holy and acceptable to Him (see Romans 12:1-2). Our bodies are parts of Christ's body and must therefore be set apart for His exclusive use.

Recall the Truth Cycle we encountered at the beginning of this book: information—observation—revelation—implication—application—transformation, and so forth. What could be the implications of this Scripture if we truly understood and believed it? I am one spirit with Jesus Christ? My body is a part of Christ's body? Notice that it's all in present tense, implying a present reality, not a future promise or possibility.

This astounding revelation is not the product of twisting and misinterpreting one passage of Scripture. This is not eisegesis (putting into or reading one's own ideas into Scripture); it is exegesis (bringing out of Scripture)—supported by a host of other unambiguous passages. As shown below, the same truth is taught throughout the New Testament.

"Why, no one ever hated his own flesh! On the contrary, he feeds it well and takes care of it, just as the Messiah does the Messianic Community, *because we are parts of his Body*" (Ephesians 5:29-30 CJB). Just as no one hates his own body, Jesus cherishes and nourishes those of us who are members of the Messianic community—the Church—because we are members of His body! Paul applies this great truth to husbands and wives, comparing that union to the union of Christ and His Church and instructing husbands to love their wives as their own bodies—as Christ does His own body, the Church.

In teaching the Corinthians about spiritual gifts, the Holy Spirit through Paul declared, "For just as the body is a unity and yet has many parts, and all the parts, though many, form [only] one body, so it is with Christ (the Messiah, the Anointed One). *For by [means of the personal agency of] one [Holy] Spirit we were all, whether Jews or Greeks, slaves or free, baptized [and by baptism united together] into one body, and all made to drink of one [Holy] Spirit... Now you [collectively] are Christ's body and [individually] you are members of it,* each part severally and distinct [each with his own place and function]." (1 Corinthians 12:12–13, 27 AMPC). He instructed them to fulfill their assigned functions while recognizing the importance of other members of that body.

Observe how believers become members of Christ's Body: upon repenting of their sins and trusting Christ, they are baptized into that body by the Holy Spirit. Once in the Body, they are made to drink of the same Spirit! Drink a spirit? The answer is a categorical yes! Jesus was speaking of the Holy Spirit when He shouted, "If anyone is thirsty, let him come to Me and *drink*! He who believes in Me [who adheres to, trusts in, and relies on Me], as the Scripture has said, 'From his innermost being will flow continually rivers of living water'" (John 7:37–38 AMP). The Holy Spirit is central in the revelation of the Indwelling. We will discuss the indwelling of the Spirit in the next chapter. I encourage you to keep thirsting for more of Him and to keep drinking!

Jesus Christ is repeatedly declared to be the Head of His Body, the Church: "And He (God) has put all things under His feet and has appointed Him *the universal and supreme Head of the church [a headship exercised throughout the church], which is His body,* the fullness of Him Who fills all in all..." (Ephesians 1:22–23 AMPC).

Observe that Christ's body is indwelt and filled by "the fullness of Him who fills all in all." Christ doesn't trickle into the members of His body in fractions or percentages: He *fills* every part. There is no member of His Body who is not indwelt by Him in His fullness. And He is also the universal and undisputed Head over all principalities and powers! Jesus Christ is the Head of the Body of which you are member—a bona fide *part*—and He lives in you in all of His fullness. You may not realize or maximize this glorious indwelling, but it is true.

Now, everyone knows that a head is not separate from other parts of the body. Decapitation equates to death. We do not call the head one name and the rest of the body by another name. They are one. The same life that is in the head is in the body. There is a flow of vitality throughout the whole body, which is interconnected. As we have seen with the analogy of the vine and the branches, the Head and the Body are one; they are inseparable.

Jesus can never again revert to His pre-Cross state when He was alone as God's Son in glory. Now and forever He has a body of which we have become members. He had a choice: He could have remained as the eternal Son, the Word by whom the Father created all things, but then He would have remained *alone*—like a grain of wheat, until it falls to the ground and dies (see John 12:24). But in His desire *to bring many sons to glory*, He took an irreversible step: He chose to take on flesh—to receive the body prepared for Him by the Father—so that through His death and resurrection we can become integrated into His Body through faith. His Body has become our contact point, our entryway into the very life of God, thereby connecting humanity to divinity!

"*Since the children share a common physical nature as human beings, he became like them and shared that same human nature*; so that by his death he might render ineffective the one who had power over death (that is, the Adversary) and thus set free those who had been in bondage all their lives because of their fear of death" (Hebrews 2:14-15 CJB).

Jesus partook of human nature so that humans can partake of divine nature! He became as we are so we can become as He is. The eternal Son became the Incarnate Word so that we can become sons of God. The Son of God became the Son of Man so that the sons and daughters of men can become children of God. Now and forever, Jesus Christ sits at the right hand of the Father *with a glorified human body.* And one of these days those of us whom He now indwells will also receive a body as glorious as His. Oh, the wonder of the love of God!

This is our heritage as believers. We are not ordinary church members gathering once a week to sing nice songs, clap hands, and drop some offerings in church coffers. We are one with Jesus Christ. We are one with Him in His crucifixion, His death, His resurrection, His triumph over Satan and all principalities and powers, and His exaltation. When the Head was crucified, His Body was crucified. When the Head died, His Body died. When the Head was buried, His Body was buried with Him. When the Head rose from the dead, His Body rose with Him. And when the Head was exalted, His Body was exalted with Him. We are seated together with Him in heavenly places, far above all principalities and powers. The Head cannot be seated someplace and the Body be somewhere else: the Body will always be where the Head is—for the simple reason that they are one. He lives in us, and we live in Him. We are members of His Body. He is our life, and He is our guaranteed hope of glory!

The Yoke of Christ

Jesus invites us to take His yoke and assures that His yoke is easy and His burden light. I love the clarity the Amplified Classic translation brings to the passage: "Come to Me, all you who labor and are heavy-laden and overburdened, and I will cause you to rest. [I will ease and relieve and refresh your souls.] *Take My yoke upon you* and learn of Me, for I am gentle (meek) and humble (lowly) in heart, and you will find rest (relief and ease and refreshment and recreation and blessed quiet) for your souls. For My yoke is wholesome (useful, good - not harsh, hard, sharp, or pressing, but comfortable, gracious, and pleasant), and My burden is light and easy to be borne." (Matthew 11:28-30 AMPC)

The yoke of Christ has been largely misunderstood by some who imagine (and teach) taking up that yoke to be some hard, strenuous exercise in discipleship predicated on self-denial and an ascetic lifestyle. This is far from the truth. While we are called to live separately from the world and to deny ourselves in following the Master, the yoke is actually what makes these things possible. The key lies in understanding the true nature of the yoke.

The yoke is primarily an instrument of union: it joins. Everything else about a yoke issues from this primary function. To be yoked with Christ is to be joined to Him—to be engrafted into Him, to be vitally connected to Him. From 1 Corinthians 6:17, quoted earlier, we learn that we become *one with Him in spirit*. The yoke of Christ is not an oppressive and restrictive "chain" or "shackle" around our necks: it is the union of our spirits with Him, made possible by His Holy Spirit within us. Thus, His invitation for us to take His yoke is an invitation to the glorious possibilities of oneness with Him! It is out of this union—our being joined to Him and becoming one with Him—that we find rest for our souls. This is the rest imparted into our souls by the indwelling Lord: we enter into His rest and share His peace. It is the rest that only His presence can give—the New Covenant equivalent of God's promise to Moses: "My Presence will go with you, and I will give you rest" (Exodus 33:14).

You can now understand why His yoke is easy and His burden light. His indwelling presence makes the self-denial, sufferings, or persecutions of the Christian life light and easy to bear. The believer can be at absolute peace, full of joy, and even sing in the midst of the storms of life. This is because the indwelling Christ bears the burdens He places on us from within us! Jesus is absolutely unlike the Pharisees, who would tie up heavy loads, hard to bear, and place them on people without lifting even a finger to help them (see Matthew 23:4). Christ is not a taskmaster; He indwells us and bears His own burdens from within us.

This same principle is applicable to Christ's call to take up the Cross and follow Him. The Cross is an instrument of death. Its primary purpose is the crucifixion of the old life, so Christ's new life can blossom in us. In taking up the Cross we identify with His death: we are crucified with Him, die with Him, are buried with Him, and are raised to life with Him. Then, like Paul, it is no longer we who live but Christ who lives in us (see Galatians 2:20). And as He indwells us, bearing the Cross of the daily Christian walk and witness becomes a joy.

Paul is a great example of the consequences of taking up the yoke of Christ and bearing His burden. The litany of his suffering for Christ and the gospel is daunting indeed:

> I have worked much harder, been in prison more frequently, been flogged more severely, and been exposed to death again and again. Five times I received from the Jews the forty lashes minus one. Three times I was beaten with rods, once I was pelted with stones, three times I was shipwrecked, I spent a night and a day in the open sea, I have been constantly on the move. I have been in danger from rivers, in danger from bandits, in danger from my fellow Jews, in danger from Gentiles; in danger in the city, in danger in the country, in danger at sea; and in danger from false believers. I have labored and toiled and have often gone without sleep; I have known hunger and thirst and have often gone without food; I have been cold and naked (2 Corinthians 11:23–27).

No one could describe a yoke that brought these untold sufferings as "easy" or these burdens as "light." In fact, they were practically unbearable. No human being could survive even a quarter of them in their own strength. But Paul bore them all and declared that he was more than a conqueror "in all these things" (see Romans 8:37). His secret can be found in his admonition to Timothy: "Join with me in suffering for the gospel, *by the power of God*" (2 Timothy 1:8). It was God's power that sustained him in the midst of these trials: *it was Christ bearing the burdens from within Paul*—the indwelling Christ gave Paul superhuman strength for his superhuman assignment—so much so that Paul described everything he suffered as light affliction: "For our **light and momentary troubles** are achieving for us an eternal glory that far outweighs them all. So we fix our eyes not on what is seen, but on what is unseen, since what is seen is temporary, but what is unseen is eternal" (2 Corinthians 4:17–18).

As the Amplified translation (AMPC) renders verse 17, "For **our light, momentary affliction (this slight distress of the passing hour)** is ever more and more abundantly preparing and producing and achieving for us an everlasting weight of glory [beyond all measure, excessively surpassing all comparisons and all calculations, a vast and transcendent glory and blessedness never to cease!]."

Momentary affliction? Slight distress of the passing hour? How?

It was the Indwelling at work: God was at work in Paul, both to will and to do His good pleasure and to bear the consequences of His ministry from within His servant.

Here's how The Message renders Paul's attitude in the face of all the seemingly impossible trials he faced: "So we're not giving up. How could we! Even though on the outside it often looks like things are falling apart on us, on the inside, where God is making new life, not a day goes by without his unfolding grace. **These hard times are small potatoes** compared to the coming good times, the lavish celebration prepared for us. There's far more here than meets the eye. The things we see now are here today, gone tomorrow. But the things we can't see now will last forever" (verses 16–18).

You can rest in the same assurance. The Christ who indwells you will walk with you and within you in your path of obedience. He will still be resident in you when you face whatever might arise from your commitment to Him. Trials and afflictions will come, but His abounding grace will make them seem like small potatoes. Tests will come, but so will your testimonies be multiplied. He will go with you wherever He sends and pay the bill for whatever He commands. By virtue of His indwelling, you will find His yoke easy and His burden light.

Christ Indwells the Church

The Lord Jesus Christ indwells His Church, His Body, of which He is the Head. This indwelling is an extension of His indwelling every member of the Church. Thus, He is in each of us, and He is among us.

In the Revelation he received on the Island of Patmos, John saw Jesus holding seven stars in His right hand and walking in the midst of the seven lampstands. Jesus explained that revelation to John: "The mystery of the seven stars that you saw in my right hand and of the seven golden lampstands is this: The seven stars are the angels of the seven churches, and the seven lampstands are the seven churches" (Revelation 1:20).

Christ is in us, individually and collectively. We must continually acknowledge and honor His presence among us.

"Again I tell you, if two of you on earth agree (harmonize together, make a symphony together) about whatever [anything and everything] they may ask, it will come to pass and be done for them by My Father in heaven. *For wherever two or three are gathered (drawn together as My followers) in (into) My name, there I AM in the midst of them.*" (Matthew 18:19–20 AMPC).

Christ at Home

We need to pay close attention to the statements in Scripture. In attending to them, we see things we might otherwise overlook; we consider the implications of truths that we would otherwise miss. Here is one of them: "All who keep His commandments [who obey His orders and follow His plan, *live and continue to live, to stay and] abide in Him, and He in them. They let Christ be a home to them and they are the home of Christ.*] And by this we know and understand and have the proof that He [really] lives and makes His home in us: by the [Holy] Spirit Whom He has given us" (1 John 3:24 AMPC).

The fact that Jesus Christ lives in you is a proven fact; it is not a wild, unsubstantiated assertion. The Holy Spirit within you is the undeniable proof that He lives in you. His Word in you is another.

The Indwelling Word

Christ indwells us by His Word. He is the living Word.

"In the beginning was the Word, and the Word was with God, and the Word was God. He was with God in the beginning. Through him all things were made; without him nothing was made that has been made. In him was life, and that life was the light of all mankind" (John 1:1-4).

As His Word dwells in us richly, *He,* the Word's living embodiment, indwells us richly: "Let the word of Christ dwell in you richly in all wisdom, teaching and admonishing one another in psalms and hymns and spiritual songs, singing with grace in your hearts to the Lord" (Colossians 3:16 NKJV).

He is the living bread. As we feast on Him, His life, presence, and power abound in us: "I am the bread of life. Your ancestors ate the manna in the wilderness, yet they died. But here is the bread that comes down from heaven, which anyone may eat and not die. I am the living bread that came down from heaven. Whoever eats this bread will live forever. This bread is my flesh, which I will give for the life of the world" (John 6:48-51).

Feast on Him. Gaze on Him continuously in the mirror of the written Word, the Bible. This will guarantee your transformation into His likeness—from one degree of glory to another.

I Can Do All Things

It is in the light of the Indwelling that Scriptures like Philippians 4:13 become even more priceless. I invite you to read the following words and receive them as truth you can bank on: "I can do all things [which He has called me to do] through Him who strengthens and empowers me [to fulfill His purpose—*I am self-sufficient in Christ's sufficiency; I am ready for anything and equal to anything through Him who infuses me with inner strength and confident peace*]" (AMP).

You can say the same thing with Paul: "I have strength for anything through Him who gives me power" (WEYMOUTH). This is the common heritage of the family of God's children.

Note, however, that Christ's strength is not merely an external empowerment—it is an *infusion:* you are ready for anything, and equal to anything through Him who infuses inner strength into you!

My mind runs to the infusions I used to give patients in the hospital in my years of active medical practice. For a variety of indications, doctors often have to give infusions—of fluids, food, blood components, or whole blood to patients. The infusions are given straight into the bloodstream of the individual needing them. And many times, to the extent that medical science can help a person, these infusions revitalize the individual, leading to recovery.

Now picture yourself receiving an infusion from Jesus Christ. It's an infusion of His life. It's an infusion of His grace and power. He infuses His wisdom into you. He so infuses His peace into you that you retain an untroubled heart in a troubled world. He so infuses His joy into you that you rejoice and praise Him even in the midst of difficult circumstances. His own strength is being infused into your innermost being. What can come up in life that you can't handle—with such a glorious infusion running ceaselessly into your spirit?

The centurion was not worthy to have Christ under his roof (see Matthew 8:8), but grace has made us worthy to host Him in our hearts. He is a permanent, eternal resident in us; we are His temple. We are His branches. We are members of His Body.

Remember, the Christ in you is not in any way inferior to the Christ who walked around Capernaum and Jerusalem. He is the same yesterday, today, and forever. He is the Lord, and He does not change. The same One who opened blind eyes, loved the unlovable, fed and healed the multitudes, stilled the storm, and now sits at the Father's right hand dwells in you, and you in Him. Your life is now hidden with Christ in God (see Colossians 3:3).

Abide in Him. Keep enjoying the nourishing sap flowing from the true Vine, whose branch you are. You will bear much fruit. And your fruit will abide and abound.

9

The Indwelling Spirit

A Transforming Encounter

The Holy Spirit *entered* into me as a young student in medical school, and His coming changed everything.

I was brought up in a religious environment. My parents and grandparents (with whom I spent a chunk of my preteen years) were ardent church folks. It was not until my second year in the university that I understood that religion didn't save. I received Jesus Christ as my Lord and Savior and became a new creature.

However, my Christian life was a struggle. I was up sometimes and down at others. I struggled to read (and understand) the Bible. I struggled to pray. I would be in a prayer meeting and the leader would mention an item for prayer and then invite all to pray. As others prayed and poured out their hearts, I could only utter a few sentences and then ran out of words. I wondered how they could pray so fervently and passionately.

Things changed when a special program was organized in the fellowship I attended, to minister the baptism of the Holy Spirit to those who had yet to receive Him. We were encouraged to spend the day in prayer and fasting as a way of preparing our hearts for the infilling of the Spirit. We gathered later that evening for the service, which began with worship and a strong teaching from the Word. The speaker explained that while every believer has the Holy Spirit in a measure, Jesus promised an outpouring of the Spirit, which happened on the day of Pentecost and subsequently became available for all who believe. He showed clearly that the promise of the Holy Spirit was not just for the apostles but for every believer. He quoted Acts 2:39: "For the promise is for you and your children and for all who are far off—for all whom the Lord our God will call."

It was then time to pray for those who desired the infilling of the Holy Spirit. The atmosphere in the hall was charged; we were so full of expectation. People began to speak in unknown tongues as hands were laid on them. Some prophesied! Suddenly I was filled with the Holy Spirit and began to speak in tongues—before anyone laid hands on me! There was such power (and joy) surging in my spirit! I prayed and prayed and prayed and prayed!

Things had and have never been the same. I was a reserved church boy, but now a new boldness came upon me. I began to share the gospel with other students. Some would weep when they heard the gospel and come to Christ in genuine repentance. The Bible, hitherto a boring and unattractive book, came alive. Insight poured out of passages that even seemed obscure. My Bible was painted in diverse colors as I shaded passages that spoke deeply to me. I would sit up into the wee hours of the night studying the Word—while my roommates slept—and then awake, refreshed, after sleeping only a few hours, to prepare for classes. New songs welled up from deep within my spirit (and have never stopped since then). An ability to communicate the truth in writing began to manifest: I wrote articles, developed study outlines, and later began to write books.

The indwelling Spirit has made the greatest possible difference in my life. I have seen lives transformed by the preaching of the Word and hearts ignited with fresh fire. I have seen people healed of their diseases, demons cast out, and captives set free. I have received amazing answers to prayers. I have received words of wisdom and knowledge and enjoyed the guidance of the indwelling Spirit, especially at the junctions of life. Following the Spirit's leading, I moved on from active medical practice to preach the gospel to the ends of the earth and to help multiply laborers for the global harvest. These manifestations of the indwelling Spirit continue in my life on a daily basis—especially as I commune with the Lord and stir up the gift of God in my life.

Other believers may have experienced the Holy Spirit in their own unique ways, but every Spirit-filled child of God can testify to the difference His indwelling makes. His matchless help abounds to us even as we continue to grow in our daily walk with the Lord and experience His ongoing work in our lives.

The indwelling Holy Spirit is God's provision for the abundant, triumphant, fruitful life. He is the One who gives life; the flesh profits nothing. He is the divine seal of ownership in every believer, our guide and counselor, our helper for every infirmity, and our power for fulfilling divine purpose. The Father has given us His own Spirit: the same Spirit who raised Christ from the dead and now indwells Him also indwells us. In this chapter, we will discover the infinite possibilities of His indwelling.

THE INDWELLING IN THE OLD TESTAMENT

In the Old Covenant, God filled certain chosen individuals with His Spirit, to empower them for some specific assignments they were to perform. This is the Indwelling. God knew there was no way they could do or be what He wanted them to do or be without the enabling of His Spirit.

However, what we see in isolated instances in the Old Testament has become the common heritage of all of God's children in the New Testament.

We will look at some instances of the Spirit's indwelling in the Old Testament and then focus on this astonishing inheritance in the New.

Bezalel: Master Craftsman

The Spirit filled Bezalel and made it possible for him to recreate heavenly realities on earth: "Then the LORD said to Moses, 'Look, I have specifically chosen Bezalel son of Uri, grandson of Hur, of the tribe of

Judah. *I have filled him with the Spirit of God*, giving him great wisdom, ability, and expertise in all kinds of crafts. *He is a master craftsman,* expert in working with gold, silver, and bronze. He is skilled in engraving and mounting gemstones and in carving wood. *He is a master at every craft!*" (Exodus 31:1-5 NLT).

Bezalel was called by God for the onerous task of replicating a heavenly reality on earth: he had the responsibility to make the tabernacle, the blueprints for which God showed to Moses on the mountain, according to the heavenly pattern. Bezalel and his helper, Oholiab, could work as engravers, designers, embroiderers in blue, purple, and scarlet thread on fine linen cloth, and weavers; they excelled as craftsmen and as designers. (See Exodus 35:35 NLT).

But there was no way Bezalel could accomplish this task in his own strength or by his training, if he had any. So God did something: He filled him with the Spirit of God. God granted him the Indwelling. The Spirit of wisdom and understanding, of counsel and might, of knowledge and of the fear of the Lord took up residence inside Bezalel. When Brother Bez worked, people saw the masterpieces he created, at a time when tools were rudimentary. What they could not see was that it was not really Bezalel working; it was the Spirit working through him.

It is noteworthy that Bezalel was not filled with the Spirit of God to preach. He was anointed to make things. The Indwelling of the Spirit made him a master craftsman—a technologist!

It bears repeating: many believers have spiritualized what God has generalized. To them, the ministry of the Holy Spirit is limited to the spiritual. They do not expect Him to make them craftsmen or specialists in information technology or expert physicians or successful businessmen. Biblically, however, we see that the Spirit knows no such differentiation. He is the Spirit of all true and beneficial wisdom, whether in spiritual, material, military, or financial affairs. Indeed, He is God! He is not only our "spiritual" helper; He is our Helper in every area and for everything.

The Indwelling of the Spirit is the key to making what you are called to make—making disciples, making money for kingdom advancement through business, making software or blueprints and designs for buildings or products for the marketplace. Depend on Him. Ask His help. His wisdom and creative ability flowing through you will bring forth ideas and products that will cause people to marvel.

There Is a Spirit in Man

When the friends of Job fell silent after exhausting their comfortless rhetoric, Elihu stepped in. He was much younger than the others in the group and had listened to them as they tried to show Job how his sins must have brought on his calamities:

"So Elihu, son of Barachel, the descendant of Buz, replied to Job, 'I am young, and you are old. That's why I refrained from speaking and was afraid to tell you what I know. I thought, "Age should speak, and experience should teach wisdom." However, ***there is in humans a Spirit, the breath of the Almighty, that gives them understanding.*** People do not become wise merely because they live long. They don't understand what justice is merely because they're old'" (Job 32:6-9 GW).

The insight from this young man is profound. He came to a realization (from observing Job's friends and Job himself) that wisdom is not an automatic accompaniment of age and that understanding does not necessarily come from experience. It is the spirit in man—the inspiration of the Almighty within them that gives them wisdom.

There is a spirit in man! There is a spirit in you, and it is none less than the Spirit of the Almighty. He has answers to all the seemingly insoluble problems of life. He can throw light on any matter, no matter how dark.

This revelation is capable of making the youngest individual the wisest—if they will open themselves up to the Spirit's work within them, and to the Word of His wisdom. They become wiser than their teachers, the aged, and their enemies (see Psalm 119:98-100).

Solomon was not the oldest or most experienced person in his time, but he was the wisest—because God filled him with wisdom and understanding. Kings came from distant kingdoms to seek his wisdom, bringing with them the wealth of their domains. He ruled over many kingdoms, not by war or by conquest but by God-given wisdom.

There is a spirit in man! Let that phrase ring within your heart. And that Spirit has the capacity to inspire you and fill you with insight and understanding.

The Spirit Entered Ezekiel

We find great manifestations of the Indwelling in the workings of the Spirit in the life of the prophet Ezekiel.

Ezekiel was granted a revelation of the glory of God. It changed his life and ministry. He described the vision in detail in the opening chapter of his book. A detailed study of his vision has been undertaken in our training course, *Divine Protocols—Principles & Protocols of God's Kingdom Government*, available at www.eternityministries.org and www.amazon.com.[12]

Among other things, Ezekiel observed four living creatures. They went only where the spirit indwelling them was going, and they did not turn aside from the direction preset by the Spirit. Each of them had wheels, and the wheels did exactly what the living creatures did—because *the same spirit that was in the living creatures was in the wheels* (see Ezekiel 1:19-21; 3:12-14; 10:15-17). The Indwelling made it possible for the wheels to do exactly what the living creatures did.

Things get really interesting when Ezekiel stops being a mere spectator to this heavenly spectacle. The same Spirit who was in the living creatures and the wheels *entered into Ezekiel*: "Then the Spirit **entered me** when He spoke to me, and set me on my feet; and I heard Him who spoke to me" (Ezekiel 2:2 NKJV).

The prophet goes on, "Then **the Spirit lifted me up**, and I heard behind me a loud rumbling sound as the glory of the LORD rose from the place where it was standing. It was the sound of the wings of the living creatures brushing against each other and the sound of the wheels beside them, a loud rumbling sound. **The Spirit then lifted me up and took me away**, and I went in bitterness and in the anger of my spirit, with the strong hand of the LORD on me" (Ezekiel 3:12-14).

As soon as the same Spirit that was in the living creatures *entered into* Ezekiel—indwelt him—the Spirit began to do in Ezekiel what He had done in the living creatures and the wheels. Ezekiel was lifted up—

something he could never have done by himself! And then the indwelling Spirit took the prophet away!

The Indwelling is the only way believers can be like their living Lord, Jesus Christ. It's the only way we can live as He lived and do the works He did. There is no other way we can stand where He stood; be bold where He was bold; rebuke what He rebuked; heal what He healed; and, ultimately, be lifted up at the rapture, as our Master was lifted up. But now, *the same Spirit who was in the Lord Jesus Christ has entered into the believer.*

This indwelling by the Spirit was what made everything the apostles did possible. The same Spirit who was in the Lord Jesus was now working in them, speaking through them, healing the sick, revealing secrets, etc. They turned the world upside down.

The Spirit of Elijah Rests on Elisha

We see a similar picture in the impartation of the spirit of Elijah to Elisha.

About the time Elijah was to be taken up to heaven, he told Elisha to ask him to do something for him. Elisha asked for a double portion of Elijah's spirit, to which Elijah replied, " 'You have asked a difficult thing . . . yet if you see me when I am taken from you, it will be yours—otherwise, it will not' " (2 Kings 2:10). Elisha remained focused and fulfilled this condition: he saw Elijah taken up to heaven in a whirlwind by a chariot of fire with horses of fire.

"He took the cloak that had fallen from Elijah and struck the water with it. '*Where now is the LORD, the God of Elijah?*' he asked. When he struck the water, it divided to the right and to the left, and he crossed over. The company of the prophets from Jericho, who were watching, said, '*The spirit of Elijah is resting on Elisha.*' And they went to meet him and bowed to the ground before him" (2 Kings 2:14–15).

This was a transforming experience for Elisha: something happened to him on that other side of the Jordan, and the sons of the prophet accurately discerned it.

The consequences of this impartation of the spirit upon Elisha were dramatic. Elisha's question at the brink of the Jordan is instructive: as he struck the water with the mantle he asked, *"Where is the Lord God of Elijah?"* He was invoking the same God that worked in Elijah to work on his behalf—to do for him and through him, the very things He did in and through Elijah! And sure enough, as Jordan had divided when Elijah struck it with his mantle, it now divided for Elisha. "When **he also** had struck the water, it was divided this way and that; and Elisha crossed over" (2 Kings 2:14 NKJV). The coming of the Spirit had now made it possible for *him also*—the regular farmer from Abelmeholah—to do the same things that the renowned Elijah did! He went on to perform about double the number of miracles Elijah did—including raising the dead.

Believer, if you have received the baptism of the Holy Spirit, the Spirit of Jesus Christ now rests on you! He not only rests on you, He *indwells* you—fills you. The same Spirit who came on Him at His baptism, filled Him throughout His earthly life, and eventually raised Him from the dead now indwells you.

Without seeing Jesus, you trusted in Him. By faith, you saw Him die on your behalf and then rise triumphantly from the dead; and you died and rose with Him. By faith, you saw Him as He ascended into heaven in a cloud—in the same way Elisha saw Elijah taken up by a whirlwind. By faith, you now see Him seated on high at the right hand of the Father, and you are seated there together with Him in the heavenly places. And now He has poured His very own Spirit into your heart.

The Pharisees and Sadducees made an identical statement (to the one the sons of the prophets had made about Elisha) when they saw the apostles doing great wonders after the Holy Spirit's outpouring. They instinctively recognized the transformation that had taken place in these ordinary Galileans: "When the Council saw the boldness of Peter and John and could see that they were obviously uneducated non-professionals, they were amazed and realized what being with Jesus had done for them!" (Acts 4:13 TLB). There could be no other explanation for the wonders they were performing. And they were right: Peter and John had not only been with Jesus but were now *indwelt* by Jesus! He was the One at work in them!

After the Holy Spirit rested on Jesus, following the temptation in the wilderness, Jesus returned to Galilee in the power of the Spirit. At a visit to the synagogue in Nazareth, He stood and read from the book of Isaiah: "The Spirit of the Lord is on me, because he has anointed me to preach good news to the poor. He has sent me to proclaim freedom for the prisoners and recovery of sight for the blind, to set the oppressed free, to proclaim the year of the Lord's favor" (Luke 4:18–19).

Every student of Scripture will agree that believers in the New Testament could say the same things. By the Spirit that rested on them, they preached the good news to the poor and brought liberty to captives and healing to untold multitudes; they proclaimed the acceptable year of the Lord. The same Spirit who worked in Jesus was at work in them.

As surely as the spirit of Elijah rested on Elisha, the Spirit of Jesus Christ now rests on and indwells the believer. In fact, according to Romans 8:9, anyone who does not have the Spirit of Christ does not belong to Him at all. That Spirit will do in you all that He did in Christ. Believe it and expect it. Just as Elisha asked "Where is the LORD God of Elijah?" as he faced the Jordan, and the waters were divided for him, *you too* will stir up the Spirit as you face the challenges of life and see God do amazing things.

An Excellent Spirit

Daniel was a beneficiary of the Indwelling. An excellent Spirit resided in him.

When King Nebuchadnezzar had his second dream, his soothsayers and astrologers could not tell him the meaning. Nebuchadnezzar himself recalled the incidence: "At last Daniel came before me (his name is Belteshazzar, according to the name of my god; *in him is the Spirit of the Holy God*), and I told the dream before him, saying: Belteshazzar, chief of the magicians, because *I know that the Spirit of the Holy God is in you,* and no secret troubles you, explain to me the visions of my dream that I have seen, and its interpretation" (Daniel 4:8-9 NKJV). Nebuchadnezzar knew that a spirit resided inside Daniel! And Daniel, though horrified by the impending doom signified by the dream, proceeded to accurately interpret it.

When King Belshazzar blanched with fear, bewildered by the inde-cipherable writing on his wall, the queen pointed him to someone who could solve the problem: "There is a man in your kingdom *in whom is the Spirit of the Holy God.* And in the days of your father, light and understanding and wisdom, like the wisdom of the gods, were found in him; and King Nebuchadnezzar your father – your father the king – made him chief of the magicians, astrologers, Chaldeans, and sooth-sayers. Inasmuch as *an excellent spirit*, knowledge, understanding, interpreting dreams, solving riddles, and explaining enigmas were found in this Daniel. . . now let Daniel be called, and he will give the interpretation" (Daniel 5:11–12 NKJV).

This is remarkable indeed. Even the heathen knew that there was a Spirit inside Daniel. It is possible to read the excellent "Spirit" men-tioned here with a small *s*—that is, as referring to Daniel's own spirit being excellent, but there is no conflict: the excellence manifesting in his life was from a higher source—the Spirit of God operating in Him.

Daniel served diverse kings and kingdoms. Under King Nebuchad-nezzar, Daniel was found to be ten times better than his peers. Even after one kingdom overthrew another, Daniel was too valuable not to retain or promote. "Then this Daniel, *because of the extraordinary spirit within him*, began distinguishing himself among the commis-sioners and the satraps, and the king planned to appoint him over the entire realm" (Daniel 6:3 AMP).

Daniel's spirit was in tune with the Spirit of God; he received reve-lations of the end times and prophesied of events that are unfolding in our time—thousands of years after he lived.

Oh, the power of that phrase in the queen's statement to Belshaz-zar: "There is a man in your kingdom..." This king neglected the man in the kingdom who had a connection with heaven—who had answers to knotty issues. No wonder his kingdom was terminated.

"There is a man in your kingdom . . . There is a man in your orga-nization . . . There is a man in your country . . . There is a man in your government . . . There is a man in your institution . . . in whom is the Spirit of the Holy God."

How desperately every kingdom, country, government, corpora-tion, and family needs men and women of the Indwelling! They will dissolve the doubts of our generation and solve riddles and enigmas in society, business, governance, medicine etc.—all by the operations of the gifts and graces of the indwelling Spirit.

I Will Put My Spirit Within You

As seen above, while the Indwelling was limited to some persons in the Old Testament, God promised a time when He would put His Spirit within each of His people, would pour out His Spirit on all humanity: "I will sprinkle clean water on you, and you will be clean; I will cleanse you from all your impurities and from all your idols. *I will give you a new heart and put a new spirit in you*; I will remove from you your heart of stone and give you a heart of flesh. *And I will put my Spirit in you* and move you to follow my decrees and be careful to keep my laws" (Ezekiel 36:25-27).

However, for God to fulfill this promise a dwelling place needed to be prepared in the hearts of people for the Spirit. This is why we read (following the promise of the Spirit in John 7:37-38) that the Holy Spirit was not yet given, because Jesus had not yet been glorified (v. 39). Jesus completed His work and is now glorified. And having received the gift of the Spirit, He has poured Him out on His people.

THE INDWELLING IN THE NEW TESTAMENT

John the Baptist was filled with the Holy Spirit from his mother's womb (see Luke 1:15). Thus his mother, Elizabeth, was carrying a double indwelling while she was pregnant with John! She was indwelt physically by baby John, who was indwelt by the Holy Spirit! If one had seen Elizabeth, there would have been no external indication of what she carried within; she would have looked exactly like any other pregnant woman. But when Mary (who was pregnant with the Lord Jesus Christ—indwelt by the incarnate Word) visited her, the baby in Elizabeth's womb leapt for joy, and Elizabeth herself was filled with the Holy Spirit and began to prophesy (vv. 41-45). The Spirit within both her and her baby began to manifest! Similarly, believers may look quite ordinary, but the mighty Holy Spirit indwells them.

As mentioned earlier, the matter of the Spirit's indwelling is so serious in the New Covenant that we are told that anyone who does not have the Spirit of Christ does not belong to Him: "You, however, are not in the realm of the flesh but are in the realm of the Spirit, if indeed the Spirit of God lives in you. And if anyone does not have the Spirit of Christ, they do not belong to Christ" (Romans 8:9). The Amplified Bible is very emphatic in its rendition of this verse: "However, you are not [living] in the flesh [controlled by the sinful nature] but in the Spirit, if in fact the Spirit of God lives in you [directing and guiding you]. But *if anyone does not have the Spirit of Christ, he does not belong to Him [and is not a child of God]*."

What the Bible is saying here is serious. It makes the Indwelling the true test of any claim of belonging to Christ: anyone without the Holy Spirit *inside* is not a child of God. In other words, the proof that you are a child of God is that there is Someone—the Holy Spirit—living *inside* you.

Christ promised the Indwelling of the Spirit: He told His disciples, "I will ask the Father, and he will give you another advocate to help you and be with you forever—the Spirit of truth. The world cannot accept him, because it neither sees him nor knows him. But you know him, for *he lives with you and will be in you*" (John 14:16-17). They had not been filled—indwelt—by the Spirit at this time; He was *with* them but was going to be *in* them.

Jesus was very clear in using precise prepositions to differentiate the present relationship of the Holy Spirit with the apostles from what was coming. To be "with" and "in" are two very different things. "He lives with you now and *later* will be in you" (John 14:17b NLT).

As can be seen from Acts of the Apostles and the epistles, the Lord fulfilled this promise. The Holy Spirit went from just being *with* believers to being *in* them.

They were filled with the Holy Spirit on the day of Pentecost (Acts 2:1-4).

They were repeatedly filled with the Spirit following Pentecost (Acts 4:31; 13:52).

They were severally described as being full of the Holy Spirit: this was said specifically of Peter, Stephen, Barnabas, Paul, and several others (Acts 4:8; 6:3-5; 7:55; 11:24; 13:9). It is interesting to note that, just as Jesus was *full* of the Holy Spirit (Luke 4:1), these believers were also said to be *full* of the Holy Spirit. They had become filled with the same Holy Spirit who filled the Master! And the consequences were just as amazing!

In the New Testament, we discover the following about the believer's indwelling by the Holy Spirit:

- **God has sent the Spirit of His Son—the Spirit of adoption—into the heart of every believer:**
  "And because you [really] are [His] sons, ***God has sent the Spirit of His Son into our hearts,*** crying, 'Abba! Father!' Therefore, you are no longer a slave (bond servant) but a son; and if a son, then also an heir through [the gracious act of] God [through Christ]" (Galatians 4:6-7 AMP).

  "For you have not received a spirit of slavery leading again to fear [of God's judgment], but ***you have received the Spirit of adoption as sons [the Spirit producing sonship]*** by which we [joyfully] cry, 'Abba! Father!'" (Romans 8:15 AMP).

- **Believers are described as temples of the Holy Spirit:**
  "Don't you know that you yourselves are God's temple and that ***God's Spirit dwells in your midst***?" (1 Corinthians 3:16).

- **They have the Holy Spirit's anointing resident in them:**
  "But you have an anointing from the Holy One, and all of you know the truth" (1 John 2:20).

  "The anointing you received from him remains ***in*** you" (1 John 2:27).

  It is sad to see believers who have the anointing of the Holy Spirit within them running after (and being abused and exploited by) "anointed" men of God. They neglect the resident anointing that

God deposited within their spirits and quite often fall prey to predators on pulpits.

- **They are led by the Holy Spirit:**
"For those who are led by the Spirit of God are the children of God" (Romans 8:14).

When the Bible says that believers are to be led by the Holy Spirit, it is necessary to understand how He does it. The Holy Spirit leads believers from within them, not from outside. He communicates the will of the Father to the child of God. He can speak through others to the believer, but even this will be confirmed by His witness in their hearts.

- **They have the witness of the indwelling Holy Spirit that they are God's children, heirs of God and joint heirs with Christ:**
"The Spirit himself testifies with our spirit that we are God's children. Now if we are children, then we are heirs—heirs of God and co-heirs with Christ, if indeed we share in his sufferings in order that we may also share in his glory" (Romans 8:16–17).

- **They are to be continually filled with the Spirit:**
"Do not get drunk with wine, for that is wickedness (corruption, stupidity), but be filled with the [Holy] Spirit and constantly guided by Him" (Ephesians 5:18 AMP).

The reason for this is that there is always room for more of the Holy Spirit in our lives. Only Jesus Christ had the Spirit without measure (see John.3:34). But every believer can experience deeper and greater flows of the river of the Spirit.

There is nothing ambiguous or figurative about these verses of Scripture. They are clear statements of fact inspired by the Holy Spirit Himself and must be taken as literally as they are stated: the Holy Spirit lives *inside* the believer! It is His indwelling that makes every aspect of the Christian life possible.

The Indwelling Helper

One of the names of the Holy Spirit revealed in Scripture is "Helper": "If you [really] love Me, you will keep and obey My commandments. And I will ask the Father, and He will give you another *Helper (Comforter, Advocate, Intercessor—Counselor, Strengthener, Standby)* to be with you forever—the Spirit of Truth, whom the world cannot receive [and take to its heart] because it does not see Him or know Him, but you know Him because He (the Holy Spirit) remains with you continually and will be in you" (John 14:15-17 AMP).

The Holy Spirit now indwells us and helps our infirmities and weaknesses: "In the same way, the Spirit helps us in our weakness. We do not know what we ought to pray for, but the Spirit himself intercedes for us through wordless groans" (Romans 8:26).

There is no infirmity or weakness the Holy Spirit cannot help. Whether in the place of prayer or in other areas of life, all that beneficiaries of the Indwelling need do is to seek help from this omnipotent, indwelling Helper, and they will never be stranded in life.

Who can't the Holy Spirit help? Can anyone be beyond the help of the Spirit of the living God? He helped the many infirmities of the apostles—ordinary tax collectors, fishermen, and "unlearned and ignorant men" (Acts 4:13 KJV)—to such an extent that their lack of professional training became inconsequential in the light of the mighty power that was manifesting through them. The Holy Spirit can help *anyone* and *everyone*, no matter their deficiencies and inabilities.

Where can't the Holy Spirit bring appropriate help? He is the omnipresent One, a very present help in trouble. Don't limit Him to church or your quiet times. He is available to help in the wilderness, in the city, on a mission field, at an exam, in a laboratory, in an airplane, at work, at home, or abroad.

What can't the Holy Spirit help with? He can help spiritually or academically, mentally and physically, naturally or supernaturally. He can help with our walk and work, with family matters, financial issues, or health issues. One word of wisdom from the Spirit can turn around the direst financial circumstance! He can help us with information or transformation, with little or much; He can help with ideas and opportunities. He can help with anything; He can help with everything.

When can't the Holy Spirit help a person? He can help all through time and for all eternity. He is Lord of all. He can help in both good and bad times. He can help in thriving or depressed economies. He can help early or late. He is totally unlimited in His ability to help us.

The wonder of wonders is that this almighty Helper *indwells* us. But most believers do not actively seek His help, or, worse, ignore Him altogether. How can He be present and we fail to *attend* to Him? And while we are frustrated and overwhelmed by the varied issues of life, the indwelling Comforter, Counselor, Helper, Intercessor, Advocate, and Strengthener awaits our invitation and cry for help.

Within you lives the great Intercessor, the One whose unerring intercession cannot be turned down by the Father. There is an all-knowing Counselor *resident* in you! The Comforter has come—and He lives in your heart! The Strengthener has taken possession of you; He longs to infuse His strength and power into every fiber of your being.

But the help of the Holy Spirit must be actively cultivated. He is the Intercessor, but He needs our cooperation to intercede. He is the Counselor, but He will not speak if we are not listening. He longs to help, but He does not force His help on anyone. As people of the Indwelling, we must seek to know our Helper and to fellowship with Him deeply, until we know His voice and can continually stir up His mighty power that is available to help us in our times of need. We must be willing to wait patiently for His help.

The Life-Giving Spirit

One of the special privileges enjoyed by people of the Indwelling is described in Romans 8:11: the Holy Spirit quickens—gives life—to their mortal bodies.

"But if the Spirit of him who made Jesus come again from the dead is **in you**, he who made Christ Jesus come again from the dead will in the same way, **through his Spirit which is in you**, give life to your bodies which now are under the power of death" (BASIC ENGLISH).

"If the Spirit of God, who raised Jesus from death, ***lives in you***, then he who raised Christ from death will also ***give life to your mortal bodies by the presence of his Spirit in you***" (GNT).

The Spirit of the Person who raised Jesus from the dead dwells in you. Can you grasp this? *The Spirit who now lives in you is the same Spirit who raised Jesus Christ from the dead.* This is not just my opinion: it is what this verse and several others declare.

As we have established with The Truth Cycle, every *revelation* of Scripture has an *implication* and an *application*. What are the implications of having the same Spirit who resurrected Christ from the dead living in us? What are the possibilities contained in such an inheritance?

No matter what might be wrong with your body, if you are reading this you are still alive. Jesus was dead, yet after three days in the grave the Spirit of God quickened Him when God raised Him from the dead. Even during His earthly ministry, it was by the power of the Holy Spirit that Jesus raised Lazarus and others from the dead. Now that Spirit who raised Christ Himself from the dead can pour His almighty life into your mortal body and drive out every disease and weakness. Amen!

Concerning the two witnesses of God in Revelations 11, after they had been dead for three and half days, "***the spirit of life from God entered into them, and they stood upon their feet***; and great fear fell upon them which saw them" (Revelation 11:11 KJV).

The truth that spirits can impart life and physical strength to a person is taught clearly in the Bible. Consider the following:

- When God made man, it was the entrance of the spirit—the breath of life—into him that made man a living being (see Genesis 2:7). The entrance of this living breath was what gave life, strength, and mobility to an otherwise lifeless lump of clay!
- According to Proverbs 18:14, "The spirit of a man will sustain his infirmity; but a wounded spirit who can bear?" (KJV). A strong spirit can sustain a broken body for a long time, but a whole body cannot survive a broken spirit for a second.
- The working of the Spirit imparted physical strength to both Daniel and Ezekiel (Daniel 10:19; Ezekiel 2:2; 3:24).
- It was by the power of the Holy Spirit that the apostles did all the

astounding miracles found in the book of Acts, including raising the dead (Dorcas, Eutychus, etc.) and bringing healing to sick and broken bodies.

- The legion of demons in the demoniac imparted so much physical strength to him that no one could subdue him; he had so much power that even when chained hand and foot he broke the iron chains to pieces. He lived among the tombs and cut himself repeatedly with dirty stones, but he survived every infection and infestation—with little or nothing to eat! The legion of demons in him gave him power (see Mark 5:1-15).

- Seven sons of a certain Jewish chief priest learned a hard lesson when they commanded an evil spirit to come out of a man in the name of "Jesus, whom Paul preaches" (Acts 19:13). They were using a name they had no relationship with. "The evil spirit answered them, 'Jesus I know, and Paul I know about, but who are you?' Then the man who had the evil spirit jumped on them and overpowered them all. He gave them such a beating that they ran out of the house naked and bleeding" (Acts 19:15-16). How could one man so overmaster seven men as to have them run, naked and bleeding? It was the superhuman strength of one evil spirit working in him that gave him such power.

- The Spirit of God coming on Samson gave him superhuman power, enabling him to do humanly impossible things—like carrying a city gate on his shoulder up a hill or killing a thousand armed Philistines with a donkey's jawbone (see Judges 15:14-16; 16:1-3). Samson was an ordinary-looking person. It was not an extraordinary physique but the Spirit who came on him that gave him power. It is noteworthy that Samson was not *indwelt* by the Spirit: the Spirit only came *on* him from time to time. *That same Spirit that came mightily on Samson now resides permanently inside believers.* This is sober truth, and it has astounding implications. If the Spirit could do such mighty things in someone He came upon, He can certainly do more in those whom He indwells.

Why should it sound incredible that the Holy Spirit can impart life and strength to your body? He created that body in the first place. He is God; He is omnipotent, all powerful. Why can't He impart power to His own temple, your body, which is His own dwelling place? You will surely be "strengthened and reinforced with mighty power in the inner man by the [Holy] Spirit [Himself indwelling your innermost being and personality" (Ephesians 3:16 AMPC).

This same Spirit of life from God that raised Jesus from the dead now lives in you. You wouldn't be a child of God if He didn't dwell in you. Now that He is in you, rivers of His life will flow through your mortal body. He guarantees healing for your body and strength for all your days.

Eventually, when the time comes for us to leave earth, we shall be changed. Mortality will put on immortality, and death will be swallowed by life. This event is described in detail in 1 Corinthians 15:35–58, but is beyond the scope of our present study. However, *our final transformation into the likeness of our risen Lord will be the work of the indwelling Spirit!* Nothing new will enter believers when the trumpet sounds: it will be the manifestation of the indwelling One—in the twinkling of an eye and in the fullness of His blazing life—that accomplishes the transformation of our bodies to incorruptibility. The last trumpet will be the divine signal for this explosion of life that "will transform our lowly bodies so that they will be like His glorious body" (Philippians 3:21). Glory to God!

Rivers of Living Water

Jesus spoke of the Holy Spirit as rivers of living water flowing from the inmost depths of those who believe in Him. This is an amazing picture of the Indwelling: the river flows from deep within, indwelling and refreshing the believer and bringing blessing wherever it flows.

"Now on the last and most important day of the feast, Jesus stood and called out [in a loud voice], 'If anyone is thirsty, let him come to Me and drink! He who believes in Me [who adheres to, trusts in, and relies on Me], as the Scripture has said, "***From his innermost being will flow continually rivers of living water.***"' But He was speaking of the [Holy] Spirit, whom those who believed in Him [as Savior] were to receive afterward. The Spirit had not yet been given, because Jesus was not yet glorified (raised to honor)" (John 7:37–39 AMP).

Jesus has now been glorified. "Exalted to the right hand of God, he has received from the Father the promised Holy Spirit and has poured out what you now see and hear" (Acts 2:33). The promise of the Spirit's outpouring is no longer something that is to happen in the future. The promise has been fulfilled! You live in the day when the river is flowing. There is no excuse for thirst or dryness. The Holy Spirit has been poured out by the Father. And if you have been born of God, He indwells you.

All Rivers Are Not Equal

People of the Indwelling must, however, note that *not all rivers are equal.* The depth, breadth, length, and force of rivers vary greatly. Some rivers are like the seasonal wadis that abound in dry regions. They come alive during the rainy seasons but dry up shortly thereafter, leaving only a sandy or rocky riverbed where once there was water.

But some rivers—like the Nile, the Mississippi, the Yangtze, and the Amazon—flow deep and wide, long and strong. Their full and forceful waters traverse several states or countries and literally sustain the economies of the cities and nations through which they flow.

The Syrian general Naaman had to be reminded that all rivers are not equal. The Jordan, to which the prophet Elisha directed him to go and dip seven times, was not quite like the Abana and the Pharpar, rivers of Damascus. (Naaman's story is found in 2 Kings 5). The Jordan River was the place of destiny for him—the place where his leprosy (and pride!) would be permanently cured and his name become forever etched into Scripture.

What is the depth of the river of the Spirit flowing in you presently? How strong are the river currents? How long and wide does the river within you flow? Could this be all that God desires for your life?

Hunger for more of God's river! The Spirit of God longs to fill you more, possess you more, lead you more, teach you more, and manifest more of His gifts and power through you. The currents of the Spirit's river can be deeper, wider, stronger, and longer in your life. These mighty springs will pour through you to bless and nourish individuals, congregations, and nations. There will be life wherever the river flows.

"For I will pour out water on him who is thirsty, and streams on the dry ground; I will pour out My Spirit on your offspring and my blessing on your descendants" (Isaiah 44:3 AMP).

Wherever The River Flows . . .

God showed a river to Ezekiel—a picture of the river of His Spirit (see Ezekiel 47:1–12). It flowed from the very throne of God—from under the threshold.

> Going on eastward with a measuring line in his hand, the man ***measured*** a thousand cubits, and then led me through the water, and it was ankle-deep. Again he measured a thousand, and led me through the water, and it was knee-deep. Again he measured a thousand, and led me through the water, and it was waist-deep. Again he measured a thousand, and it was a river that I could not pass through, for the water had risen. It was deep enough to swim in, a river that could not be passed through (Ezekiel 47:3–5 ESV).

As the man measured a thousand cubits each time and brought Ezekiel through, the depth and width of the river continued to increase until it became a mighty river that could not be crossed without knowing how to swim. And wherever the river flowed, life came: "***Wherever the river flows, life will flourish***—great schools of fish—because the river is turning the salt sea into fresh water. Where the river flows, life abounds" (Ezekiel 47:9 MSG).

Life flourishes wherever the river of the Spirit flows. Life comes to individuals, churches, and whole denominations when the river flows into them—no matter how dead they were hitherto. That river that carries the very life of God flows deep within your spirit.

How I love the clause "He measured a thousand . . ." God doesn't just pick us up and toss us into the river. We could drown if we are brought to depths for which we aren't prepared. He *measures* according to the degree of our capacities and hunger. As He does, the water rises and keeps rising until it becomes a mighty river to swim in. Ask Him to measure another thousand in your walk with Him—to take you further and deeper in your experience of the river until the pure and holy currents of that river bear you in their living embrace. Ask Him to take you further and farther than you have ever been before.

There Is a River

"There is a river whose streams make glad the city of God, the holy place where the Most High dwells. **God is within her**, she will not fall; God will help her at break of day" (Psalm 46:4-5).

I believe this Scripture alludes to the river of the Holy Spirit. Even in the midst of the chaos described in Psalm 46—nations raging, mountains quaking, and earth being removed—the streams of that river, flowing deep within the believer, make glad the "city" of God. They are the source of unending joy that spring from the inmost beings of the people of the Indwelling. Even in the face of great challenges, the streams keep flowing, flooding the heart with joy unspeakable and peace that passes understanding.

Notice that the river flows in "the holy place where the Most High dwells." And because God is within her, indwelling her—His tabernacle, His temple—she will not be moved. She cannot fall while the Most High indwells her, with multiplied streams of the river flowing within. Her Helper is near; God will help her right early.

If you are filled with the Holy Spirit, remember that there is a river within you. It is one that cannot run dry, because its waters flow from the sanctuary. All you need to do is keep dredging the channels—to keep removing everything that hinders the flow—so that the river can flow clean and deep and wide from within your spirit. Streams of life, healing, peace, joy, power, grace, and love will pour out of that indwelling river and water your life, making you a blessing to many.

The Spirit of Profit

In God's kingdom dynamics, the Indwelling is the guarantee of profit for our Master. Only by the operation of His Spirit *from within our lives* can we bear abiding and abounding fruit for God.

We see this clearly illustrated in Paul's encounter with the slave girl at Philippi (Acts 16). The girl was possessed by a spirit—the spirit of Python, a demonic spirit that enabled her to tell fortunes. By doing this she brought much profit to her masters.

But Paul himself was also possessed by a Spirit—the Holy Spirit was resident in him. He was a beneficiary of the Indwelling. He also brought much profit to his Master—by the Spirit who was in him.

Now the slave girl and Paul could have gone on in their separate lives, each carrying what they carried within and each bringing profit to their master through the spirit that possessed them. But matters came to a head one day in Philippi. It was a clash of spirits: the spirit of divination in the girl was confronted by the Holy Spirit in Paul. Python lost his place in the girl and was cast out. But the casting out of the spirit was tantamount to the end of profit for the girl's owners. The spirit that brought them profit was gone. And "when her masters saw that ***their hope of profit was gone,*** they seized Paul and Silas and dragged them into the marketplace to the authorities" (Acts 16:19 NKJV). They were beaten and imprisoned, but God sent a powerful earthquake that shook the foundations of the prison and brought them out.

Whether in the kingdom of darkness or in the kingdom of light, the Indwelling is the secret of profit. There can be no profit of any sort for God in a life—the profit of holy, grateful, and fruitful living or of effective ministry—without the indwelling of the Holy Spirit.

"The manifestation of the Spirit is given to every man to ***profit*** withal" (1 Corinthians 12:7 KJV).

Pursue the full dimensions of the Indwelling. Study His working in the lives of people (historical and contemporary) who are, or were, greatly used by Him. Cultivate a continuous consciousness of the Indwelling. Walk in the Spirit and seek His gifts and power. Your profit will be obvious to all. The Indwelling will guarantee it.

Stirring Up the Spirit of Power

We have received a spirit of power, of love and sound mind: "For the Spirit which God has given us is not a spirit of cowardice, but one of power and of love and of sound judgement" (2 Timothy 1:7 WEYMOUTH). We have not received a spirit of timidity; therefore, fear will have no dominion over us. Fear has to do with punishment; however, Christ has become our righteousness, so we have confidence before the Father. The One who indwells us is not afraid of anything: there is nothing and no one He cannot handle. This should encourage you to face life boldly—in continual dependence on the greater One who is with you, for you, and within you. He will imbue you with self-control and pour His love for God and others into your heart.

As beneficiaries of the indwelling of the Spirit, we might expect every benefit of this indwelling to be released automatically. But that is not how God designed the victorious life to operate. It is as we consciously *walk* in the Spirit—cultivate the fellowship of the One who indwells us—that His virtues are released in our lives.

"That is why I would remind you to *stir up (rekindle the embers of, fan the flame of, and keep burning) the [gracious] gift of God, [the inner fire] that is in you . . .* For God did not give us a spirit of timidity (of cowardice, of craven and cringing and fawning fear), but [He has given us a spirit] of power and of love and of calm and well-balanced mind and discipline and self-control" (2 Timothy 1:6–7 AMPC).

Stir up the Spirit who dwells in you. He is a Spirit of power, of love, and of a sound mind. Fear and timidity shall have no dominion over you. As you stir the Spirit by spending time with Him in prayer, in the Word, in fellowship with other believers, and by following His leading, you will walk in the power and gifts of the indwelling Spirit.

"By this we come to know (perceive, recognize, and understand) that we abide (live and remain) in Him and He in us: because He has given (imparted) to us of His [Holy] Spirit" (1 John 4:13 AMPC).

As this study of the Indwelling is not merely academic, this could be a good time to pause and undertake a spiritual exercise—to stir up the mighty Spirit who resides within you. Fan the coals to flame again. Pray in the Spirit; pray in your understanding. Speak God's Word over your life and your circumstances. The Father has given you a Spirit of power, of love, and of a sound mind. Reject everything He didn't give you—fear, worry, depression, sicknesses, despair etc. Faith will rise in your heart as you stir up the Spirit!

PART THREE

To enjoy the fullest potentials of the Indwelling, it is crucial to keep in perpetual view the finished work of Jesus Christ, which made the Indwelling possible in the first place. As we gaze upon Him and what He did for us, we will walk in the reality of our redemption rights and privileges. This section of *The Indwelling* is provided towards accomplishing this objective.

Jesus Christ is himself . . . the property of every believer. Believer, canst thou estimate what thou hast gotten in Christ? . . . **All that Christ, as God and man, ever had, or can have, is thine**—*out of pure free favour, passed over to thee to be thine entailed property forever. Our blessed Jesus, as God, is omniscient, omnipresent, omnipotent. Will it not console you to know that all these great and glorious attributes are altogether yours? Has he power? That power is yours to support and strengthen you, to overcome your enemies, and to preserve you even to the end. Has he love? Well, there is not a drop of love in his heart which is not yours; you may dive into the immense ocean of his love, and you may say of it all, "It is mine." Hath he justice? It may seem a stern attribute, but even that is yours, for he will by his justice see to it that all which is promised to you in the covenant of grace shall be most certainly secured to you.*

And all that he has as perfect man is yours. As a perfect man the Father's delight was upon him. He stood accepted by the Most High. **O believer, God's acceptance of Christ is thine acceptance; for knowest thou not that the love which the Father set on a perfect Christ, he sets on thee now? For all that Christ did is thine.** *That perfect righteousness which Jesus wrought out, when through his stainless life he kept the law and made it honourable, is thine, and is imputed to thee.*

—Charles H. Spurgeon, *Morning and Evening,*
entry for January 3; *emphasis added*

10

With Open Faces

*A generation of believers has arisen who have never seen
the place where their price was paid.*

Beholding Calvary

God's call is sent to all and is clearly stated in His Word, the Bible. Oftentimes, however, God speaks to us individually to communicate His will for us with respect to our specific service to Him.

I remember very clearly what the Lord told me when He called me to preach the gospel. It was at a Christian program that was being held at the university campus where I was a medical student. I was in the middle section of the auditorium, towards the front. A renowned preacher had been invited and was ministering powerfully under the anointing of the Holy Spirit. As he did, many of the brethren began to fall down under the power of God! I had never experienced this up till this point in my life; I knew it was genuine but decided I was never going to fall just for falling's sake.

Suddenly, as I stood praying, I was overcome by God's power and fell down. While I was on the floor, I heard a voice speaking to me; the words were audible, distinct, and unmistakable: *"Behold Calvary; behold the day of My judgment. Thou shall be an evangel of My love."*

169

I cried and cried and cried. I prayed desperately, asking the Lord to reveal His finished work on Calvary, and the day of His judgment to me. I knew then that my life could never take the path of the regular medical doctor. My life purpose and direction were forever settled.

These were my marching orders; they are permanently etched into my spirit. In beholding Calvary I would see the finished work of Christ that purchased our redemption; in seeing the day of His judgment I would see the eternal destiny of the unsaved and develop a burning compassion for the lost. These two great forces would then propel me towards the fulfillment of His purpose in and through my life—to help others enter into their purchased redemption and ignite their hearts to win the lost.

Seven hundred years before Jesus was born, the prophet Isaiah described His suffering in unambiguous detail, and the role that *beholding* Him would play for those who will enjoy the benefits of His atoning sacrifice.

The Lord's Suffering Servant

"See, my servant will prosper; he will be highly exalted. But many were amazed when they saw him. His face was so disfigured he seemed hardly human, and from his appearance, one would scarcely know he was a man. And he will startle many nations. Kings will stand speechless in his presence. For they will see what they had not been told; they will understand what they had not heard about" (Isaiah 52:13–15 NLT).

The prophecy of the Suffering Servant actually begins in Isaiah 52, as shown in the verses above. Isaiah's vision of the Servant continues in chapter 53:1–6:

Who has believed our report? And to whom has the arm of the Lord been revealed? For He shall grow up before Him as a tender plant, and as a root out of dry ground. He has no form or comeliness; and when we see Him, there is no beauty that we should desire Him. He is despised and rejected by men, a Man of sorrows and acquainted with grief. And ***we hid, as it were, our faces from Him***; He was despised, and ***we did not esteem Him***. Surely He has borne our griefs and carried our sorrows; yet we esteemed Him stricken, smitten by God, and afflicted. But He was wounded for our transgressions, He was bruised for our iniquities; the chastisement for our peace was upon Him, and by His stripes we are healed. All we like sheep have gone astray; we have turned, every one, to his own way; and the Lord has laid on Him the iniquity of us all. (NKJV)

In these verses (and others in Isaiah 53), we see how God was at work in Christ, effecting redemption for lost and oppressed humanity. The master plan of redemption was being played out as Jesus Christ became the atoning sacrifice for our sins, sicknesses, and sorrows. But the response of the beneficiaries of God's great redemptive work was and is astounding. The very people for whom God took on flesh and paid the ultimate sacrifice could not see what God was doing. And their totally inappropriate response ensured that they missed out on the benefits of the finished work of Christ.

The Response

The prophetic utterance of the response of the people as the Suffering Servant stood in our place is intertwined with the things the Servant experienced.

- As He bore our sorrows and griefs, carried our sicknesses and pains, and was despised, *we esteemed Him not*.
- "His face was so disfigured he seemed hardly human, and from his appearance, one would scarcely know he was a man." But our response was to conclude that *there was no beauty about Him that we should desire Him*.
- The Man of Sorrows was acquainted with griefs not His own, because the sins, sicknesses, and pains He bore were ours. Yet instead of gazing in wonder and gratitude at Him as He took our curses, *we*

hid, as it were, our faces from Him—We turned our backs on him and looked the other way (see NKJV, NLT).

• It was our weaknesses he carried; it was our sorrows that weighed him down. *And we thought his troubles were a punishment from God, a punishment for his own sins!*

Unclaimed Benefits of Redemption

What Isaiah prophesied centuries earlier was exactly what was done to the Suffering Servant. And this was why they missed out on the benefits of redemption.

There are things that belong to us because we belong to Christ. But the vast majority of us live beneath our covenant redemption benefits— like those who live in penury, unaware of millions of dollars assigned to their names in unclaimed dividends accounts. How it must grieve Christ to see His people bearing the griefs and sorrows He already bore with finality on our behalf. Why should we carry what Christ has already carried for us? Why should we be defeated by what He already defeated? And why should we not have comprehensive shalom—total wholeness and peace—after He took the chastisement to bring us peace?

If we are to maximize Calvary and walk in our full redemptive rights and privileges, we cannot have the same attitude as those who saw no beauty in Him and thus despised and rejected Him.

We Did Not Esteem Him

"He was despised, and we did not appreciate His worth or esteem Him" (Isaiah 53:3b AMP). To esteem is "to prize; to set a high value on; to regard with reverence, respect or friendship" (Webster). While the Servant was suffering in our place, Isaiah emphatically declared that *we esteemed Him not.* The Servant didn't amount to much in the eyes of the people as He hung on the Cross. The record of His crucifixion in the

Gospels is filled with the mockeries of those present. No wonder they devalued and sold Him for 30 pieces of silver (see Matthew 27:9-10). That was how much He was worth in their eyes.

If those of us who are now offered the full redemption Jesus Christ purchased repeat the same mistake as those who witnessed His suffering, how can we possibly enjoy the benefits of redemption? How can we benefit from His finished work if we do not esteem His Cross as worthy of our focused gaze, meditation, and highest sacrifice?

There Was No Beauty about Him That We Should Desire Him

How beautiful is the Savior in our eyes? Our standards for measuring beauty are warped and twisted from true reality. The fathers in this pilgrim way saw the beauty of the Man of Calvary. Even in His bruised and battered state, tears would flow as they gazed at the greatest wonder in the universe—God suffering for the sins of His creatures. And as they were enraptured in His immeasurable loveliness, joy unspeakable and peace indescribable flooded their souls. Healing virtue poured from the Cross to their spirits and bodies, and the assurance of His presence blanketed them with grace. Songs such as "When I Survey The Wondrous Cross," "Man of Sorrows," and "Amazing Grace" testify to their persistent gaze on Calvary. They sang songs such as "I Stand Amazed," written by Charles H. Gabriel:

> I stand amazed in the presence
> of Jesus the Nazarene,
> and wonder how he could love me,
> a sinner, condemned, unclean.
>
> *How marvelous! How wonderful!*
> *And my song shall ever be:*
> *How marvelous! How wonderful*
> *is my Savior's love for me!*

For me it was in the garden
he prayed: "Not my will, but thine."
He had no tears for his own griefs,
but sweat-drops of blood for mine.

In pity angels beheld him,
and came from the world of light
to comfort him in the sorrows
he bore for my soul that night.

He took my sins and my sorrows,
he made them his very own;
he bore the burden to Calvary,
and suffered and died alone.

When with the ransomed in glory
his face I at last shall see,
'twill be my joy through the ages
to sing of his love for me.

Such were the songs and confessions of our forebears in the faith. They wondered ceaselessly at the Cross of Christ and basked in the glorious redemption He purchased. But a generation of believers has now arisen who have never seen the place where their price was paid. These days, the Cross doesn't mean much to the average Christian—or even preacher. Instead of beholding His beauty, we are attracted and mesmerized by fleeting fancies and vanities. A lost world enchants us with its fading beauty.

David, a man after God's heart, declared in verse four of the 27th psalm, "One thing have I asked of the Lord, that will I seek, inquire for, and [insistently] require: that I may dwell in the house of the Lord [in His presence] all the days of my life, *to behold and gaze upon the beauty [the sweet attractiveness and the delightful loveliness] of the Lord* and to meditate, consider, and inquire in His temple" (AMPC).

Do we desire Him? Do our hearts and flesh cry out for our risen Lord? What are the dominant desires of our hearts? Our desires show up in our preaching and praying. Out of the abundance of our hearts flow diverse revelations and prayer requests, primarily focused on fulfilling our needs and wants.

Those who will enjoy the full benefits of redemption will be those who are continually captivated by His beauty.

> Oh Lord, You're beautiful
> Your face is all I seek
> For when Your eyes are on this child
> Your grace abounds to me.
>
> —Keith Green

We Hid Our Faces . . .

Of all the things that God's people did as the Savior paid our price, I believe this, more than any other, made it impossible to walk in the fullness of redemption rights and privileges. Isaiah had proclaimed a few chapters earlier (Isaiah 45:22), "***Look to Me***, and be saved, all you ends of the earth! For I am God, and there is no other."

Comprehensive salvation, which includes forgiveness of sins, healing for our bodies, and deliverance from the oppression of the enemy, requires that we *look* at the Savior. Looking in this sense is not a fleeting or occasional glance but a continuous gaze on the Master. "Those who look to him are radiant; their faces are never covered with shame" (Psalm 34:5). *Saving virtue is released when our faces are towards His face*: in this face-to-Face communion, there is a flow of divine power that brings total deliverance.

Serpent on the Pole

For their healing and deliverance from the lethal affliction of the fiery serpents, God instructed Moses, "'Make a snake and put it up on a pole; ***anyone who is bitten can look at it*** and live.' So Moses made a bronze snake and put it up on a pole. Then when anyone was bitten by a snake *and looked at the bronze snake*, they lived" (Numbers 21:8-9).

If they looked anywhere else other than at the bronze serpent on the pole, they died. If they looked at their wounds, they died. If they looked at one another, they died. If they focused on the serpent that bit them and pursued and killed it, they still died. Even if they looked at Moses, they died! Life and healing lay in the upward look at the serpent on the pole. They looked and lived.

Amazingly, this bronze serpent on the pole that God used to bring healing to the Israelites in the wilderness typified Christ. It was a foreshadowing of how Jesus would be lifted on the Cross when He took upon Himself our curses. If there is healing in the type—the shadow—then there must be healing in the reality which that shadow represents. If they looked on a bronze serpent and were healed, we can certainly expect to be healed as we look on Christ. The shadow cannot be more powerful or beneficial than the reality.

The Lord Jesus Himself declared, "Just as Moses lifted up the serpent in the desert [on a pole], so must [so it is necessary that] the Son of Man be lifted up [on the cross], in order that everyone who *believes* in Him [who cleaves to Him, trusts Him, and relies on Him] may not perish, but have eternal life and [actually] live forever!" (John 3:14-15 AMPC).

Note that *believing* in Christ is the direct equivalent of the Israelites' *look* at the serpent on the pole. *To look is to believe.* Those who looked at the serpent on the pole did that because they believed what God had told Moses—i.e., that they would be healed if they looked. Those who believe in Christ do so because they look to what He did on the Cross as their hope of salvation.

Total Redemption

There are those who wonder (or even deny outright) that the finished work of Christ included both forgiveness of sins and healing for all. The truth is that Jesus took upon Himself both our sins and our sicknesses. Isaiah declared emphatically that He *took* our infirmities and *carried* our diseases and that by His stripes we have been healed (see Isaiah 53:4-6). The Holy Spirit confirmed this through Matthew many years later: "When evening came, many who were demon-possessed were brought to [Jesus], and he drove out the spirits with a word and healed all the sick. This was to fulfill what was spoken through the prophet Isaiah: *"He Himself took our infirmities and bore our sicknesses."* (Matthew 8:16-17 NKJV).

Any sacrifice that can procure eternal life must, by that very fact, be capable of imparting and extending physical life. How can anyone who cannot keep a person alive for 80 years claim he can confer eternal life? Someone might argue that eternal life is for the soul, but anything or anyone that can heal the soul must be able to heal the body. Saving or healing the soul is far more difficult, after all, than healing the body. The Christ who purchased salvation also abolished death and brought life and immortality to light through the gospel (see 2 Timothy 1:10). He could not have had the ability to impart immortality if He had been unable to handle mortality. To bring immortality is far more difficult than to heal mortality! The same sacrifice that purchased eternal life for us also has power to heal our physical bodies and impart strength to us for doing God's will on earth. Amen.

From the foregoing, we see the shocking disservice that those who *hid their faces* from the Suffering Servant did to themselves. Instead of gazing at the Son as He became accursed with our curse—like the bronze serpent on the pole—they turned their faces away! How Isaiah must have wondered at this strange response. Hide your face from the serpent on the pole? How would you be healed? From where else could healing virtue flow to your mortal wounds?

The same thing that caused humanity to wander from God in the first place came back to cheat the people out of redemption's privileges when deliverance finally came. "All we, like sheep, have gone astray, each of us has turned to our own way," lamented the prophet in Isaiah 53:6. After turning their own way, they turned their backs on Him and hid their faces from Him.

Hid their faces from *what*?

They hid their faces from the greatest event in the history of the universe. The only Son of the King of the universe was dying as a sacrifice on a hill in their neighborhood, and they hid their faces! Something that had never happened since the foundation of the world (and would never be repeated for all eternity) was happening in their lifetime, and their response was to hide their faces.

They hid their faces from witnessing the despoiling of principalities and powers and the total and irrevocable defeat of the devil. It was at that Cross that Jesus disarmed principalities and powers and crushed the head of the serpent. Satan was present at the Cross, and there Jesus bruised the enemy's head! [Satan's head could not have been bruised in absentia!]. Since they "hid their faces" and didn't see where Jesus defeated the devil and his cohorts, the enemy Jesus overcame would continue to despoil and devastate those who turned away from the Savior.

They hid their faces and turned away when the Master uttered the three defining words of full redemption: *It is finished!* Since they didn't see when the Master finished what was finishing them, the adversary Christ finished could continue to work on finishing them.

They hid their faces on the day that God laid down His life for the redemption of man.

All of heaven was watching the same event they turned away from. The Father God had His eyes on Calvary's hill. Where else could a father sacrificing his son look? Where was Abraham looking when Isaac was on the altar except at the altar? The Father had consigned His only begotten Son on the altar for man's redemption, and His eyes were on that altar! Abraham had been halted by the voice from heaven even as he was about to bring the knife plunging into the heart of his beloved son, but there was no substitute on the day God's own Son willingly gave Himself up on the altar! *God endured the agony from which He had spared Abraham*—only it was infinitely worse. His eyes were on that Cross when the beneficiaries of His supreme gift turned away and despised the very sacrifice that would procure their redemption.

The Father has never removed His eyes from Calvary's Cross. It's an eternal reference point for Him, and it must become ours. As far as God is concerned, Calvary is not merely a historical event. To us who live in time and speak of the past, the present, and the future, the crucifixion of Christ is a past event that happened about 2,000 years ago on a hill outside Jerusalem. We look *back* to it, but God is not a human being; He doesn't look back to anything: everything lies before Him. He inhabits eternity; He fills the eternal past, time past, the present, future time, and the eternal future with His presence, *simultaneously*. God is as much in the past as He is in the present; He is as much in the past as He is in the future. On this blessed day, He sees the creation of the world, the fall in the garden, the death of Christ on the Cross, His resurrection, and the last day, not chronologically along a timeline but all at the same time. He doesn't see sequentially as time-bound humans do, but simultaneously. As we come to Him through Christ, He sees Christ taking our place as our substitute—He sees everything together. The Father has never removed His eyes from the Cross where His Son purchased redemption. We must look where He is looking.

The angels watched in amazement. It is our conviction that the total attention of all residents of heaven (if they can behold events on earth) was riveted on the Cross the day Jesus died. Even the unbroken attention of the hordes of hell was on that Cross, and the Man on it. But the human beings who were to benefit from that supreme sacrifice hid their faces and turned away!

What were they looking at? Where are we looking?

They Shall Look on Him Whom They Pierced

The Jews hid their faces from the Messiah, but one day they will look on the One they pierced. They will gaze on the One they once rejected and esteem the One they once despised. They will mourn deeply and grieve bitterly as they look on the One they long neglected and ignored—the One who bore their griefs and carried their sorrows.

In Zechariah 12:10—13:1, we read how God will intervene for the salvation of Israel in the last days:

> "And I will pour out on the house of David and the inhabitants of Jerusalem a spirit of grace and supplication. ***They will look on me, the one they have pierced,*** and ***they will mourn for him as one mourns for an only child, and grieve bitterly for him as one grieves for a firstborn son***. On that day the weeping

in Jerusalem will be . . . great. . . . The land will mourn, each clan by itself, with their wives by themselves. . . . *On that day a fountain will be opened to the house of David and the inhabitants of Jerusalem, to cleanse them from sin and impurity*".

According to this amazing prophecy, Israel will eventually come face-to-face with that One from whom they once hid their faces. They will look on the Suffering Servant: they will see the place where redemption was purchased and will mourn and grieve that it took thousands of years for them to see it. Oh, the needless pains and anguish of the nation that once spurned the Messiah!

As they begin to look on the One they pierced, "On that day *a fountain will be opened* to the house of David and the inhabitants of Jerusalem, to cleanse them from sin and impurity" (Zechariah 13:1). This would be the direct equivalent of their fathers looking at the bronze serpent on the pole that Moses had lifted up in the wilderness. Now, as a repentant nation gazes at the One they pierced, they too will look and live. The fountain of the redeeming blood that flowed on Calvary will be opened to God's people, and salvation will come. The fountain will bring redemption, healing, and shalom to Israel.

There is a fountain that opens to all who look on the One who was pierced. The great law of the fountain is that it opens only when you look; if you keep looking, it keeps opening and springing forth. The fountain that will open to Israel on that day when they eventually look at Him whom they had pierced is already open to those of us who now look to Him in faith. It is a fountain of all the benefits of our full redemption. It is a fountain of all the covenant blessings of the blood of the Lamb. It is a fountain of life and power, flowing full and free from the Cross, where the Savior crushed the head of the serpent and despoiled all principalities and powers. An inexhaustible fountain filled with all the blessed consequences of Calvary pours its endless blessings to those who gaze with open faces on the One who was wounded for their transgressions and bruised for their iniquities—by whose stripes they have been healed. They look to Him and are radiant, and their faces will never be ashamed (see Psalm 34:5).

Through the prophet Isaiah, God had told Israel and all the nations of the earth to *look to Him* and be saved. There is no other way to enter into and enjoy the great privileges of redemption than looking at Him who was lifted up, that He may draw all to Himself—and to abundant life.

With Open Faces

In the light of the preceding revelation, we see the wonder of 2 Corinthians 3:18: "But we all, ***with open face*** beholding as in a glass the glory of the Lord, are changed into the same image from glory to glory, even as by the Spirit of the Lord" (KJV).

Isaiah prophesied how "we hid, as it were, our faces from Him." But a new reality beckons those of us who cherish Him and the glorious redemption He purchased on our behalf. We desire Him. We gaze on Him with unveiled faces. Where else should we look? Our hearts have been captivated by His beauty. All else that may have seemed glorious to us has lost its attraction—by virtue of the glory that excels! Our driving desire is to know Him and to be transfigured into His likeness. We want to dwell in His presence and behold His beauty. And as we do so, we ourselves are being transfigured into His likeness. His great redemption works in us, not only to forgive our sins and heal us but to change us from one degree of glory to another, until we reach the full measure of the stature of Christ Himself.

Unlike those Isaiah spoke about, we *esteem* Him. We esteem what He did for us on the Cross. We esteem Him worthy of our trust, our worship, our all. We agree wholeheartedly with Isaac Watts:

> Were the whole realm of nature mine;
> That were an offering far too small.
> Love so amazing, so divine;
> Demands my soul, my life, my all.

From One Degree of Glory to Another

A closer look at 2 Corinthians 3:18 reveals an amazing truth: the transformation that comes from gazing at our crucified, risen, exalted Lord with open faces is *from one degree of glory to another*: "And all of us, as with unveiled face, [because we] continued to behold [in the Word of God] as in a mirror the glory of the Lord, are constantly being transfigured into His very own image in ever increasing splendor and *from one degree of glory to another*; [for this comes] from the Lord [Who is] the Spirit" (AMPC) .

You see, there are degrees of glory—all glory is not on the same level. The glory of the Creator is not on the same level as the glory of creatures. The best way to understand this is to view glory as an unending ladder with different rungs. The rungs of a ladder are at different levels. God's glory is at the infinite top of the ladder.

"There are also heavenly bodies [sun, moon and stars] and earthly bodies [humans, animals, and plants], but the glory and beauty of the heavenly is one kind, and the glory of the earthly is another. There is a glory and beauty of the sun, another glory of the moon, and yet another [distinctive] glory of the stars; and *one star differs from another in glory and brilliance*" (1 Corinthians 15:40-41 AMP).

According to this Scripture, there is a vast difference in the glory inherent in, and emanating from, the stars: all stars are glorious, but they are not all at the same level of glory—one star differs from another star in glory. Believers are compared to stars (see Daniel 12:3-4). Thus, while all believers have access to the fullness of glory available in Christ, they do not all function at the same level of glory. The reason is that on this side of eternity they can change their levels of glory only by transformation into Christ's likeness. This is why the possibilities they enjoy are vastly different: their experience corresponds to their degree of transformation into His likeness.

Something happens when we begin to gaze on the Master, and on the place where our price was paid: we begin to change in terms of degree. As we behold Him in the mirror of His Word, we go from lower to higher degrees of glory. It's a journey of ever-increasing splendor, ultimately culminating in our being transformed *into the very likeness of our Lord*.

The Truth Cycle we introduced at the beginning of this book represents the process of beholding Him in the mirror of His Word (numbers 1 to 6, as discussed in the book's introduction). First we receive His Word (information). Then we gaze on Him as we carefully observe the Word. Insights and revelations emerge, each with huge implications and applications to our lives. As we apply the Word thus received, we are transformed.

Once applied, the Word never leaves a person at the same level. It produces transformation, which opens an upward and outward spiral, and catapults the individual to a different level from where they started (see illustration at Introduction). Thus, as we continue to look at the mirror of the Word, we see new truths (information) at a higher level, from which we then observe and receive further revelations. The cycle repeats, but at a higher level. It continues to spiral upward, as shown in the introduction, moving us from one degree of glory to another.

Here is an undeniable fact: *as levels and degrees of glory change, possibilities change.* The things that are impossible at one degree are possible, normal, or even easy at a higher degree. The diagram below illustrates the relationship between our transformation and the possibilities we experience in Christ.

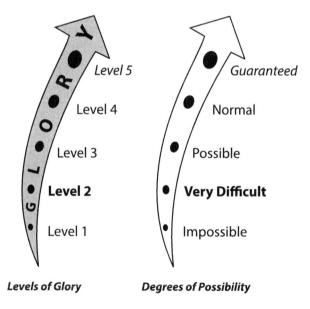

Levels of Glory   **Degrees of Possibility**

From the illustration above, we see that, as degrees (or levels) of glory change, possibilities also change. *Degrees of possibilities are directly proportional to degrees of glory.* As degrees of glory change, things that seemed *impossible* gradually begin to seem *very difficult*, but possible. Then they become *possible*, then *normal*, and finally *guaranteed*. Can you locate yourself on this scale? At what level of glory are you operating?

To understand the overwhelming authority of the Lord Jesus Christ, picture Him at the peak of this endless ladder of glory. He is the fullness of the Father's glory—the One in whom we are ascending in glory. What can be impossible to Him?

You can now see how people can be in Christ and yet their experience of His love, power and presence vary greatly. What seems impossible to someone at level 1 is quite normal and to be expected at level 4. But then there are those who have grown in their walk with the Lord, who have tasted the goodness of God's Word and the powers of the age to come. They know that God's promises are not merely possible; they are guaranteed. In their renewed minds, with the help of the omnipotent Creator of heaven and earth, all things are not just possible but guaranteed. They *know* that God cannot fail and that no word from God shall be void of power for fulfillment. By applying the Word and changing degrees, they've gone from simply believing to *knowing* the absolute dependability of God's Word and His unfailing faithfulness. They have arrived at something the Bible calls "the full assurance of faith"—the "unqualified assurance and absolute conviction engendered by faith" (Hebrews 10:22 NKJV, AMPC).

This principle (of increasing degrees leading to increasing possibilities) is true for all facets of life, both spiritual and temporal.

Academic degrees have an impact on the types of problems you can solve, and the ease with which you can do so. A university professor with a bachelors, masters, and PhD degree can solve problems in a given field that a high school graduate cannot. Possibilities change as degrees change. But if the high school graduate will focus on changing degrees, he may one day be like his professor!

Degrees of finances determine purchasing power and clout in the marketplace: all wealth is not at the same level. Salaries of federal government workers are different from those of oil company workers, but the wealth of the richest persons in the world is definitely of a different degree. This degree of wealth confers possibilities that the poor and middle class know nothing about.

Similarly, there are degrees of temperature. Degrees of temperature determine what the heat can cook, dissolve, or melt: the higher the temperature (the hotter the fire or heat), the greater the possibilities.

Yet again, degrees of information confer greater access and possibilities to those who possess them. This explains why everyone wants to know—before everyone else, and more than anyone else. This has great implications in our information age.

As surely as there are academic degrees, there are also *spiritual* degrees—in both the kingdom of light and the kingdom of darkness (see 1 Timothy 3:13 KJV). While many study and sacrifice to acquire academic degrees, they pay no attention to the procurement of higher levels of spiritual degrees. While academic degrees are desirable, spiritual degrees are superior to them. This was why Peter and John could solve a problem (as in raising the crippled man at the gate called Beautiful) that left chief priests with theological degrees stupefied. It is why a *medical* doctor can go to a *native* doctor in search of protection or solutions to other life issues. And it is why an anointed but illiterate preacher can bring healing to multitudes that medical doctors have deemed incurable. The good news is that, for believers in Christ, academic and spiritual degrees are not mutually exclusive: believers can grow in both!

Higher spiritual degrees guarantee higher levels of possibilities, access, vision, power, and manifestations. As you transition from one degree of glory to another, the things that were impossible to you at lower degrees of glory become normal at higher levels. The things that once held you bound or stood like insurmountable mountains crumble as you ascend the ladders of glory. This transformation comes as we gaze upon the Lord *with open faces*—as we continually behold Him in the mirror of His Word and allow His Spirit to work in us.

The level of possibilities you will enjoy in Christ is directly proportional to your degree of transformation into His likeness. The infinite possibilities in Christ are accessible only as you go from one degree of glory to another.

It is important to note that our transformation into Christlikeness is by degrees, not by a sudden leap unto perfection. Our coming into Christ was a *translation*: God translated us out of the kingdom of darkness into the kingdom of His dear Son (see Colossians 1:13). But our growth in Christ is by *transformation*—from one degree of glory to another. So keep changing by degrees—keep increasing in the degrees of peace, grace, love, patience, knowledge, power, humility, self-control, and other virtues of Christ that you manifest.

Our transformation is a function of the Indwelling. It comes by the Spirit's work within us (see 2 Corinthians 3:18). Thus the Indwelling guarantees our metamorphosis into Christlikeness. This is why insight into the operations of the Indwelling is so crucial.

There Is a Place

There is a place in God—and it belongs to the believer—where sin loses its attraction and no longer rules over the body. At this place of grace, the believer is established in righteousness and is far from the tyranny of sin and the oppression of the enemy.

There is a place where peace is normal in the midst of storms. There is a place in God where you can enjoy peace that passes all understanding, even in the midst of the greatest battles and turmoil of life.

There is a place where miracles are normal, where the supernatural is a constant.

There is a place where the manifestations of the gifts of the Spirit are abundant, not scarce—regular, not occasional. At this place, the believer flows continuously with God's awesome river; she is led by the indwelling Spirit, bears His fruit, and channels His power. Words of wisdom, prophecy, supernatural revelations, gifts of healing, and the working of miracles abound here. They are not just some promises in the Bible; they become present realities, bringing blessing to many.

There is a place where faith becomes your new default setting, and doubt is strange. At this place in God, it is easy to believe that the faithful One will keep His word. It is impossible for Him to fail. You pass from guesswork to confidence—to the full assurance of faith. You know that God is not a man, that He should lie. He can be depended upon. You count Him faithful who has promised.

There is a place where prayer is not a shot in the dark—a last resort of a desperate soul. Answers to prayer are *guaranteed* at this level of glory. You understand how Jesus could pray the way He did in front of the cave that held the rotting body of Lazarus: "Father*, I thank You that You have heard Me. I knew that You always hear* Me and listen to Me; but I have said this because of the people standing around, so that they may believe that You have sent Me [and that You have made Me Your representative]" (John 11:41–42 AMP).

Jesus wasn't guessing. He wasn't hoping that the Father would hear Him. He knew. And thus with unwavering certainty He shouted, "Lazarus, come forth!" And Lazarus did come forth—after four days in the grave! But Jesus never intended to enjoy this privileged assurance of unfailing answers from the Father all alone. He wanted it to be the heritage of every member of the family. The experience of those who walked with Him shows that they also enjoyed this unshakable confidence in the Father. I invite you to marvel at the audacity of the Apostle John's declaration below:

"And this is the confidence (the assurance, the privilege of boldness) which we have in Him: *[we are sure] that if we ask anything (make any request) according to His will (in agreement with His own plan), He listens to and hears us.* And if (since) we [positively] know that He listens to us in whatever we ask, *we also know [with settled and absolute knowledge] that we have [granted us as our present possessions] the requests made of Him*" (1 John 5:14–15 AMPC).

John speaks exactly like the Master. He was not guessing about prayer. He knew with settled and absolute knowledge that whatever he asked that was in line with the revealed will of God would be granted. He encouraged the brethren to come to the place where this would be their normal lifestyle.

We wonder why people don't pray. The answer is surprisingly simple. They would pray *if they were sure* God would answer. Who would pass over a guarantee that he or she could get *whatever* they requested? Prayer would be the most desirable activity if God's people were as sure of answers as the early disciples were. The sad root of prayerlessness is unbelief.

There is a place where the truths of Scripture are not just some nice advice from a quaint, good book but the very wisdom of God for the believer, with answers for everything in life.

Now, how do we get to such a place in God? By changing degrees! As you go from one degree of glory to another, things that were hitherto impossible become possible, then normal, then guaranteed. And this change from one degree of glory to another is made possible by the indwelling Spirit working in us and transforming us into the very likeness of the Lord Jesus Christ – as we gaze on Him with open faces.

At what degree of glory do you wish to operate in life? Are you satisfied with your present degree?

There is more in God! But much now depends on our engaging the process that births transformation. I encourage you to make a sacred and irrevocable decision that no day will pass without your changing degrees. We must aspire to the fullest expressions of our redemption privileges.

Partakers of the Inheritance

". . . giving thanks to the Father who has **qualified you** to share in the inheritance of his holy people in the kingdom of light. For he has rescued us from the dominion of darkness and brought us into the kingdom of the Son he loves, in whom we have redemption, the forgiveness of sins" (Colossians 1:12–14).

The Father has made us fit—*qualified* us—to take our portion of what belongs to us because we belong to Christ. He has *delivered* us. He has translated, transplanted, and conveyed us into a kingdom radically different from where we were before. Note the past tense in these verses: they do not speak of things God will do but of things He has done already. Now He invites you to take your portion of the inheritance He has purchased with His own blood.

But this will not work automatically. If you would take your part of the purchased inheritance, then take your eyes from your wounds, from the serpents on the ground—and, yes, from the Moseses of our time—and turn your face to our own "serpent on the pole." Turn your face to the Cross, to the place where our price was paid. See the sinless hanging there in the sinners' stead.

Gaze upon the stripes that purchased your healing. He took the chastisement of our peace, but you will remain harassed and restless *until you see where He did it.* And if you keep your eyes on Him who bore our sicknesses and carried our pains, healing virtue will flow. The fountain will be opened to you.

If you desire that Calvary and its redemptive rights and privileges would be yours to the fullest, rip off every veil and distraction and begin to esteem the One who stood in your place. Our gaze on Him must be continuous, not sporadic, and must be with open, unveiled faces—with no masks or cover-ups. Only then can we experience the transformation He promises.

Moses told Pharaoh that "not a hoof" of all that belonged to the Israelites would be left in Egypt; everyone and everything would be leaving the house of bondage (see Exodus 10:26). What was Moses going to do with hooves? Was he going to eat the shoe of a cow? I don't believe so. The point he was advocating was a "heartitude"—an attitude of the heart—that refused to let the enemy keep anything that belonged to Israel.

If you desire that not a hoof of all that Jesus purchased for you will be left for the devil, you must turn your face toward the price Jesus paid for you. Keep looking in the mirror of His Word, and keep Isaiah 53:5 before your eyes: "But He was pierced for our transgressions, he was crushed for our iniquities; the punishment that brought us peace was on him, and by his wounds we are healed." Like the Israelites, you will look and live. If they looked at a bronze serpent on a pole and healing flowed to them, think what will happen if you gaze continually upon the Son of God lifted up on the Cross, raised from the dead and exalted far above the heavens. And keep in mind—as we have already established in *The Indwelling*—that the Son, the Lord Jesus Christ, now lives in you—Christ *in* you, the hope of glory.

Arise and take your journey to the place where you belong because you belong to Christ. Your translation is not a myth, but sober reality.

Take your share of the inheritance that belongs to God's people in the kingdom of light. Maximize your redemptive benefits, rights, and privileges, and become God's channel of blessing to a world in need.

> *"Bless the Lord, O my soul, And **forget not all His benefits**:*
> *Who forgives **all** your iniquities, Who heals **all** your diseases, who*
> *redeems your life from destruction, Who crowns you with loving-*
> *kindness and tender mercies, Who satisfies your mouth with good*
> *things, So that your youth is renewed like the eagle's."*
> Psalm 103:2–5 NKJV

11

The Sense Is in the Tense

My friend Chris Akosa has a funny way of explaining the power of the Holy Spirit and the Name of Jesus. He says, "If you are full of the Holy Spirit and you say to a demon, 'Came out, in Jesus' Name!' the demon will not ask you to correct your grammar before coming out! The power of God will drive it out."

Chris is right, of course: the demon will certainly obey, but it would have been better for the anointed to also learn the rules of grammar. Communicating with human beings is very different from casting out demons.

Tenses are important. Most languages have them in one form or another. Without them, it will be difficult to communicate accurately. Misunderstanding will be rife. It will be impossible to determine if the communication is with respect to the past, the present, or the future—or whether the event has been completed or is ongoing.

In English grammar, a tense is defined as "a set of forms taken by a verb to indicate the time (and sometimes also the continuance or completeness) of the action in relation to the time of the utterance."[13]

Some experts claim that there are as many as 12 tenses in the English language, while others just emphasize the major three: past, present, and future.

Tenses are not just important in human-to-human communication; they are also vital in divine-to-human communication. What this means is that if we do not pay attention to the tenses in which God

THE INDWELLING

speaks to us, there is no way we can understand what He says. We will hear or read His word, but we will not be on the same page.

True Christianity is not first of all a call to *do* something but an invitation to rest on something that has been *done*. Thus, if we don't get into the same tense with God, the Christian life will be a continual struggle to do something we are not called to do—something that has already been done for us by Christ Jesus.

"What Is Written? How Do You Read It?"

We need to read the Bible correctly, if we are to understand it and benefit from its amazing truths and promises. We must pay attention to the tenses in God's Word—in whatever language we read it. Otherwise, we run the risk of placing past events in the future, present events in the past or future, or future events in the present.

"On one occasion an expert in the law stood up to test Jesus. 'Teacher,' he asked, 'what must I do to inherit eternal life?' '**What is written** in the Law?' he replied. '**How do you read it**?'" (Luke 10:25-26).

This exchange between Jesus and the expert in the Law gives some insight into how Jesus viewed the Scriptures. He first asked the expert *what was written* and then sought to know *how he read it.* In the New American Standard Bible, Jesus is said to have asked him, "What is written in the Law? **How does it read to you?**"

You see, what is written is already written, and it will stand forever. But how we read what is written and how it reads to us determine whether or not we understand it and what we will get out of it.

Take Galatians 3:16 for instance: "The promises were spoken to Abraham and to his seed." The Scripture does not say "and to seeds," meaning many people, but "and to your seed," meaning one person: Christ.' This is an example of how adding a single letter *s* can change the whole meaning and intent of Scripture. If we read 'seeds' (plural) instead of 'seed' (singular) in this verse of Scripture, we end up with a totally different meaning than God intended to communicate to us. This is exactly what happens if we ignore the tenses in Scripture and read future tense where the Word put a past tense.

What is written and how you read it are two very different things. It is possible to read something that is written and have an understanding completely different from what the author intended. We can approach what is written with preconceived ideas and be oblivious to plainly stated truths.

We need to get into the same tense with God. *The sense of what God says is in the tense!*

If we push into the future that which God has put in the past, we will not experience the truth in that area.

- We will continue to carry the guilt and condemnation over sins that God already forgave when we asked Him to.
- We will be waiting on God to do something He has clearly told us in His word He has done already.
- We will keep hoping that something will happen instead of standing on what has already happened.
- We will be waiting for blessings that Scripture declares are ours already.
- We will not walk in our God-given authority. Our authority is based on *done*—past or past perfect tense—not future tense. Authority can be exercised based only on established realities (something that has been done and stands done, i.e., an accomplished fact), not future possibilities. For instance, one cannot say, "I will be made CEO of this company next month; therefore, I terminate your appointment." He could be told to wait until he becomes CEO! Thus, the Lord Jesus declared, "All authority **has been given** to me in heaven and on earth. Therefore go . . ." (Matthew 28:18-19). He commissions us based on the existing reality of His universal lordship. We must come into the same tense with God to walk in the authority He has vested on us.

If we relegate to the past something God puts in the future,

- We will be running ahead of God instead of waiting for His timing.
- We will be disillusioned about why certain things have not happened, when God never said they are to happen now.

- We will be claiming promises that are not "ripe," trying to use faith to collect something we must wait in hope for.

If we place in the past or future something that God puts in the present,

- We will postpone many benefits of our redemption to the future. Instead of enjoying them now, we will assume they'll become operational when we get to heaven.
- We will miss the current moves of God.
- Our faith will be mostly historical or futuristic, not current and relevant.
- We will miss the present applications of God's Word, thinking that such truths are no longer tenable.

When we get into the same tense with God, we find that what God has done stands done—it remains for us to enter into our enjoyment of His pre-existing accomplishment.

This principle is especially true of believers in the New Testament. The overriding theme of the gospel is that *it is possible for people who have had a terrible past to have a brand new present and a glorious future.* This is the hope to which we are called, the amazing possibility we are called to embrace—that in Christ the past can be blotted out and night changed to day.

Imagine, then, what happens when the candidates and heirs of such a great salvation mix up the tenses of the truths that guarantee their liberty and heritage.

They will live in the past!

Their lives will be full of carryovers from the old life.

They will continue to accept their defunct identities as their present reality, whereas the truth is that *old things have passed away!* They are not what they used to be. They are not where they used to be. They have things they never had before. They have entered a heritage to which they were hitherto total strangers. They are new creatures in Christ— partakers of His very nature and life.

Satan's Strategy

Satan's strategy is to manipulate the tenses in the minds of believers, thereby blinding their minds to their glorious heritage. He keeps bringing up their pasts and conjuring up a future that cannot come to pass. In his craftiness and deceit, he pushes their present heritage into the future, causing them to apply hope where faith is needed to truly possess, appreciate, and appropriate the possessions that are already theirs. He creates strongholds in the minds of God's people, making them think that something the devil is doing cannot be undone by what Christ has done on the Cross.

It's an old strategy that worked well for the devil in the Garden of Eden. He put into the future something that Adam and Eve possessed in the present. He promised them something they already had and by mixing up the tenses in their minds opened them to his lies. They were toppled from their inestimable heritage—and all humanity with them.

A closer look at what happened at the fall is very instructive.

> Now the serpent was more crafty than any beast of the field which the LORD God had made. And he said to the woman, "Indeed, has God said, 'You shall not eat from any tree of the garden'?" The woman said to the serpent, "From the fruit of the trees of the garden we may eat; but from the fruit of the tree which is in the middle of the garden, God has said, 'You shall not eat from it or touch it, or you will die.'" The serpent said to the woman, "You surely will not die! ***For God knows that in the day you eat from it your eyes will be opened, and you will be like God, knowing good and evil.***" When the woman saw that the tree was good for food, and that it was a delight to the eyes, and that the tree was desirable to make one wise, she took from its fruit and ate; and she gave also to her husband with her, and he ate. Then the eyes of both of them were opened, and they knew that they were naked; and they sewed fig leaves together and made themselves loin coverings. (Genesis 3:1-7 NASB)

Observe the things the serpent offered Adam and Eve if they would but heed his hisses:

- Their eyes would be opened.
- They would be like God.
- They would know good and evil.

Adam and Eve already had everything the devil offered them—with the exception of the evil. *They were everything the devil had said they would become.* What the devil put in the future as a desirable possibility was, in fact, their true identity and present reality.

Their physical eyes were already opened; God did not create them blind. How could they have seen the serpent or the trees if they had been blind? Their spiritual eyes were open. Adam's spiritual eyes were opened so widely that he had amazing insight into what God was doing while he was asleep—when Eve was being created. He awoke from his deep sleep with an accurate prophecy: "This is now bone of my bones and flesh of my flesh; she shall be called 'woman,' for she was taken out of man" (Genesis 2:23).

How did he know she was bone of his bones and flesh of his flesh, and that she had been taken out of him? Adam and Eve could hear and recognize God's voice; they could fellowship with Him in the Garden in the cool of the day. The only thing their eyes were not open to was evil: they were blind to it.

Satan said they would be like God. Adam and Eve were like God already. Indeed, God had set out to make them like Himself. The manifesto for man's creation was clear: "Then God said, '**Let us make mankind in our image, in our likeness**, so that they may rule over the fish in the sea and the birds in the sky, over the livestock and all the wild animals, and over all the creatures that move along the ground.' So **God created man in His own image**; in the image of God He created him; male and female He created them." "God created human beings; **he created them godlike**, reflecting God's nature. He created them male and female" (Genesis 1:26–27 NIV; v. 27 MSG).

So what was the devil talking about? Adam and Eve were *godlike* already. How else would they become like God? And what does the devil know about being like God? Interestingly, it was when they listened to the devil that they became *unlike* God—they became *like* the devil—like the one they listened to. You become like the one you listen to. This is why you must keep listening to God, not to people or your problems or the devil. Let God's voice keep ringing in your heart; faith will rise in your spirit.

The devil even had the nerve to prefix his lies with "For God knows . . ." (Genesis 3:5). How did he know what God knows? Who authorized him to speak for God? Even if there were nothing else to do, Adam and Eve could have said, "Hold on, serpent. Where did you get what you are saying from? We need to confirm this new information from God. We can talk about it further after we have asked God, but until then shut up and slither away." But they accepted the devil's testimony on face value—a tragic error.

By relegating to the future something that was theirs in the present, the devil brought his evil future to bear on humanity. *Satan used a nonexistent future to collect a glorious present!* He hoodwinked Adam and Eve. He mixed up the tenses to confuse their senses. He still does that today.

Adam and Eve could have simply dismissed the devil if they had stood in the reality of their present status and refused to listen to his spurious promises. They could have told him, "We are like God already! He made us in His own image, serpent! We don't need to eat anything to become like God! We don't need a fruit to open our eyes! Our eyes are open already! We can see everything we need to see! We can see God, and we can see His beautiful creation!"

Masterstroke

Satan tried the same old trick with the Last Adam—the Lord Jesus Christ. At the temptation, he promised that something that already belonged to Jesus Christ would become His—if He would but yield to his lies. But the Master dealt him a blow that still resounds through time.

Let's take a closer look at the events at Christ's temptation (Luke 4:3-14).

"The devil said to Him, 'If You are the Son of God, tell this stone to become bread'" (v. 3).

Observe here that Satan applied an *"if"* to something that had no *ifs* about it. He still does that today—attributing *ifs* to solid realities, questioning facts that ought never to be questioned. He posits *ifs* with regard to the eternal and unchanging truths of Scripture and projects doubt about the exceedingly great and precious promises of a God who cannot lie. "If you are a child of God . . . If God really loves you . . . If you were really healed . . . If your prayer was really answered . . . What if it doesn't work out . . . ? What if you fail . . . ?"

"If you are the Son of God . . ." That's like saying to a human being, "If you are a human being, do something to prove you are." Both the speaker and the hearer know that a human is being addressed. What might the speaker be aiming to achieve by such a request?

"But Jesus answered, 'It is written: "Man shall not live by bread alone"'" (v. 4). The Master cut the enemy to size with unchanging truth: man was to live by every word of God, and He Himself *was* that Word made flesh. He didn't need anything the devil had to offer.

"The devil led him up to a high place and showed him in an instant all the kingdoms of the world. And he said to him, 'I will give you all their authority and splendor; it has been given to me, and I can give it to anyone I want to. If you worship me, it will all be yours'" (vv. 5-7). Note that Satan shows Jesus Christ all the kingdoms of this world—in a moment of time. The devil is showing the creature to its Creator! He flashes before Christ the kingdoms that Christ Himself created!

Then the devil promises to give all authority to the One who already has all authority in heaven and on earth. He is promising power and authority to the Mighty God, the Prince of Peace, Emmanuel—God with us!

Satan claims that earth, its kingdoms, and all authority *has been delivered to him!* Note that he puts his spurious claim *in the past perfect tense*—the right tense for him in order to exercise his "rights"! At the same time, he denies Christ's present identity and authority as the Owner of earth, declaring such ownership a possibility—if Christ would only worship him.

Some preachers have interpreted this Scripture to indicate that

Satan held the legal right over earth—that it was delivered to him by Adam when the latter succumbed to his temptation in the Garden—and thus had the right to give it to whomever he chose. This assertion is true, but it is not the whole truth. The complete truth is that the Adam who sold the earth, the devil who bought it, and the earth that was sold *all belonged to God.* It's as though a slave in a house bought an item belonging to the Master from a fellow slave in the house! Seller, buyer, and the item all belong to the Master, and all remain within the house! And it was an illegal and unauthorized transaction to begin with!

The Bible repeatedly declares (from Genesis through Revelation), that God owns the earth and all it contains. As he blessed Abraham, Melchizedek called God "possessor of heaven and earth" (Genesis 14:19 KJV). This was just 11 chapters after The Fall (in Genesis 3). David declared, "The earth is the LORD's, and everything in it, the world, and all who live in it; for he founded it on the seas and established it on the waters" (Psalm 24:1-2). David's prayer in 1 Chronicles 29:11-13 sums it up well:

> Yours, O Lord, is the greatness, the power and the glory, The victory and the majesty; For all that is in heaven and in earth is Yours; Yours is the kingdom, O Lord, And You are exalted as head over all. Both riches and honor come from You, And You reign over all. In Your hand is power and might; In Your hand it is to make great And to give strength to all. Now therefore, our God, We thank You And praise Your glorious name. (NKJV)

There is nothing historical about God's ownership and authority over heaven and earth. Let God's Word be true, and every demon a liar. Satan was claiming something that didn't belong to him—in the presence of the rightful Owner! He even proceeded to tell the Owner *to do something so He could own something He already owned.* What audacity!

"Jesus answered, 'It is written: "Worship the Lord your God and serve him only"'" (Luke 4:8).

Satan tried one more temptation (and even quoted Scripture to support his deceit): "Then he brought Him to Jerusalem, set Him on the pinnacle of the temple, and said to Him, 'If You are the Son of God ... throw yourself down from here. For it is written ...'" (Luke 4:9-10).

Both Christ and the devil knew the reality: Christ was (and is) the eternal Son of God. Why didn't the devil ever tempt anyone else with "If you are the Son of God ...?" He was questioning *a present reality* in the hope that the One he was tempting would heed his lies and do something—to become what He already was and always had been! In effect, *the devil was telling Christ to do something so He could become something He already was!* This is exactly what he does to believers today. He either denies outright or relegates their present reality to an uncertain future and then invites them to do something so they could earn or become something that Christ's finished work has already purchased for them.

Jesus answered, "It says: 'Do not put the Lord your God to the test'" (Luke 4:12).

After whipping the devil with the Word, "Jesus returned to Galilee **in the power of the Spirit**, and news about him spread through the whole countryside" (Luke 4:14).

There is a strong connection between identity and power. Jesus would not have returned *in the power of the Spirit* if the devil had succeeded in redefining His identity by getting Him to listen to his lies. Jesus overcame because He knew who He was. He stood in His eternal identity. He didn't need to prove anything: He was the Son of God, and the devil knew it.

Do you know who you are, or are you waiting for others to tell you?

The devil knows the heritage of believers. He has access to the Bible, and He knows that the Word cannot be broken. He knows what Jesus Christ did to him on the Cross. He knows that he and his principalities and powers were crushed at Calvary. But he will continue to take advantage of believers who do not know that he is a defeated foe—and thus put his defeat as a future possibility—something that is yet to happen. This will end when they come to agree with God—when they get into the same tense with God.

Proverbs 12:26 intrigues me: "The righteous is more excellent than his neighbour: but the way of the wicked seduceth them" (KJV). Since the opening clause of the verse states a fact, the righteous ought to be content, to hold firmly to his more excellent identity and not to sell himself short. But then we read that, despite his being more excellent than his neighbor, "the way of the wicked seduces" the righteous. It draws him—intending to take him from the Way to another way, from his more excellent heritage to destruction. The purpose of the seduction is to uproot the righteous from his present identity—to an empty future—to "cast him down from his excellency" (see Psalm 62:1-7 KJV).

Adam and Eve were far more excellent than the devil and the serpent he used to seduce them. However, Satan failed woefully with the sinless Son of God—as he certainly will with any child of God who agrees with God by putting what Christ has done for them in the proper tense.

12

The Past Tense of God's Word

Christianity is not primarily about getting God to do something. It's about believing what He has done. It's about entering an existing reality—and deriving your identity from that reality. The problem of faith for most believers will be resolved, if we can just get into God's tense—come to agree that what God calls done, is done indeed.

For instance, if we agree with God's past tense (what His Word says about our situation), our present tense (our current situation) will soon be in the past, and what God stated in past tense will become our present experience. This is actually the true meaning of faith—that despite our present, often pressing situations, we choose to agree with God's past tense declarations (what His Word says concerning us). Indeed, God's past tense is a 'sentence' on our present tense: what God calls done will ultimately override our present circumstances, if we believe. He calls us to come into agreement with His Word.

If we are not to pray amiss, we must pray in the right tense. Otherwise, instead of giving thanks for what God has done, we will continue to bombard heaven with our prayers and fasting—for God to do what He has already done for us!

The sense is in the tense! We will proceed to briefly examine several Scriptures that reveal what God has *done* for us.

Reconciled!

"Therefore, if anyone is in Christ, he is a new creation; old things have passed away; behold, all things have become new. Now all things are of God, *who has reconciled us to Himself* through Jesus Christ, and has given us the ministry of reconciliation." (2 Corinthians 5:17–18 NKJV).

God has reconciled us to Himself through Jesus Christ. This means that if you have received Christ, you have been *reconciled* to God. It's been done. There is no existing quarrel between God and you. The chief source of the trouble, sin, has been taken away in Christ. So you have peace with God. Now you can stand before God as if there were never a problem. God is not accusing you of anything: He is not the accuser of the brethren—that is the devil's ministry.

Reconciliation opens the door to infinite possibilities. With reconciliation come righteousness, access, and boldness.

Dead—to Sin, the World, and Our Old Master

Jesus solved the sin problem—by becoming sin for us and being nailed to the Cross. And since He did it all on our behalf, his action on our behalf is reckoned to our account. When He was condemned, we were condemned with Him. When He was crucified, we were crucified with Him, and when He died, we died. When He was buried we were buried with Him. And when He rose, we also rose with Him.

"Since, then, *you have been raised with Christ,* set your hearts on things above, where Christ is seated at the right hand of God. Set your minds on things above, not on earthly things. For *you died,* and your life is now hidden with Christ in God" (Colossians 3:1–3).

"For we know that *our old self was crucified with him* so that the body ruled by sin might be done away with, that we should no longer be slaves to sin—because anyone who has died has been freed from sin" (Romans 6:6–7).

Our old self *was crucified* with Christ. The verse doesn't tell us to do something to free ourselves—it tells us what has been done on our behalf. Our part is to believe and proclaim it in the face of every temptation.

Accepted in the Beloved

"He chose us in Him before the foundation of the world, that we should be holy and without blame before Him in love, having predestined us to adoption as sons by Jesus Christ to Himself, according to the good pleasure of His will, to the praise of the glory of His grace, by which He has made us ***accepted*** in the Beloved" (Ephesians 1:4-6 NKJV).

Notice the tense—it's past tense. You are accepted. You are not hoping that God will accept or welcome you. You have been accepted—by the One who matters most, and where it matters most!

What if someone or a group doesn't accept you? It would be good if they did, but as long as you are walking in the light it doesn't really matter. It's not a problem. Your identity does not derive from their approval or rejection. Your destiny is not in their hands. Their opinions are secondary, not primary! Praise the Lord!

How restless many are because they are not accepted into some circles! If only they could belong to the clique or the inner circle! But now they are excluded, rejected as unqualified and unfit to belong.

Christ has borne our rejection. He was rejected so we could be accepted. He was forsaken so we could be received. On the Cross, the Father turned His face away from His suffering Son, so He could turn it toward His wandering sons and daughters. He was despised so we could be esteemed—from the dunghill to be joint heirs with Christ Himself.

Our hearts will never rest until we receive this revelation. We are accepted in the Beloved: we have been accepted and stand accepted—by the Father of our Lord Jesus Christ. Get in the right tense with what God has done for you.

He Has Blessed Us

"Praise be to the God and Father of our Lord Jesus Christ, who has blessed us in the heavenly realms with every spiritual blessing in Christ" (Ephesians 1:3).

Keep the tense in view. This is not a prayer for blessing: it is a statement of fact. The Father has *blessed us already* with every spiritual blessing.

It might seem as though the blessings are limited to *spiritual* blessings, of no relevance to our material needs. However, *spiritual blessings are the parents of physical blessings*; it was the invisible spiritual that created the visible, material world. Therefore, if we will but acknowledge the spiritual blessings with which we are already blessed, they will produce tangible material benefits to address our every need.

He Has Delivered Us

God has delivered us. Note the tense—the sense is in the tense. I have provided the reference for this undeniable truth (Colossians 1:13) from several translations, to bring utter clarity to the truth at hand. It is impossible to read these plain statements of Scripture and not be gripped by the reality being proclaimed. If you are truly in Christ, God is not planning to, or going to, deliver you from the power of Satan. He has done it already. And whomever the Son sets free is free indeed. I invite you to read the following Scriptures and marvel:

CEV: "God **rescued us** from the dark power of Satan and brought us into the kingdom of his dear Son."

BBE: "Who has made us *free from the power of evil* and given us a place in the kingdom of the Son of his love."

ESV: "*He has delivered us* from the domain of darkness and transferred us to the kingdom of his beloved Son."

AMP: "He has **rescued us and has drawn us** to Himself from the dominion of darkness, and has **transferred us** to the kingdom of His beloved Son."

According to this Scripture, you have been *delivered* from the power of the devil. You are free from him. It is true that you will still have to walk on earth where he roams, but he has no authority over you. And deep in his twisted soul, he knows it. He knows that while he walks about like a roaring lion seeking whom to devour, the real Lion, the Lion of the tribe of Judah, resides within you. What can a fake lion do to the real Lion? "Shall iron break the northern iron and the steel?" (Jeremiah 15:12 NKJV).

He Has Translated Us

Take a closer look at the second part of Colossians 1:13, quoted above from several translations. God did not rescue us out of the dominion, authority, and control of Satan and his kingdom of darkness and then leave us in limbo—hanging in no man's land. He removed us from one kingdom and relocated us into another of a very different kind: ". . . who hath delivered us from the power of darkness, ***and hath translated us*** into the kingdom of his dear Son" (KJV).

Translation is powerful. It uprooted Enoch from earth and transplanted him into heaven. It plucked Elijah from Israel and relocated him to heaven. It has transferred you into a kingdom with amazing benefits.

The sons of the prophets pestered Elisha after Elijah was taken up to heaven. They insisted on going to look for Elijah. Elisha told them the score: Elijah had been translated. He had been taken up to heaven by a chariot of fire and horses of fire. Elisha had seen it. He had received the mantle that fell from the revered prophet. But the sons of the prophet were not content to receive truth from a faithful eyewitness. Here's the exchange between them and Elisha (2 Kings 2:16-18 MSG):

> They then said, "We're at your service. We have fifty reliable men here; let's send them out to look for your master. Maybe God's spirit has swept him off to some mountain or dropped him into a remote ravine."
>
> Elisha said, "No. Don't send them."
>
> But they pestered him until he caved in: "Go ahead then. Send them."
>
> So they sent the fifty men off. For three days they looked, searching high and low. Nothing.
>
> Finally, they returned to Elisha in Jericho. He told them, "So there—didn't I tell you?"

God's Spirit cannot take you from somewhere to nowhere. He is not the author of confusion: better to leave Elijah alone than to take him up and then dump him on a mountain or in a gulley somewhere. But unbelief set sons of the prophets searching in the forest for a man who had been translated to heaven! Like those who sought the resurrected Savior in the grave, they were looking for the living among the dead.

You are no longer *who* you used to be, and you are no longer *where* you used to be. God did not make you a new creation and leave you in an old location. After recreating you, He translated you into a different kingdom. You cannot be ruled by two kingdoms at the same time. It is either that you are still in the kingdom of the devil, or you are in the kingdom of God's beloved Son.

You see, when kingdoms change, everything changes. *The realities of the new kingdom become the new normal.* This is why you must now renew your mind to align with the new realities of the new kingdom into which you have been translated. You must now settle down to discover the operational protocols of the new kingdom to which you belong.

When kingdoms change, languages, customs, and values all change. Agendas change. Priorities change. The new kingdom works differently and will not tolerate the ways of the old. This was what happened when King Nebuchadnezzar conquered the kingdom of Judah and carried Daniel and others captive to Babylon. It was impossible to operate the protocols of Judah in the kingdom of Babylon. So Daniel and his friends had to be tutored in the ways of Babylon. To be able to stand before King Nebuchadnezzar, they had to master the protocols of Babylon.

The great challenge for believers in Christ is how to delete the protocols of the kingdom of darkness and "install" the protocols of the kingdom of God. When we were under the dominion of darkness, the last "programmer," Satan, had so downloaded his viruses into our minds that we responded effortlessly to his lies, afflictions, and diseases. He could manipulate us at will by remote control. But we are in a new kingdom now. Old things have passed away. We are no longer under his authority. Jesus now commands our destiny, and we must use the divine "antivirus" of God's Word to reformat and renew our minds.

The subject of kingdom protocols is so vital; it has been discussed in detail in our book *Divine Protocols*. I urge you to obtain this resource so you can learn how things work in the kingdom to which you belong.

You will also discover your awesome privileges as a bona fide citizen of the kingdom of God.

You see, your lot is a function of the kingdom to which you belong and in which you dwell. For instance, those in Singapore cannot be dominated by the realities of Afghanistan. Citizens and permanent residents of the United States of America do not share the same heritage as those who live in areas ravaged by terrorists. Their cases are different because they belong to different "kingdoms." The power cuts that are rife in Africa have nothing to do with the American who lives in New York. His situation is very different!

So with you, child of God: your case is different because you have changed kingdoms. The Father has rescued you from the kingdom of darkness and translated you into the glorious kingdom of His Son Jesus Christ. You are no longer where you used to be. Things that used to be your master no longer have power over you.

Some modern-day sons of prophets (akin to the ones Elisha dealt with) are trying to locate translated believers in strange places. They fill the redeemed people of God with fear. They use their prophecies and spurious utterances to convince believers that they are still under the dominion of curses, of demons, witches, and wizards, and can only be set free when the prophet or man of God prays some prophetic prayers and commands fire on the altars holding them captive. They are hoping to find translated "Elijahs" on some strange mountains or in some strange valleys.

Refuse to agree with any suggestion that you are still where you used to be. You have been translated. This has been done already. You are in a kingdom where Satan and his demons have no authority. They are of darkness, and you are now light in the Lord. Satan is severely allergic to light. *There is absolutely no way the prince of darkness can cross over into the kingdom of light and pluck you out of the hand of the Prince of Peace.* That's impossible. Your times are in God's hands; you are engraved on the palms of His hands, and no one is able to pluck anything out of His hand. The devil knows it. And his oppression over you will end when it becomes a settled reality in your spirit. You shall know this truth, and it shall make you free.

He Has Given Us . . .

"His divine power **has given us** everything we need for a godly life through our knowledge of him who called us by his own glory and goodness. Through these **he has given us** his very great and precious promises, so that through them you may participate in the divine nature, having escaped the corruption in the world caused by evil desires" (2 Peter 1:3-4).

Or, as rendered in the Amplified Bible, "For his divine power **has bestowed on us** [absolutely] everything necessary for [a dynamic spiritual] life and godliness, through true and personal knowledge of Him who called us by His own glory and excellence. For by these **He has bestowed on us** His precious and magnificent promises".

This passage does not speak of something God will give us but of things *He has given us* already—everything we need for life and godliness, as well as very great and precious promises. He has made us participants in the divine nature! He has graciously *bestowed* these amazing blessings on us already. We must keep it in the right tense.

By His divine power, He *has given us* everything we need for life and godliness. This must be your confession henceforth: instead of talking about your need, say, "God has given me everything I need for life and godliness." Keep saying it until it settles in your spirit just as it is settled in heaven. Get into the right tense with God. Unbelief makes us cry and beg for things that God has given us already—and we call it prayer! You have everything you need for life and godliness. They are yours as you increase in the knowledge of the One who has called you.

You are an heir of exceedingly great and precious promises of a God who cannot fade or fail. The Message translation calls them "absolutely terrific promises"—"your tickets to participation in the life of God." You are the heir of these promises; you are not an orphan. The omnipotent Yahweh has given you absolutely terrific promises; He is waiting for you to claim them. They cover everything you can possibly need in your journey through earth—spiritual, physical, financial, emotional, etc. You need to discover them. You need to stand on them. And you can be sure that the One who promised is faithful, and He will fulfill them. But first, you need to agree with His Word.

Spirit of Power

"That is why I would remind you to stir up (rekindle the embers of, fan the flame of, and keep burning) the [gracious] gift of God, [the inner fire] that is in you by means of the laying on of my hands [with those of the elders at your ordination]. For *God did not give us* a spirit of timidity (of cowardice, of craven and cringing and fawning fear), but [*He has given us* a spirit] of power and of love and of calm and well-balanced mind and discipline and self-control." (2 Timothy 1:6-7 AMPC).

If God did not give you a spirit of timidity and fear, then you have no right to have it. It's not yours. As a child of God, you have no reason to collect or keep something that the Father did not give you. You can reject it.

On the contrary, God has given us a spirit of power and of love—a spirit of sound, calm, and well-balanced minds, and of discipline and self-control. This is the Spirit who indwells you, and He will manifest these qualities in you as you acknowledge Him.

Received

We receive what God has given to us.

"For you have not received a spirit of slavery leading again to fear [of God's judgment], but *you have received the Spirit* of adoption as sons [the Spirit producing sonship] by which we [joyfully] cry, 'Abba! Father!' The Spirit Himself testifies and confirms together with our spirit [assuring us] that we [believers] are children of God" (Romans 8:15-16 AMP).

"Now *we have received, not the spirit of the world, but the [Holy] Spirit who is from God*, so that we may know and understand the [wonderful] things freely given to us by God" (1 Corinthians 2:12 AMP).

You have received the Holy Spirit, not the spirit of this age. He makes it possible for you to realize, comprehend, appreciate, and *apprehend* the many blessings lavished on us by God's favor.

We have received reconciliation through the atonement, with its amazing benefits: "Not only is this so, but we also boast in God through our Lord Jesus Christ, through whom we have now **received reconciliation**" (Romans 5:11). All those who receive this reconciliation are now reconciled to God. The separation is over.

Pay attention to what you have already received from God, not what you are expecting to receive. What you have received is so astounding that, were you to realize this truth, you would be full of endless gratitude to God. And as you acknowledge the divine deposits and overflow with thanksgiving, everything else will be added to you.

The Name Above All Names

Jesus has given us His Name. The almighty, irresistible Name that the Father gave Him following His exaltation has been given to the Church. The same Name by which we are saved has now become our family inheritance—the heritage of every believer.

In that name we receive forgiveness of sins and cast out devils; we can lay our hands on the sick and they will recover. We receive answers to our prayers—we draw from Jesus' unlimited account in the Bank of Heaven with the Father. As you read the following Scriptures, you begin to get an idea of the power of the Name that has been given us. I invite you to read them meditatively:

- "These signs will accompany those who have believed: *in My name* they will cast out demons, they will speak in new tongues; they will pick up serpents, and if they drink anything deadly, it will not hurt them; they will lay hands on the sick, and they will get well" (Mark 16:17–18 AMP).
- "And I will do [I Myself will grant] whatever you ask in My Name [as presenting all that I AM], so that the Father may be glorified and extolled in (through) the Son. *[Yes] I will grant [I Myself will do for you] whatever you shall ask in My Name [as presenting all that I AM].*" (John 14:13–14 AMPC).
- "At that time you won't need to ask me for anything, for you can go directly to the Father and ask him, and *he will give you what you ask for because you use my name.* You haven't tried this before, but

begin now. Ask, using my name, and you will receive, and your cup of joy will overflow. . . . ***Then you will present your petitions over my signature!*** And I won't need to ask the Father to grant you these requests, for the Father himself loves you dearly because you love me and believe that I came from the Father" (John 16:23–27 TLB).

- "In that day you will not [need to] ask Me about anything. ***I assure you and most solemnly say to you, whatever you ask the Father in My name [as My representative]***, He will give you. Until now you have not asked [the Father] for anything in My name; but now ask and keep on asking and you will receive, so that your joy may be full and complete" (John 16:23–24 AMP).

When we come before the Father in that Name, we are presenting all that Christ is, all that He has accomplished; not our own righteousness or achievements. We ask the Father to grant our requests on the basis of Jesus' standing with Him, i.e., what Christ means to Him. You see, then, why it is impossible to come in that Name and be disappointed. *Jesus is too respected in Heaven, too regarded by the Father, too honored in the Father's presence for you to come in His name and be rejected.*

Take that mighty Name into the conflicts of life. Confront the devil and his cohorts with that Name. They know the Name; it is the Name of the prevailing Lion of the Tribe of Judah—the One who overcame them and crushed their heads—who now indwells you! They stand helpless before the Name—before the Name that you have *received*!

"For this reason also [because He obeyed and so completely humbled Himself], ***God has highly exalted Him and bestowed on Him the name which is above every name***, so that at the name of Jesus every knee shall bow [in submission], of those who are in heaven and on earth and under the earth, and that every tongue will confess and openly acknowledge that Jesus Christ is Lord (sovereign God), to the glory of God the Father" (Philippians 2:9–11 AMP).

Every knee must bow to that Name. It's not optional; it is compulsory. Every tongue must confess—frankly and openly—that Jesus Christ is Lord. He is Lord of all, not just Lord of the spiritual. He is Lord of the local and the global, Lord of the celestial and terrestrial, Lord of the material, Lord of the political, and Lord of the financial. His authority covers all aspects of life—for all time and eternity—and includes everyone and everything, everywhere in the universe—in heaven, on earth, and under the earth. Nothing is exempted from the authority of this Name. Jesus Christ is not a church reverend—with his authority limited to church matters. He is not a departmental savior who is an expert in one department and a rookie in another. He is Lord of all.

The reason that Name seems impotent in the mouths of many believers is that they have never seen the true *size* of the Owner of the Name. A name is as powerful as the owner of the name. Therefore, without a revelation of *the colossal size of Jesus Christ*—His supreme exaltation by the Father, His absolute triumph and irresistible authority—mentioning His Name will not produce much result.

A comprehensive study of this glorious Name is beyond the scope of this book. The reader is encouraged to investigate the boundless treasures encased in the Name. In this regard, I highly recommend E. W. Kenyon's book *The Wonderful Name of Jesus* and our training program, *The Understanding Life Study Course* (book and audio teachings), which reveal Jesus' standing before the Father—the basis of the authority and power vested in His Name.

Obtained . . .

Another word used to describe what has come to us because of our union with the Lord Jesus Christ is "obtained." It stipulates what belongs to us in Christ.

An Inheritance

"In Him also **we have obtained an inheritance**, being predestined according to the purpose of Him who works all things according to the counsel of His will" (Ephesians 1:11 NKJV).

I heard of a boy from a certain tribe who was named Bwanhot, meaning "empty-handed" in their local language. I wondered how and why someone would have given such a name to his son.

You are not empty-handed, child of God. God forbid that. You obtained a vast and incorruptible inheritance when you received Jesus Christ as Lord. In the same way Paul prayed for the Ephesians, ask God to open your eyes to your inheritance in Christ (see Ephesians 1:15–23). Research that inheritance. Discover what belongs to you because you belong to Christ, and walk in the light of it.

Mercy

God told Moses, "'I will have mercy on whom I have mercy, and I will have compassion on whom I have compassion.' It does not, therefore, depend on human desire or effort, but on God's mercy" (Romans 9:15–16).

Life is not by power or by might; no one can become or receive anything apart from the mercy of God. The good news is that in Christ God's mercy towards us is not an arbitrary, unpredictable, or occasional expression, but our eternal heritage. We have become permanent recipients of God's mercy. What else will God do with someone who abides in Christ if not show her mercy?

We have *obtained* or *received* mercy from God. The unchanging divine attitude towards every believer is an attitude of mercy. No good father looks at his children any other way. "Which in time past were not a people, but are now the people of God: which had not obtained mercy, but now have **obtained** mercy" (1 Peter 2:10 NKJV).

Paul details his own journey of mercy in his first letter to Timothy: "And I thank Christ Jesus our Lord who has enabled me, because He counted me faithful, putting me into the ministry, although *I was formerly* a blasphemer, a persecutor, and an insolent man; but *I obtained mercy* because I did it ignorantly in unbelief... However, for this reason *I obtained mercy*, that in me first Jesus Christ might show all longsuffering, as a pattern to those who are going to believe on Him for everlasting life" (1 Timothy 1:12, 13, 16 NKJV).

Observe what Paul was *formerly*—someone who blasphemed and persecuted and was shamefully and outrageously and aggressively insulting toward believers (see v. 13, AMP). But he became a new creature in Christ. Old things passed away. His old identity was dead. Instead of being a candidate for judgment and condemnation, he was now an object of God's mercy. When issues arose, Paul could give his opinion as one that had "*obtained mercy* of the Lord to be faithful" (see 1 Corinthians 7:25 KJV).

Consider Romans 9:22–24: "What if God, although choosing to show his wrath and make his power known, bore with great patience *the objects of his wrath*—prepared for destruction? What if he did this to make the riches of his glory known to the *objects of his mercy*, whom he prepared in advance for glory—even us, whom he also called . . . ?"

In this Scripture, Paul speaks of some people as objects of wrath, but of believers as objects of mercy—"even us" whom God called, and prepared beforehand for glory.

Apart from obtaining mercy, we have actually become *objects of mercy*. That connotes a permanent state of favor as we walk in the light. Nothing else can be poured into an object, or vessel, of mercy—as long as that vessel continues to walk in fellowship with the Father. An object of mercy can *expect* the mercy of God in every situation and for every need. Even if an object of mercy falls into sin, she can ask for mercy—and God is faithful and just to forgive our sins and cleanse us from all unrighteousness.

I encourage you to pause and make this confession right now: "I have obtained mercy from the Lord. I am an object of God's mercy. God will show mercy to me in every situation. Goodness and mercy will follow me all the days of my life." Then thank the Father for His abiding mercy on your life; it belongs to you because you belong to Christ.

A Faith of Equal Privilege

Peter addresses his second epistle "to those who have received (*obtained an equal privilege of*) *like precious faith* with ourselves in and through the righteousness of our God and Savior Jesus Christ" (2 Peter 1:1 AMPC).

According to this foremost apostle, every believer has obtained "a faith of equal standing"—"a faith that is as valuable as ours, a faith based on the approval that comes from our God and Savior, Jesus Christ" (ESV, GW).

What Peter is saying is that *the faith we obtained is exactly the same as the one he, John, Paul, and all other apostles obtained.* It's not inferior. This is remarkable. Our faith in Christ is as precious, as valuable, and as powerful as Peter's and Paul's! Our faith can do everything that the faith of the apostles did—if we will nourish it and grow it to its full potential. Glory to God!

We discover a very important truth from Ephesians 4:4–6: "There is one body and one Spirit, just as you were called in one hope when you were called; one Lord, **one faith**, one baptism; one God and Father of all, who is over all and through all and in all". According to this Scripture, there's only one faith, not two or three or seven, but one faith. There is no different, higher class faith for super-apostles and great men and women of God, and another lower, inferior faith for the Christian masses. It's one faith. We are also told that the Father is above *all,* is in *all*, and works through *all*—not just great preachers of the gospel.

We discover why God would give a faith of equal possibilities to both apostles and disciples: it's because He is fair! "This letter is from Simon Peter, a slave and apostle of Jesus Christ. I am writing to you who share the same precious faith we have. ***This faith was given to you because of the justice and fairness of Jesus Christ***, our God and Savior" (2 Peter 1:1 NLT).

God gave us a faith with the same potential as Peter's and John's, *because of the justice and fairness of Jesus Christ.* It would have been unfair for God to give us a faith of a lesser standing than theirs and then expect us to live as they did, face the same adversary they did, and accomplish the same Great Commission. How could He have done this to us and remained fair? How could He be the Father of us all and then give some of His children a lesser inheritance than He gave to others? No, the Father would never do that. He grants a faith of equal privilege to everyone who comes to Christ. Everything, then, depends on what we do to grow our faith to its fullest potential. As with the Thessalonians, whose faith grew exceedingly (see 2 Thessalonians 1:3), our own faith can so grow that we will experience and manifest the fullest possibilities of the indwelling Christ.

In the parable of the pounds (minas) told by the Lord Jesus (see Luke 19:11-27), the master gave a mina to each servant. However, *the servants did different things with what they were given, resulting in different outcomes.* Using the seed capital given him by the master, a diligent servant made ten more minas, while a lazy one buried his one mina and loafed around till his master returned. If the two servants were to have gone to market—the diligent with eleven minas and the slothful with one—their purchasing power would have been vastly different. Their financial possibilities would not have been the same; the eleven minas of the diligent would have accomplished far more than the undeveloped mina of the idle. But the lazy servant could never have rightly blamed his poor outcome on anyone but himself, since the master was not unfair in the allocation of the minas.

God has given you the same faith that He gave to the apostles; it's the same faith that every great servant of God, historical and contemporary, has received. It's a faith that can save the lost, heal the sick, raise the dead, open blind eyes, reveal secrets, birth revival, and shake cities. It's a faith that can turn the world upside down. It could be said of us, as it was of Paul and the other apostles, "These men who have caused trouble all over the world have now come here" (Acts 17:6). Why should we possess such a faith of equal privilege and do nothing with it? What will you do with this faith of amazing possibilities? What will it accomplish in your life?

If we abide in the mercy we have obtained, become established as objects of mercy (not occasional recipients of favor), and apply this precious faith to the incredible inheritance we have obtained, we will be astounded by the possibilities.

In Time Past . . . but Now

The life of a child of God is sharply divided into two segments: past and present. Of course, there is a glorious future ahead, but the believer had a past, which was dealt with by the finished work of Christ in which he has trusted. That past is no longer operational. He is now a new creature in Christ. Notice the tenses in the following Scriptures:

"And you hath he quickened, **who were** dead in trespasses and sins; Wherein **in time past** ye walked according to the course of this world, according to the prince of the power of the air, the spirit that now worketh in the children of disobedience" (Ephesians 2:1–2 KJV)

You were dead in trespasses and sins. You are no longer like that. You are alive now.

In time past you followed the course of this world and were controlled by the prince of the power of the air (the devil). But that was then—it's what you *were,* not what you *are.* Something happened that terminated the devil's authority over you. You are no longer a child of disobedience.

"Wherefore remember, that ye being **in time past** Gentiles in the flesh, who are called Uncircumcision by that which is called the Circumcision in the flesh made by hands; That **at that time** ye were without Christ, being aliens from the commonwealth of Israel, and strangers from the covenants of promise, having no hope, and without God in the world: **But now** in Christ Jesus ye who sometimes were far off are made nigh by the blood of Christ" (Ephesians 2:11–13 KJV).

The more I look at these Scriptures, the more I am convinced that many of us are not reading our Bibles properly. We mix the past with the present and postpone our present heritage to a millennial future.

See what the passage says: *at that time*—before you were saved— you *were* (notice the past tense), without Christ. You *were* a stranger from the covenants of promise, and *were* without hope and without God in a dangerous world. That's what you *were.*

But now!

"**But now** [at this very moment] in Christ Jesus you who once were [so very] far away [from God] have been brought near by the blood of Christ" (Ephesians 2:13 AMP). You are no longer far away from God. You have been brought near. You don't need to scream in order for Him to hear you. You can pray to Him in a whisper—from where you are, seated with Christ at His right hand in heavenly places—and He will answer you. You can call Him "Abba! Father!"

God brought you near to Himself by the blood of His Son Jesus Christ, not by anything you did. You are so near, in fact, that He lives in you, and you in Him. You can now come boldly to the throne of grace and find help in time of need. You cannot be stranded in life. The greater One lives in you! "Which *in time past* were not a people, *but are now* the people of God: which had not obtained mercy, *but now* have obtained mercy" (1 Peter 2:10 NKJV).

Redemption changes everything. You were once hopeless, but now you brim with hope and a confident expectation regarding the future. You rest in God's all-sufficiency. You know that you are more than a conqueror through Him who loved and loves you. This is your present heritage.

Consider Ephesians 2:19: "So then *you are no longer* strangers and aliens [outsiders without rights of citizenship], *but you are* fellow citizens with the saints (God's people), and are [members] of God's household" (AMP).

You are no longer what you used to be—an outsider, exile, migrant, and alien excluded from the rights of kingdom citizens. Now you belong. You are a new creature in Christ. You are an insider now. You share citizenship with the saints. The Father has made you fit to take your portion of the inheritance of the saints in the light. Glory to His name!

Profitable!

Onesimus was *"formerly"* unprofitable to Philemon, his master. But redemption changed that. Onesimus was now a new creature in Christ. He was now profitable to his master, Philemon, and to Paul (Philemon 1:11).

Maybe you were unprofitable to yourself, to your family, and to society at large. You were a problem requiring solution! That was in time past—formerly. That's your history. But now. . .! You are a new creature—a brand new person. You are loaded with possibilities. God has given you everything you need for life and godliness. You are a solution now. Hallelujah!

Onesimus had to stand on his new identity (see Philemon 1). He was a slave; now in Christ he had become a freeman and a *brother* to his former master. Imagine the huge shift necessary in Onesimus's thinking for him to acknowledge and walk in this new identity. He had charges to answer before his master; now all charges against him were forgiven—quashed!—and Paul could send him back to Philemon without fear of reprisals. The book of Philemon is a real study of how to get used to our new identity in Christ.

How will you judge yourself? Will it be by your history or by your heritage in Christ? Stand on your new identity.

How God Speaks Today

Many believers do not understand how God speaks to us now. They are filled with what their man of God or prophet or pastor has told them. "Bishop said . . . Prophet declared. . . Papa said . . . ," etc. However, "*in the past* God spoke to our ancestors through the prophets at many times and in various ways, but *in these last days* he has spoken to us by his Son, whom he appointed heir of all things, and through whom also he made the universe" (Hebrews 1:1–2).

Notice the tenses—they tell us how God spoke *in the past* and how He speaks to us *in these last days*. How can we hear God if we don't even know how or through whom He is speaking currently?

Keep your eyes on Jesus, and your ears open to His Word. He is God speaking to you, stirring your heart to lay hold on your inheritance. He is Emmanuel, God with us, God in us. He calls you to gaze upon His finished work so you can enjoy your boundless redemption privileges.

He Himself Took . . . and Carried . . .

"When evening came, they brought to Him many who were demon-possessed; and He cast out the spirits with a word, and healed all who were ill. This was to fulfill what was spoken through Isaiah the prophet: 'He Himself *took* our infirmities and *carried away* our diseases" (Matthew 8:16–17 NASB).

The only reason Jesus took our infirmities is so that we could be free from them—He did it to grant us that, being delivered from all that had held us down and in bondage, we should serve God without fear, in righteousness and true holiness.

Why should you carry what Jesus has carried for you? He carried away our diseases. That's past tense. It's done—and He did it for you. The sense is in the tense: Jesus is not going to carry or take away that disease or sickness. He has done that already. If you will agree with God and start thanking Him for what He has done, you will see the manifestation of the greatest miracles of your life.

By Whose Stripes You Were Healed

Observe the tense in Peter's statement of what Christ has done for us: "Who Himself bore our sins in His own body on the tree, that we, *having died to sins*, might live for righteousness—by whose stripes you were *healed*" (1 Peter 2:24 NKJV).

You have died to sin—the text says it: "having died to sins"! It also says that "you *were* healed." Keep the tense close to your heart. God understands grammar. He knows what He is talking about. He could have assigned this reality to the future if that had been where he wanted it. But He put it in the past tense, as an accomplished fact. And because it is done already, you can stand in faith *now* to claim it as yours. "*Now* faith is. . . " In what tense do you put your healing?

It sounds foolish to confess that we were healed while the pain is wracking the body or the swelling is very tangible, visible, and tender. According to our version of reality, the presence of symptoms equates to the absence of healing.

God is not denying what we feel when He asks that we agree with His Word. He is asking us to agree—to consider Him faithful, to acknowledge what He has done for us in Christ—so that it can manifest in our lives. We must believe in order to see or experience. The evidence of His Word is superior to the evidence of our senses and feelings. The visible reality may be the presence of symptoms, but there is a greater reality—the unfailing Word of God. That Word is an overarching reality over all other realities, and it will subsume and swallow them—if we will hold to it steadfastly.

Stand on these great truths. You have died to sin. You have been healed—Jesus took your infirmities and carried your diseases. Confess it repeatedly. If you stand on Scripture, Scripture will stand for you.

He Has Qualified and Made Us Fit

"Giving thanks to the Father, *Who has **qualified and made us fit** to share the portion which is the inheritance of the saints (God's holy people) in the Light*" (Colossians 1:12 AMPC).

This must be the icing on the cake. I was tempted to put it at the beginning—so you wouldn't exclude yourself from the glorious inheritance that God has *qualified* you to enjoy. We were certainly unfit to partake of the inheritance of the saints in the light. We were in the kingdom of darkness, but God's great heart reached out to us in our unworthy state, cleansed us from our sins, and made us worthy to take our share of the inheritance!

Let nothing persuade you otherwise. If God has qualified you for something, then you must be qualified indeed. Who can disqualify someone whom God has qualified? Who can declare unfit someone the Holy One has pronounced fit? Take your eyes away from yourself and dare to believe what God has done for you. Then, with newborn boldness, take your portion of the inheritance.

Religion is man's effort to be qualified to receive from God. It manifests itself in seeking to be justified by good works—trying to earn God's approval by being good enough. But there is nothing we could ever do to be good enough before God. All our righteousness and good works are like filthy rags before His unapproachable holiness.

We often feel as though we have not prayed enough, fasted enough, given enough, sacrificed enough, been good enough, etc., to enjoy God's highest and best. But the divine testimony in Colossians 1:12 should put our hearts at rest. We have been qualified by the One who matters most. We have been declared fit where it matters most. Faith rises from our spirits to lay hold on the exceedingly great and precious promises of our great Father God.

13

The Present Tense of God's Word

A Know-So Salvation

I was raised in a church denomination that taught that people could not know for sure if they were saved while they were still alive. They held that only after death could anyone discover whether they were saved or lost, i.e., whether they had eternal life. All a person could do in this life was to believe to the best of their ability, do as much good as possible, and hope for the best. It was after I got saved and began to read the Bible for myself that I realized how wrong they were. They couldn't grasp the present tense of God's Word—that there are certain things that are ours *now*—things we can be assured beyond doubt belong to us.

Ours is a know-so salvation; it is rooted in God's unbreakable Word, not guesswork. There are several definite things the Word tells us that we have—things that are ours here and now because of our union with the Lord Jesus. These things belong to us as people of the Indwelling. They are ours *in the present,* not as a future promise or possibility. We will explore several of them in this chapter. The list that follows is not exhaustive; I encourage you to embark on a voyage of discovery, targeting Scriptures that declare our present heritage in Christ.

We Have . . .

We Have Redemption

"In Him **we have redemption** through His blood, the forgiveness of sins, in accordance with the riches of God's grace" (Ephesians 1:7).

We have redemption—we have been redeemed, bought back—from the curse, and from Satan's dominion. This truth is repeated in Paul's letter to the Colossians: "in whom **we have our redemption,** [because of His sacrifice, resulting in] the forgiveness of our sins [and the cancellation of sins' penalty]" (Colossians 1:14 AMP).

Redemption has multidimensional consequences. Our price has been paid; therefore we are free from what legally bound us. Also, the price of our redemption is an accurate indicator of our value to the Father. Redemption restores us to the Father's family and favor. And we have that redemption *now.*

There are aspects of God's redemptive plan that are yet to be made manifest for the simple reason that they are further down the road on the divine timetable. For instance, the redemption of our bodies is a blessed hope cherished by the people of the Indwelling. But because we are redeemed, we are even now indwelt by the Spirit, who will execute that final transformation!

It is interesting to note the tense in which Jesus completed our redemption. As He hung on that Cross, having satisfied every demand of justice and having fulfilled every prophecy of Scripture concerning His redemptive work, "Jesus said, '*It is finished.*' With that, he bowed his head and gave up his spirit" (John 19:30).

"*It is finished.*" That is as clear as it can be. These were the last words Jesus uttered before He bowed His head and dismissed His Spirit. Nothing was left undone. The chastisement necessary for our peace was upon Him. The price of full atonement and a perfect redemption had been paid. We must keep these three awesome words in perpetual view: *It is finished*; they hold the key to maximizing the benefits of Calvary.

Christ has redeemed us—from the curse of the broken law and from the hand of the enemy. That is an accomplished fact, not a future possibility. We must walk in our redemption benefits as a settled and current reality, not a future expectation.

"Therefore the redeemed of the LORD shall return, and come with singing unto Zion; and everlasting joy shall be upon their head: they shall obtain gladness and joy; and sorrow and mourning shall flee away" (Isaiah 51:11 KJV).

We Have Eternal Life

As God's children, we have eternal life. Eternal life is the very nature of God Himself—His own kind of life. This life of God is ours *now*. We will carry that same life in our recreated spirits to heaven. Our bodies will be changed so that mortality can put on immortality, but our spirits are already alive with the life of Christ Himself.

"And this is the testimony: God **has given us** eternal life, and this life is in His Son. **Whoever has the Son has life**; whoever does not have the Son of God does not have life" (1 John 5:11-12).

God's testimony is clear: He has given us eternal life, and that life is in His Son. The question, then, is simple: Do you have the Son? If you have the Son, then you have life. He is your life!

Scripture declares, "I write this to you who believe in (adhere to, trust in, and rely on) the name of the Son of God [in the peculiar services and blessings conferred by Him on men*], so that you may know [with settled and absolute knowledge] that you [already] have life, yes, eternal life*" (1 John 5:13 AMPC). "He who believes and trusts in the Son and accepts Him [as Savior] **has eternal life [that is, already possesses it]**" (John 3:36 AMP). "He who believes [in Me as Savior—whoever adheres to, trusts in, relies on, and has faith in me—already] **has** eternal life [that is, **now possesses** it]" (John 6:47 AMP).

There is no ambiguity about the meanings of these verses. If you have the Son you have life. You have put your faith in Him; you possess eternal life—now. Glory to God!

It may seem presumptuous for someone who is still on earth to claim that he has eternal life. Why not wait until you finish the race successfully before making such a claim?

The truth is that *only those who have eternal life can live eternally in heaven.* We will be carrying heaven in us when we go to heaven: if anyone does not have the Spirit of Christ resident within—indwelling him—he doesn't belong to Him at all. And when He comes to take His ransomed ones home to glory, His Spirit's life in us will be the proof that we are His. Going to heaven will be the final component of our translation: we have been translated from darkness into light, from the kingdom of Satan into the kingdom of God, and finally we will be translated from earth to heaven, where we belong.

An Inheritance

"In Him also **we have obtained an inheritance**, being predestined according to the purpose of Him who works all things according to the counsel of His will" (Ephesians 1:11 NKJV).

Following this declaration, Paul prayed for believers that

> the God of our Lord Jesus Christ, the Father of glory, may grant you a spirit of wisdom and of revelation [that gives you a deep and personal and intimate insight] into the true knowledge of Him [for we know the Father through the Son]. And [I pray] that the eyes of your heart [the very center and core of your being] may be enlightened [flooded with light by the Holy Spirit], so that you will know and cherish the hope [the divine guarantee, the confident expectation] to which He has called you, the riches of His glorious inheritance in the saints (God's people), and [so that you will begin to know] what the immeasurable and unlimited and surpassing greatness of His [active, spiritual] power is in us who believe. . . (Ephesians 1:17–19 AMP).

Our present need is for our eyes to be enlightened—flooded with light—so we can know the riches of the glorious inheritance of the saints. The prayer asks God to give us something (His Spirit of wisdom and revelation) that will help us see what He has already given us! Hallelujah!

We have what God says we have. We are what He says we are. We can do what He says we can do. If we don't believe that, we make Him out to be a liar, and His truth is not in us.

We Have a High Priest

"Since **we have a great high priest** who has ascended into heaven, Jesus the Son of God, let us hold firmly to the faith we profess. For we do not have a high priest who is unable to empathize with our weaknesses, but we have one who has been tempted in every way, just as we are—yet he did not sin. Let us then approach God's throne of grace with confidence, so that we may receive mercy and find grace to help us in our time of need" (Hebrews 4:14-16).

We have a great High Priest. We are well represented in heaven; right at the throne room of the universe and at the right hand of the Father, we have a High Priest interceding for us! And He is not a high priest who is "out of touch with our reality" (MSG) but who has been tempted and tried in every way that we are. Except for our sin, He's been in our shoes; He knows our struggles and weaknesses. As our high priest He pleads and intercedes for us, not against us.

You can now see why we can approach the throne of grace with bold-ness and complete confidence. It has nothing to do with what we have merited, but with what our High Priest has done for us. We are accepted before the Father on His ticket. And our High Priest ever lives to make intercession for us. "He holds His priesthood unchangeably, because He lives on forever. Therefore He is able also to save to the uttermost (com-pletely, perfectly, finally, and for all time and eternity) those who come to God through Him, since He is always living to make petition to God and intercede with Him and intervene for them" (Hebrews 7:24-25 AMPC).

Our case is very different from that of the Israelites. They had high priests who were beset with personal weaknesses and failures—like Aaron and the Levitical priests. They had to first make atonement for their own sins before they could be of any use to the people! But of how much use could they have been, loaded down with their own shortcomings?

Our case is different. Our High Priest is "holy, blameless, unstained by sin, separated from sinners, and exalted higher than the heavens" (Hebrews 7:26 AMPC).

We Are . . .

There are several things God declares that we are—now, in the present. We are not to try to become these things, or to make a strenuous effort to achieve them. We simply believe what He says about us, and by believing enter into the reality of our inheritance.

We are who He says we are. We have what He says we have. We can do what He says we can do.

We Are God's Children Now:

"Beloved, **we are [even here and] now** children of God, and it is not yet made clear what we will be [after His coming]. We know that when He comes and is revealed, we will [as His children] be like Him, because we will see Him just as He is [in all His glory]" (1 John 3:2 AMP).

We Are Chosen and Holy:

"But **you are a chosen people, a royal priesthood, a holy nation, God's special possession**, that you may declare the praises of him who called you out of darkness into his wonderful light. Once you were not a people, but **now you are the people of God**; once you had not received mercy, but now you have received mercy" (1 Peter 2:9–10).

We Are His Workmanship—His Handiwork, His Masterpiece, Now

"For **we are God's handiwork**, created in Christ Jesus to do good works, which God prepared in advance for us to do" (Ephesians 2:10).

We Are More Than Conquerors Now:

"Yet in all these things *we are more than conquerors* and gain an overwhelming victory through Him who loved us" (Romans 8:37 AMP).

We Are Complete in Him Now:

"For in Him the whole fullness of Deity (the Godhead) continues to dwell in bodily form [giving complete expression of the divine nature]. And you are in Him, made full and having come to fullness of life *[in Christ you too are filled with the Godhead - Father, Son and Holy Spirit* - and reach full spiritual stature]. And He is the Head of all rule and authority [of every angelic principality and power]" (Colossians 2:9-10 AMPC).

   We are complete in Christ, and He is complete in us. We have come to fullness of life in Him. In Him we have life, and have it more abundantly. Because we are in Him, we are filled with what fills Him: we too are filled with the Godhead—Father, Son, and Holy Spirit!

We Are as He Is in This World:

"In this [union and fellowship with Him] love is completed and perfected with us, so that we may have confidence in the day of judgment [with assurance and boldness to face Him]; because *as He is, so are we in this world*" (1 John 4:17 AMP).

   What an amazing statement! This would be incredible if it were not God's Word forever settled in heaven. As He was (and is) the begotten of the Father, so are we. As He was (and is) indwelt by the Father, so are we. As He was (and still is) filled with the Holy Spirit, so are we. As He is the light of the world, so are we. As He was sent by the Father, so has He sent us. As He is seated at the right hand of the Father, so are we seated together with Him! As He had authority over all principalities, powers, and demons, so has He given us authority over all the works of the enemy. And when He shall appear, we shall be like Him. Glory to God!

This is not wishful thinking. It's a revelation of who we are in Christ—of what belongs to us because we belong to Him. We must meditate on these truths until they take root in our hearts, dominate our thinking, and begin to manifest through us—to the glory of God and the blessing of many.

He Gives Us . . .

The Victory

"But thanks be to God! *He gives us the victory* through our Lord Jesus Christ" (1 Corinthians 15:57). This truth is re-echoed in 2 Corinthians 2:14: *"But thanks be to God, who always leads us as captives in Christ's triumphal procession and uses us to spread the aroma of the knowledge of him everywhere."*

These Scriptures are in the present tense. God *gives us* the victory, and He does it through our Lord Jesus Christ—the indwelling Christ who is also seated at the right hand of the Father interceding for us. And He *always* leads us in triumph in Christ. We are part of a triumphal procession. We cannot be part of Christ's triumphal procession and walk in defeat. We have been integrated into Christ's victory parade!

God gives us the victory because the victory belongs to Him. David knew this, and thus declared, *"Yours, O Lord, is the greatness, the power and the glory, the victory and the majesty; For all that is in* heaven and in earth is Yours; Yours is the kingdom, O Lord, and You are exalted as head over all. Both riches and honor come from You, and You reign over all. In Your hand is power and might; In Your hand it is to make great and to give strength to all" (1 Chronicles 29:11–12 NKJV).

David got the victory over Goliath, over the house of Saul, and over the fierce Philistines and other dreaded warriors he faced in battle because God gave him the victory. The victory is the Lord's. The kingdom, power, glory, majesty, and greatness are all His. Riches and honor belong to Him. And He can give any of these to whomever He chooses. Now, in Christ, He has chosen us as subjects of His kingdom and objects of His love. He gives us the victory—always, not occasionally—and then uses us to spread the fragrance of His knowledge in every place. What a heritage!

All Things Richly to Enjoy!

"Command those who are rich in this present world not to be arrogant nor to put their hope in wealth, which is so uncertain, but to put their hope in God, **who richly provides us with everything for our enjoyment**" (1 Timothy 6:17).

God gives us all things richly to enjoy!

Some want to paint God as a sadist—a killjoy. They see Him as a stern and sour, cosmic policeman bereft of fun and enjoyment. The word *enjoy* seems foreign to many believers: in their religious minds, *enjoying* must be carnal—an indication that one has not died to the flesh. After all, the way to eternal life is narrow and hard! Enjoyment is for unbelievers; the believers' promised lot on earth is tribulation; their enjoyment will be in the world to come!

But God's Word is clear: He *gives us* all things richly to enjoy! This is present tense, not future. Here is how some other translations communicate this amazing generosity of our gracious God:

" . . . God, who richly and ceaselessly provides us with everything for our enjoyment" (AMP).

"Tell them to have faith in God, who is rich and blesses us with everything we need to enjoy life" (CEV).

" . . . God, who generously gives us everything for our enjoyment" (GNT).

This is not the picture of God that most believers have in their heads. They dare not utter it but think of Him as stingy and difficult to get anything from. One must pray laboriously and believe assiduously to receive the simplest of His blessings. As far as they are concerned, "God gives us all things richly to *endure!*"

Do you know the God who "richly and ceaselessly provides us with everything for our enjoyment"? Is that your inner picture of your heavenly Father? Oh, that you will get a *biblical* revelation of our Father God and His overwhelming generosity.

We must renew our minds. One way to do this is to proclaim these truths continually—whether or not we feel like it.

It must be noted, however, that the divine provision is not for us to compete with the world or accumulate vain perishables in an age that is passing away. This present earth and all it contains are destined for fire. While enjoying God's bountiful provisions, we are to abound in good works, to bless the poor, and to deploy the resources for advancing His kingdom. We are to lay up treasures in heaven, not on earth, where moth and rust corrupt and thieves break in and steal. We are called to be His kingdom treasurers!

Life to Your Mortal Body

"But if the Spirit of Him who raised Jesus from the dead dwells in you, He who raised Christ from the dead will also give life to your mortal bodies through His Spirit who dwells in you" (Romans 8:11 NKJV). This statement of what the Holy Spirit will do is to be experienced beginning now. It declares what the Holy Spirit will do in us now and in the future—He gives life to our mortal bodies.

This is one of those promises that we are apt to postpone to the future, as in, the Holy Spirit will give life to our mortal bodies at last—at the time of rapture, when we get to heaven. But the text says no such thing.

The Holy Spirit dwells in us now. He gives life to our mortal bodies now. He will continue this sacred ministry in us until it climaxes at the sound of the last trumpet—when our mortal bodies will be changed and become immortal.

Imagine the infinite possibilities of having the same Spirit of Him who raised Jesus from the dead living in us. We explored this in chapter 9, "The Indwelling Spirit." *The same Spirit who raised Jesus Christ from the dead dwells in you!* He will do in us what He did in Christ. If He could raise Christ from the dead, then there is no part of our bodies He cannot flood with the life of God. What infirmity can survive such a "lethal" dose of life?

"We who are alive are always being given over to death for Jesus' sake, so that ***his life may also be revealed in our mortal body***" (2 Corinthians 4:11). The very life of Jesus Christ *manifested*—revealed—in our bodies! This is not a redemption benefit to be enjoyed during the millennium, for then we will no longer have mortal bodies. This is our present heritage. Christ is in you; He is the Vine and you are a branch. The same life that is in the Vine is pouring into you, a branch! What a heritage—the life of Jesus Christ manifesting in our bodies as we walk on earth.

The Lord Is . . .

The Lord Is My Shepherd Now:

"The LORD is my shepherd, I lack nothing" (Psalm 23:1).

You see, "***you were*** like sheep going astray, ***but now*** you have returned to the Shepherd and Overseer of our souls" (1 Peter 2:25). He is the good Shepherd—the One who laid down His life for the sheep. We are secured by our Shepherd. This great Shepherd of the sheep makes us complete in every good work to do His will, working in us what is well pleasing in His sight (see Hebrews 13:24-25). Bless His Name!

The Lord Is My Helper Now:

This changes everything. It assures my outcome in the battles of life. Nothing compares to the blessedness of enjoying the guaranteed help of the almighty Creator of heaven and earth. It is impossible for a person who is helped by God to fail. Consider Hebrews 13:5-6:

> Let your character or moral disposition be free from love of money [including greed, avarice, lust, and craving for earthly possessions] and be satisfied with your present [circumstances and with what you have]; for **He *[God] Himself has said,*** I will not in any way fail you nor give you up nor leave you without support. [I will] not, [I will] not, [I will] not in any degree leave

you helpless nor forsake nor let [you] down (relax My hold on you)! [Assuredly not!]. *So we take comfort and are encouraged and confidently and boldly say,* "The Lord is my Helper; I will not be seized with alarm [I will not fear or dread or be terrified]. What can man do to me?" (AMPC).

I have highlighted some parts of this amazing Scripture for emphasis. God says as insistently as possible, *"I will not, I will not, I will not in any degree leave you helpless nor forsake nor let you down nor relax My hold on you."* In the original language, there are three negatives in verse five, hence the repetition of "I will not" in the Amplified translation quoted above. How else can God say it for us to know He means what He is saying?

In the light of what God has said, we take comfort and boldly declare the reality of God's ever-present help: we will not be afraid, for what can man or demons do to us? *We speak on the basis of what God has spoken.* Because He Himself has said . . . , we take courage and boldly say . . . We have heard what the faithful One said that He is our helper and that He will never let go of us, so we say boldly, "The Lord is my helper; I will not fear. What can man do to me?"

Many of us are saying things that are out of harmony with what God has said about us, our situations, our past, our present, and our future. We speak, not in tune with God's unfailing Word but in line with our apparent circumstances. So, instead of soaring over them in faith and confident assurance and seeing the unfailing Word prevail over them, we allow them to overwhelm us.

God is your helper. That's a present reality: He is helping you *now* as you read these lines. And He has committed Himself to help you for the rest of your life. Whom should you fear?

"The LORD is my Light and my Salvation—whom shall I fear? The LORD is the refuge and fortress of my life—whom shall I dread?" (Psalm 27:1 AMP).

The Greater One Is in Me Now:

"You, dear children, are from God and have overcome them, because *the one who is in you is greater than the one who is in the world* (1 John 4:4,). This verse proclaims the Indwelling. There is someone in the world, but there is also Someone in the believer. And the One who indwells us is greater than the one who indwells the world.

The greater One is in us—now! He will not come into us when we get to heaven. He is much more than *for* us in the battles of life. He is much more than *with* us when we face our "Goliaths"—as He was *with* David when he confronted the giant from Gath. If a shepherd boy the Lord was *with* could topple Goliath, think what could happen if those He dwells *in* would dare to maximize His indwelling! He is *in* us—now—and He will be in us forever. His indwelling guarantees our victory.

Notice that this verse is addressed to "little children"; it proclaims the victory of "little children" over the mighty spiritual forces that rule this present age. How could little children win such a victory? What could be their source of power to prevail in such titanic warfare against the hosts of hell? Little children don't normally win battles; thus their victory must be from a source other than themselves. And it is: they overcome *because* He who is in them is greater than he who is in the world.

Jesus is called God's holy servant (some translations say "holy child") in Acts 4:27 and 30. He overcame because the Father—the greater One—indwelt Him. He declared in John 14:11, "I am in the Father and the Father in me." Later, in verse 28 of the same chapter, He called the Father the greater One: "I am going to the Father, for the Father is greater than I." Now the same greater One—the Father—who dwelt in Jesus also indwells you, the believer.

Isaiah 12:6 comes to mind: "Cry out and shout, O inhabitant of Zion, for *great is the Holy One of Israel in your midst!*" (NKJV). Here all the inhabitants of Zion, beneficiaries of God's saving grace, are told to cry out, to raise a shout of victory. The reason is given: the One who is greater than the greatest and higher than the highest—the Holy One of Israel—was in their midst. His presence was more than enough reason to shout!

You too have come to Mount Zion, to the city of the living God, to the heavenly Jerusalem, and to an innumerable company of angels (see Hebrews 12:22). The living God was in the midst of Israel as a nation, but in the New Covenant He is literally "in the midst" of each of His redeemed children, and in the midst of His Church. He lives within you—in the midst of your heart! And as with Israel, His indwelling presence is more than enough reason for you to wake up shouting every day of your life.

It is this great One—the Holy One of Israel—who indwells His people. He is the One the apostle John had in mind when he wrote, "He who is in you is greater than he who is in the world."

You may look like a feeble little child when compared to the challenges facing you—to that sickness or financial need or project, or to the great vision God has given you. But the greater One resides in you now. Remember this truth at every juncture of life. Remember it in the face of every temptation or trial. The fact that the greater One lives in you guarantees your victory.

The Lord Is With Me Now:

"Behold, I am with you all the days (perpetually, uniformly, and on every occasion), to the [very] close and consummation of the age. Amen (so let it be)." (Matthew 28:20 AMPC).

The devil suggests that I will be all by myself when the events that threaten me will happen. The issues of life assume that I will be alone when they arrive. How mistaken! The Lord is with me all my days, perpetually, uniformly, and on every occasion. He is not with me today and gone tomorrow; He is not any less with me when I can't feel His presence. He is with me uniformly—in the fullness of His love, power, and grace—to the very close of the age. His presence dispels my fears and worries.

The persons of faith we read of in Scripture were blessed with that presence—Joseph, Moses, David, and Daniel, among so many. But the Lord was not more with Joseph than He is with you. Meditate on this reality. We often cry for what Moses enjoyed—the manifest presence of

God, but Moses was not a beneficiary of the Indwelling. The fact that the Father, Son, and Holy Spirit indwell you automatically guarantees His presence. He is with you because He is in you! God is not less with the believer today than He was with Moses in the wilderness, or with Daniel in the lions' den. We just haven't taken God at His Word. We haven't dared to acknowledge and cultivate that Presence.

In the thick of his troubles from idolatrous monarchs and an apostate nation, Jeremiah proclaimed, *"But the LORD is with me like a mighty warrior*; so my persecutors will stumble and not prevail. They will fail and be thoroughly disgraced; their dishonor will never be forgotten. . . Sing to the LORD! He rescues the life of the needy from the hands of the wicked" (Jeremiah 20:11-13).

God's presence was more than sufficient for His prophet. The rebellious kings who persecuted and hounded him are all gone, but the legacy of this faithful prophet continues to impact lives. God's presence and help were the secrets of his enduring ministry.

The apostle Paul knew the reality of God's all-sufficient help. As his fruitful life drew to an end, he wrote to his protégé Timothy,

> At my first trial no one supported me [as an advocate] or stood with me, but they all deserted me. May it not be counted against them [by God]! *But the Lord stood by me and strengthened and empowered me,* so that through me the [Gospel] message might be fully proclaimed, and that all the Gentiles might hear it; and I was rescued from the mouth of the lion. The Lord will certainly rescue me from every evil assault, and He will bring me safely into His heavenly kingdom; to Him be the glory forever and ever. Amen (2 Timothy 4:16-18 AMP).

The Lord was there when everyone else walked out on Paul. Demas forsook him, but the Lord stood by him. Brethren abandoned him, but the Lord didn't: He was there through thick and thin. And His help was the only reason Paul could go as far as he did in the gospel: "To this day I have had the help that comes from God, and so I stand here testifying" (Acts 26:22 RSV).

A man who lived under the Old Covenant wrote the following inspired words: "The LORD is with me; I will not be afraid. What can mere mortals do to me? The LORD is with me; he is my helper. I look in triumph on my enemies. It is better to take refuge in the LORD than to trust in humans" (Psalm 118:6–8).

Surely we are heirs of a better covenant. We cannot enjoy less than the psalmist enjoyed. The Lord is on your side, now. And He is with you, as He ever was with anyone you read about in Scripture.

By the Grace of God, I Am What I Am

"But by the grace of God *I am what I am,* and his grace to me was not without effect. No, I worked harder than all of them—yet not I, but the grace of God that was in me" (1 Corinthians 15:10).

Paul here declares what grace had done in his life. He was all he was by grace. He accomplished all he did by grace.

That's true for you too. By the grace of God, you are what you are—righteous, redeemed, and loaded with the benefits of redemption.

By the grace of God your name is written in the Lamb's Book of Life.

By the grace of God we have inherited the divine nature. He is the great I AM, but by His grace I am what I am.

By the grace of God you are an able minister of the New Testament.

By the grace of God you have accomplished all you have achieved so far.

By the grace of God your tomorrow and eternity are guaranteed.

It's all by grace. Instead of denying what grace has granted us, we ought to acknowledge that grace and grow in it. His grace is our present reality—His omnipotent benevolence, His almighty kindness—is our portion in our journey from earth to heaven, from time to eternity. And it is more than enough.

(For a detailed study of grace, see our book *Overflowing Grace*, available at www.eternityministries.org).[14]

14

The Past Tense of God's Word—
about the Devil!

There is a song of victory we used to sing in our Christian fellowship in my undergraduate days:

I have seen, seen, the downfall of Satan
Glory be to God, Glory be to Jesus!
I have seen, seen, the downfall of Satan
Glory be to God, Amen!

When I look at my front, I see Satan has fallen
When I look at my back, I see Satan has fallen
When I look at my right, I see Satan has fallen
When I look at my left, I see Satan has fallen
I have seen, seen, the downfall of Satan
Glory be to God, Amen!

We would then change the words and sing, "I have seen, seen, the victory of Jesus. . . . When I look at my front I see Jesus has conquered, when I look at my back . . ." We would dance and dramatize the words, pointing to our fronts, backs, and sides as we celebrated the victory of the Son of God over Satan and all evil forces.

Have you seen the display of the defeated devil? Have you seen Satan's *fall?* His fall is revealed in the mirror of God's Word. The vision of the defeated devil is available only at the Cross. That was where it happened. Until you see it, you will continue to give the devil authority that he no longer has over you.

It is important to note the tenses in which God speaks about the devil. If not, we won't view him correctly; we will not see him in his current state. Something happened to Satan at Calvary that forever changed his narrative in relation to the believer—but he never wants God's children to discover it. He is no longer who he used to be, and he is no longer where he used to be. We too are no longer who we used to be or where we used to be! Calvary changed both of our stories!

I Saw Satan Fall

One time Jesus sent out seventy of his disciples on a mission. They did great exploits in His name. "The seventy returned with joy, saying, Lord, even the demons are subject to us in Your name! He said to them, '*I watched Satan fall* from heaven like [a flash of] lightning. Listen carefully: *I have given you authority* [that you now possess] to tread on serpents and scorpions, and [the ability to exercise authority] over all the power of the enemy (Satan); and nothing will [in any way] harm you. Nevertheless do not rejoice at this, that the spirits are subject to you, but rejoice that *your names are recorded in heaven*'" (Luke 10:17–20 AMP).

The Message's paraphrase of the event makes for interesting reading: "The seventy came back triumphant. 'Master, even the demons danced to your tune!' Jesus said, 'I know. *I saw Satan fall,* a bolt of lightning out of the sky. See what I've given you? Safe passage as you walk on snakes and scorpions, and protection from every assault of the Enemy. No one can put a hand on you'" (Luke 10:17–19).

Remember to pay attention to the tenses. The sense is in the tense.

Notice that Jesus put Satan's fall in the past tense. It was a real event, not a figment of imagination. Other translations of Luke 10:18 show the unmistakable certainty of Satan's fall:

"Yes, returned Jesus, *I was watching and saw Satan fall* from heaven like a flash of lightning" (PHILLIPS).

"*I kept my eyes on Satan*, he replied. *He fell* like lightning from the sky" (RIEU).

"I was beholding with a calm, intent, continuous contemplation Satan having fallen *in one fell swoop* from heaven like lightning" (WUEST).

Satan *fell*, and Jesus saw it: Jesus beheld him with "*a calm, intent, continuous contemplation*" as he fell from heaven "in one fell swoop". But the disciples, who celebrated the submission of fallen demons to the name of the exalted Lord, hadn't seen it. It happened so fast—like a bolt of lightning from the sky—a fallen angel of light falling from heaven! Since they hadn't seen Satan fall, they were surprised to see his demons subject to the Name of Jesus.

Satan's fall was not a secret in the spirit realm. The hosts of heaven saw the event. Even his demons saw him fall, as they fell with him. And while they submit to him as their twisted lord, they know in the depths of their seared souls that they serve a *fallen* master.

Isaiah was given a revelation of that event, which the prophet described in detail: "How art thou *fallen from heaven*, O Lucifer, son of the morning! how art thou *cut down to the ground*, which didst weaken the nations! For thou hast said in thine heart, I will ascend into heaven, I will exalt my throne above the stars of God: I will sit also upon the mount of the congregation, in the sides of the north: I will ascend above the heights of the clouds; I will be like the most High. Yet thou shalt be brought down to hell, to the sides of the pit" (Isaiah 14:12-15 KJV).

Satan's pride and rebellion caused him to be cast out of heaven. This was before Adam and Eve came on the scene: it was a fallen Satan who seduced Adam and Eve in the garden. Satan was not content with where his Maker had placed him, so he planned a terribly ill-advised coup against the King of heaven. He was "cut down to the ground." Satan fell in three worlds—heaven, earth, and hell. After he fell from heaven, the Son of God came to earth, crushed his head, and rose victorious over principalities and powers from the grave. Satan's fall will continue when he is cast into the bottomless pit, and finally into the lake of fire (see Revelation 20:1-10). He will be brought down to hell.

He has been sentenced to a downward spiral that is eternal in duration and bottomless in depth.

Satan fell. Keep that in mind in all your encounters with him. That is his new reality. He is not who he used to be, and he is not where he used to be. He used to be up there, but he fell. He used to be powerful, but he fell. He used to have authority, but he lost it all. It should not surprise you that he, his demons, and his works are subject to the Name of the risen Lord of the universe.

*"**I have given you authority and power** to trample upon serpents and scorpions, and [physical and mental strength and ability over all the power that the enemy [possesses]"* (AMPC), Jesus said to us. Notice again that this is in the past tense. Jesus didn't say "I will give you authority over all the works of the enemy." That would have been a great promise to look forward to, but that is not what the Master said. Instead, His words were, "I have given you authority."

If He gave you authority, this means that you already have it. You possess authority over all the works of the enemy. Nothing shall by any means hurt you.

Jesus uses the word *"trample"* to describe what His delegated authority will enable believers to do to the devil and his cohorts. "Trample" is not a kind or gentle word; it connotes crushing, irresistible power. In fact, it implies scorn or contempt for what is being trampled, and pride and triumph for the person doing the trampling. Such is the authority Christ has given us over the devil and all the power of the enemy.

We often wonder why the devil seems unrestrained, doing all he is doing to steal, kill, and destroy lives, families, and nations. It's because the people to whom Jesus gave authority over him are not using their authority. If the Body of Christ will discover and walk in the authority conferred on us by the risen, exalted Christ, we will put the devil on the run. "The reason the Son of God appeared was to destroy the devil's work" (1 John 3:8). Like our Master, we sons of God will also be manifested in the different platforms He has located us, to wield His authority to destroy the works of the devil.

I know that this seems too good to be true, but it is true. This is your present reality in Christ. This is who you are—a woman or man of authority, not a helpless victim of a defeated devil. Didn't you read that Jesus Christ conquered principalities and powers and bruised the head of the serpent? Why should it surprise you—you in Christ and indwelt by the same Christ who destroyed Satan himself—that demons should be subject to you in His name?

"Rejoice that your names are **written** in heaven" (Luke 10:20). There is that past tense again. Your name is not going to be enrolled in heaven. It is written there already—now, as you read this. It is written there because you believe what Jesus Christ did for you. The Lamb paid your price. You received Him as Lord and Savior. Now your name is written in the Lamb's Book of Life—in the book of the One to whose keeping you have entrusted your soul.

Many believers are so terrified of missing heaven. They live in perpetual fear of doing something that will erase their names from the Lamb's book of life. Some who have trusted Christ even doubt that their names are there! But you can bank on it. You can be sure of your eternal destiny. Glory to His Name!

Having Despoiled Principalities and Powers

The Bible is very emphatic on the fact that Jesus *subjugated* and *disarmed* principalities and powers. And He did a great job! Following is Colossians 2:15 from some Bible translations. Together they bring out several aspects of the triumph of Christ over all evil forces:

"And **having spoiled** principalities and powers, **he made** a shew of them openly, triumphing over them in it" (KJV).

"And **having disarmed** the powers and authorities, **he made a public spectacle of them**, triumphing over them by the Cross".

"There Christ **defeated** all powers and forces. He let the whole world see them being led away as prisoners when he celebrated his victory" (CEV).

The devil is not who he used to be. He has been *disarmed and defeated*. Notice that all of this is in the past tense: Jesus has *done* it already! Jesus didn't crush Satan, his principalities and powers, and make a spectacle of them in private: the event was very public—at the Cross where

He gave His life for us and cried, "It is finished!" Then He rose again from the dead. This was how He finished the one who was finishing us.

Here's how The Message and the Phillips New Testament render the same verse (Colossians 2:15):

"He **stripped** all the spiritual tyrants in the universe of their sham authority at the Cross and marched them naked through the streets" (MSG).

"And then **having drawn** the sting of all the powers ranged against us, he exposed them, shattered, empty and defeated, in his final glorious triumphant act!" (PHILLIPS).

Meditate on what this Scripture is saying. Satan was a cosmic spiritual tyrant, but Jesus Christ *stripped* him of his sham authority and marched him naked through the streets. My brother, Charles, describes him well when he says, "Satan is dethroned, disarmed, defeated and destroyed." No wonder Satan is so full of wiles and deceit—he lost his authority, so he now uses tricks, lies, and deceit to accomplish his agenda.

With Lies . . .

It's amazing what Satan accomplishes with lies. We see a stunning example of this from the operation of his earthly agents, whom God addressed in Ezekiel 13:22: "Because **with lies** you have made the heart of the righteous sad, whom I have not made sad; and you have strengthened the hands of the wicked, so that he does not turn from his wicked way to save his life" (NKJV).

Note that the twin evils here were accomplished with lies: saddening the heart of the righteous, whom God has not made sad, and strengthening the hands of the wicked, thereby entrenching them in evil. With lies!

Here's the same truth from other Bible versions; one marvels at the myriad things the devil does to God's people—with his lies! He

- "**intimidated** with lies the heart of the upright whom I had done nothing to alarm" (NJB).
- "**confounded and confused** good people, unsuspecting and innocent people, with your lies" (MSG).

- "**discouraged** righteous people with your lies, even though I hadn't brought them any grief" (GW).

The righteous are intimidated, discouraged, downcast, and experiencing things that are neither decreed nor sent by the Father. How? Why? Because Satan is using lies to accomplish these things against the righteous, whom God has blessed!

Here is a righteous person with whom the Father is at complete peace. There is no subsisting quarrel between her and heaven. The Father deeply loves and cherishes her; He longs to hear her voice uplifted in worship, to answer her prayers, and to meet all her needs. Indeed, all heaven celebrates her salvation and walk with God. But she is sad, discouraged, confounded, and confused down here on earth. She is depressed, disheartened, and sad, but it is not the Father making her sad. What could be the problem?

It's Satan at work. *With lies* he makes the heart of the righteous sad—whom God has not made sad.

He makes the heart of the believer fearful, whom God has not made fearful.

He makes the righteous hopeless, whom God has not made hopeless. With lies, he declares impossible something that God has not declared impossible.

He uses lies to intimidate God's children and fill them with an inferiority complex—whom God has not made inferior to anybody else! With lies Satan makes joint heirs with Christ depressed—whom God has not depressed!

He makes the child of God lonely, to whom God has guaranteed His presence! With lies Satan makes beneficiaries of the Indwelling feel helpless, forsaken, and abandoned—whereas Christ, the Holy Spirit, and the Father reside within them!

He brings condemnation to the righteous, whom God has justified in Christ.

With his lies, he makes the hearts of believers troubled, worried, anxious, and fretful—the very ones to whom God has guaranteed the unsearchable riches of Christ and the supply of every need!

You see why the solution to Satan and his wiles is neither more prayer nor fasting nor shouting, but truth. There is no antidote to lies, other than truth. No wonder Jesus declared, "You will know the truth, and the truth will set you free" (John 8:32). As important as prayer is, Jesus never said, "And you shall pray the prayer and the prayer shall set you free." Indeed our primary prayer should be for the opening of our eyes so that we can know and experience the truth. God's truth—the Bible—is our God-given lie detector. Anything contrary to that Word is false. We resist Satan and his lies by standing on that Word. We refuse everything the Father has not given us. We take captive every thought, emotion, or feeling contrary to our God-given inheritance. Victory is guaranteed when we confront the enemy with the sword of the Spirit, which is the Word of God.

He Has Done All Things Well

Scripture says of Christ, "He has done everything well" (Mark 7:37). That means that when He destroyed the devil, He did it well. When He defeated principalities and powers, He did so well.

You will not be overcome by what Jesus Christ has overcome. If the devil is conquered, it means he is no longer functioning as he used to—he is now like spoiled equipment. Jesus actually bruised his head; all the devil could do was bruise Jesus' heel—a picture of the pain and anguish of the crucifixion.

We do not deny the existence of the adversary. Or that he is walking about like a roaring lion seeking whom to devour. But we make bold to say that he has no power over a citizen of the kingdom of light. He has no authority over a child of God with Christ living on the inside—a partaker of the Indwelling. Indeed, the tables are now turned. As Isaiah prophesied (see Isaiah 14:2), God has taken our captor captive and given us authority to rule over our oppressor!

Cultivate the habit of viewing and addressing the devil in the tenses in which the Word describes him. In the light of the finished work of Christ, you will see him as he is—a defeated foe.

The One Who Had the Power of Death

Up on Calvary's Cross, Jesus Christ dissolved the greatest fear of mankind: death.

"Inasmuch then as the children have partaken of flesh and blood, He Himself likewise shared in the same, that ***through death He might destroy him who had the power of death, that is, the devil***, and release those who through fear of death were all their lifetime subject to bondage." (Hebrews 2:14–15 NKJV).

Here Scripture speaks of Jesus destroying Satan. Elsewhere we read the following words: "... ***The reason the Son of God appeared was to destroy the devil's work***" (1 John 3:8). "The reason the Son of God was made manifest (visible) was to undo (destroy, loosen, and dissolve) the works the devil [has done]" (1Jn.3:8b AMPC).

If we combine the revelations of Hebrews 2:14 and 1 John 3:8, we find that *Jesus not only destroyed the works of the devil, He destroyed the devil himself!* By partaking of flesh and blood, Jesus destroyed Satan and his works, abolished death, and brought life and immortality to light through the gospel. And he released us from the fear of death.

I have noticed the mortal fear many believers have of death, especially in Africa. The prayer points that elicit the loudest and most violent prayers in church these days are those that call for prayer against death. God's precious children scream, swing neck and arms, and stomp their feet as they try to keep death at bay with their prayers! But something more than prayer was required to overcome this age-old enemy of mankind.

Jesus did it on the Cross. He died in our place. And then He rose triumphantly from the dead, showing that the power of the grave has been broken. Now we walk in victory over death by faith in what He did for us. We know that our lives are hidden in Christ and in God. We know that our times are in the hands of the Father, not in the hands of enemies, demons, or witches and wizards.

Death holds no terror for the true believer. We are neither reckless nor suicidal, nor do we wish that our days on earth be cut short, but we are not terrorized by the fear of death. As a servant of God once said, for those of us in Christ, sudden death is sudden glory. Death becomes the corridor we pass through in our final translation to eternal glory. And the Great Shepherd will be with us when we pass through that valley of the shadow of death; we need fear no evil.

A closer look at Hebrews 2:14 reveals an amazing truth—if we carefully observe the tense! It refers to the devil as *him who had the power of death*. Notice that Satan *had* (past tense) the power of death. He used to have it, and, oh, how he used it to terrorize humanity and keep people in lifelong bondage. What Jesus did "set free those who had been in bondage all their lives *because of their fear of death*"—"those who were slaves all their lives *because they were terrified by death*" (v. 15 CJB, ISV).

The fear of death is still the greatest fear in the world today. It petrifies presidents and peasants and terrifies both the rich and the wretched.

It keeps people from doing what they know to be right.

It keeps people in slavery; instead of taking a bold stand for freedom, they cower.

It keeps them from going where they know they should go.

It keeps people from pursuing their dreams and maximizing their potentials. What if I were to die?

It keeps people from standing by their convictions. What if they kill me?

It binds people in stagnation. What if I fail or am killed?

In Jesus' Name, you are released from that paralyzing fear of death. Amen!

Once the fear of death is taken away, life explodes in a blaze of glory. Possibilities multiply; new vistas open for those who dare to risk death to reach for their dreams on the horizon.

Queen Esther went before the king, Xerxes, to plead for her people, the Jews. She lost the fear of death and declared, "If I perish, I perish!" Daniel and his friends stood on their convictions and were not terrified by fiery furnaces or the lions' den. Their love and reverence for God were stronger than their fear of death.

Delivered from the fear of death, we can obey the Great Commission and go wherever the Master sends. We will promptly and gladly obey Him—whatever the cost. What if we were to die preaching the gospel? No problem. We go home to our eternal rewards. What if we are killed for taking a stand for righteousness? No problem. We go to be with Christ, which is far better! People who have eternal life can afford to lay down physical life—for the right cause.

You see, *eternal life is superior to physical life.* This is why the early Church was not fixated on long life. Long life is good, but eternal life is infinitely and incomparably better. The one who has eternal life cannot be threatened by the termination of physical life. The fear of losing physical life cannot stop such a person from pursuing eternal objectives. This explains why God could allow people like John the Baptist, Stephen, the apostles, and a host of other believers to die the way they did. Their deaths were painful, but they were bearable. They left earth but landed in heaven. It's a different story for those without Christ. Even if they were to live a thousand years on earth, they are still headed to an endless eternity in a lake of fire.

Satan no longer has the power of death. He once had it. But Jesus defeated him and took the keys of death from him. But the enemy continues to terrify those who are not established in this truth. You shall know this truth, and it shall set you free from the fear of death—*permanently.*

Jesus declared, "I am the First and the Last. I am the Living One; I was dead, and now look, I am alive for ever and ever! And **I hold the keys of death and Hades**" (Revelation 1:17-18).

Jesus holds the keys of Hades (the world of the dead) and of death itself. Notice the present tense—He *holds* the keys of death and Hades! He *has* them because He defeated and disarmed the one who *had* those keys, i.e., the devil. Therefore you cannot pass through death's door until He opens it. And He will not open it until His purpose for your life is fulfilled—until you finish your life assignment. He will hold your soul in life and not allow your feet to be moved. He who keeps you will not slumber. No one can take you out of earth without His permission. He even has to authorize the death of the birds of the air! None of them can fall to the ground without His permission! How much more you!

You no longer need to "cower through life, scared to death of death" (Hebrews 2:15 MSG). Jesus died for you. Then He rose from the dead. He is the resurrection and the life, and He lives in you. He is your life.

Now, beloved in Christ, keep the central message of this book—the revelation of the Indwelling, in perpetual view. Jesus, who disarmed and defeated principalities and powers, now lives in you. He not only sits enthroned in glory at the Father's right hand, He indwells you. What can Satan and his cohorts do to you—a carrier of their risen Conqueror?

The same Christ who destroyed both the works of Satan and Satan himself now resides within you. This is not an idea or an illusion: it is sober fact. It is the declaration of God's eternal Word that is forever settled in heaven; it is unfailing truth that you can depend on. Christ is in you, and He is your hope of glory. He is your guarantee of permanent victory for all time and eternity.

15

Agree with God

These are my people, but when I speak in past tense they speak in future tense. When I speak in present tense they speak in future tense. And when I speak in future tense they speak in present tense. Can two walk together except they agree? Can two work together except they agree?

A prophetic word received by author

To walk in the fullness of redemption benefits and to maximize the full possibilities of the Indwelling, we must first agree with God. Often, we are so focused on the manifestation of the things we desire that we neglect the process. The process requires that we agree with God *first*; then there can be a manifestation of what the Word says concerning us.

"Then Jesus said, 'Did I not tell you that *if you believe, you will see* the glory of God?'" (John 11:40).

"I would have lost heart, **unless I had believed that I would see** the goodness of the Lord In the land of the living" (Psalm 27:13 NKJV).

If you believe (present tense), you will see (future tense), the manifestation of the glory of God. We desire to see first and then believe, but that flies in the face of the divine protocol for the manifestation of God's promises. We must agree with God first. We must count Him faithful, then He will do what He promised.

Even when we pray, we must note that it is more important to listen to God than to pray. Why should God listen to what we say if we pay no attention to what He has said?

If you listen to Him, you might hear Him declare in past tense something you are praying for Him to do. He might say "Done!" while you are pleading "Do!" As believers pray and fast in an effort to get God to do, to bless, to heal, etc., God says, "Blessed . . . Healed . . . Done! I did all that already!"

"Oh God, bless me!"

"I have blessed you with all spiritual blessings in heavenly places in Christ Jesus."

"Oh God, give me money!"

"I have given you everything you need for life and godliness."

This puts prayer on a very different plane. Many of our prayers ought now to be prayers of thanksgiving and acknowledgment—thanking God for what He has done for us in Christ already and giving Him glory for what He is doing in us by His Spirit's indwelling. We should also pray prayers of inquiry—seeking to hear God's heart and mind on issues. Instead of tabling our agendas before Him, we should be sitting at His feet to hear His priorities so we can discern and fulfill His purpose in our generation. This is quite different from the crazed and frenetic prayers of desperate believers trying to obtain something that God already declares to be theirs.

How God Speaks

If we are to come into agreement with God, we need to understand *how* He speaks.

For instance, when God speaks of the marriage *supper* of the Lamb (see Revelation 19:9), we are likely to think of an evening or night meal—according to our definition of supper. But God speaks according to His eternal reference points. He inhabits eternity and speaks from eternity's perspective. Since we know that there is no night in the heavenly city, then the marriage supper of the Lamb cannot be a night meal. This is an example of how we impose our earthly definitions on heavenly realities. It's also why we must renounce every preconception if we are to receive divine revelation. God's Word must forever be its own interpreter—we understand what God means by looking at it in the light of the whole counsel of His Word.

God doesn't necessarily present things as they are; He says things as He has purposed them to be. He issues eternal decrees over matters.

As Alpha and Omega, He has both the *alpha* word and the *omega* word—He speaks first and last.

As the omniscient, omnipotent Sovereign of the universe, He calls the things that are not as though they are. We see this in His dealings with our father Abraham:

"As it is written, "I have made you a father of many nations" in the presence of Him whom he believed – God, who gives life to the dead and calls those things which do not exist as though they did; who, contrary to hope, in hope believed, so that he became the father of many nations, according to what was spoken, "So shall your descendants be."

And not being weak in faith, he did not consider his own body, already dead (since he was about a hundred years old), and the deadness of Sarah's womb. He did not waver at the promise of God through unbelief, but was strengthened in faith, giving glory to God, and being fully convinced that what He had promised He was also able to perform" (Romans 4:17–21 NKJV).

God does not speak according to what is; He speaks according to who He is. What God told Abraham was in keeping with who He is: "I have made you . . . ," not "I will make you . . ."

God does not call the things that are as they are from our perspective. This is our version of reality. Neither does He call the things that are as though they are not. He calls the things that are not as though they are: He "speaks of the nonexistent things that [He has foretold and promised] as if they [already] existed." He "speaks of future events with as much certainty as though they are already past" (v.17 – AMPC; TLB).

Faith—like Abraham's—invites us to agree with God—to agree that things that are not, which He has called as though they are, will come forth and be, though we cannot see them presently.

Abraham was strong in faith, giving glory to God. He said "Amen!" to what God said. He so believed God that he raised the knife to kill his own son in obedience to God, in the firm conviction that God was able to raise him from the dead.

Satan strives to imitate God's ability to speak things that are not into existence. So he speaks his fears, terrors, doubts, etc. into the minds of people—so they can happen in their lives. He is speaking by a twisted "faith," confessing lies in the hope that the hearers will believe them, so they can happen!

The devil, too, does not speak according to what is, but according to who he is. This is why he always speaks evil, fear, disease, discouragement, failure, etc. How could he, being evil, speak good? How could he, the author of death, speak life? How could he, being a failure, speak success? How could he, being accursed, speak blessing? Keep this in mind whenever you hear his voice: it's his version of reality, not reality. There is no truth in him; this means that he does not have capacity to speak the truth, but only lies.

The Law and the Testimony

It is easier for us to agree with God when we understand that His Word is His law and His testimony. *"The law of the Lord* is perfect, converting the soul; *The testimony of the Lord* is sure, making wise the simple" (Psalm 19:7 NKJV).

Isaiah confirms the revelation God gave to David: "Bind up the testimony, seal the law among my disciples... To the law and to the testimony! If they do not speak according to this word, it is because there is no light in them" (Isaiah 8:16, 20 NKJV).

From the witness of these Scriptures, we see that God's law is perfect and His testimony is sure. His disciples are to bind His testimony to their hearts and set His law as a seal on their spirits. Their position, popularity, wealth, celebrity status, and expertise are secondary and immaterial: if they do not speak according to this Word it is because there is no light in them. They are walking in darkness—no matter how cultured or civilized they might seem.

Listen believer: if anyone or any situation speaks about your destiny, your future, and God's purposes for your life, but does not speak according to this Word—according to what the Word says about you—it is because there is no light in them. Their counsel shall not stand. Everything contrary to God's testimony about you is a lie, and "their lies shall not be so" (Isaiah 16:6 NKJV).

What clarity believers would enjoy if they would but agree with God! It would be so easy to make decisions, to determine what is right, acceptable, or proper. They would not be confused by society's changing standards or the glamorization of abominations. They would not be confused by the devil and his agents, nor would he be able to use his lies to cheat them out of their heritage. They would be men and women of conviction—fully persuaded on every issue in life. They would have a simple formula for solving problems and sorting out issues: *What is God's testimony on the matter? What does His Word say about it?* They would then search the Scriptures and seek His face until they found out. Then they would take their stand on God's testimony.

To understand God's testimony, picture God in the witness box in a courtroom. He lifts His right hand and swears by Himself that every utterance He will make will be true and nothing but the truth. Assume, for instance, that you are the judge who is going to make a decision on the case to which God is called to testify. Now Yahweh takes the witness box and gives His testimony on the matter.

Who could cross-examine Him? Who could discredit His testimony?

What would you do? Would you continue to call other witnesses and take other testimonies after you had heard from the all-knowing, omnipotent, omnipresent Creator of heaven and earth? Or would you close the case and deliver your judgment based on God's testimony?

But we call other witnesses after God has spoken! We read His testimony in His Word, but it doesn't suffice for us. We listen to our circumstances, our environment, our fears, our woes, and our wants—as though they are surer than God's sure Word!

I would be downright foolish to call other witnesses on a matter after God had testified about it. I choose to accept His testimony as sure. "Therefore I esteem all thy precepts concerning all things to be right; and I hate every false way" (Psalm 119:128 NKJV).

Faith is agreeing with God's testimony on everything—on who He says you are, your healing, provisions, and the world at large. To believe God is to order your life and make every decision from a conviction that God cannot lie—that His Word is true and trustworthy. To the woman or man of faith, God's testimony on everything is sure—dependable, reliable, trustworthy. His testimony is so sure that you can bank on it; you can make your decisions based on it. You can cast your hopes on it—for all time and eternity.

God's Word is His testimony. In it He testifies, "By His stripes, you are healed. I am the LORD that heals you. My God will supply all your needs according to His riches in glory in Christ Jesus. I will never leave you nor forsake you. When you pass through the waters, they will not overflow you, and through the fire, you will not be burned. You can do all things through Christ that strengthens you."

Everything you read in God's Word is His testimony. And his words are sure. When you agree with God, you are standing on solid ground, and your expectation will not be disappointed.

With regard to God's Word, you see, "whoever has accepted it has certified that God is truthful" (John 3:33). When you receive God's testimony, you declare that God cannot lie: "Whoever receives His testimony has set his seal of approval to this: God is true. [That man has definitely certified, acknowledged, declared once and for all, and is himself assured that it is divine truth that God cannot lie]" (Jn.3:33 AMPC).

When you agree with God's testimony, you declare Him faithful. You label Him true. You put a stamp of authenticity on His Person and promise. Can you see how this certification causes God to ensure the manifestation of your expectation?

On the other hand, anyone who rejects God's testimony has made Him out to be a liar. A witness and his testimony are inseparable. If God's testimony doesn't amount to much to a person, they are saying that God himself doesn't amount to much. How can such a god undertake for you?

"If we accept [as we do] the testimony of men [if we are willing to take human authority], the testimony of God is greater (of stronger authority), for this is the testimony of God, even the witness which He has borne regarding His Son" (1 John 5:9 AMPC).

We accept the testimony of experts in different fields and use their testimony to make our decisions. We accept the testimony of engineers and use them to build our homes, offices, or even skyscrapers. We accept the testimony of meteorologists. We accept the testimony of doctors.

But the testimony of a God who cannot lie is infinitely greater and of supreme authority.

On what testimony will you take your stand or decide the cases of your life?

The testimony of the senses is not sure. They are fickle, changing, and unreliable.

The testimony of your eyes is not sure. Our eyes lie to us all the time!

The testimony of your feelings is unstable and changing. But the testimony of the Lord is sure—making wise the simple. Agree with it. It will make you wise unto salvation, deliverance, victory, and good success.

As we continually receive, confess, and act on God's testimony, it becomes *law* to us. It no longer sounds like the testimony of an ordinary witness in a court of law, which can be accepted or rejected. It becomes final to us—irreversible, unbreakable, and sure.

"I have taken Your testimonies as a heritage forever. For they are the joy of my heart" (Psalm 119:111).

When we accept God's testimony, we become His faithful witnesses, bearing testimony to His truth. We become His instruments for calling others to faith in His testimony. Jesus is called the faithful witness (Revelation 1:5). By accepting His testimony, our own testimony becomes dependable—like His! Our testimonies to men and devils will carry His power if they are in agreement with His own testimony. But if our testimonies are contrary to the testimony of His Word concerning ourselves and our circumstances there is no power backing them.

The sense is in the tense. We must come into the same tense with

God. Only then can we begin to make sense of what He says to us in His Word. We must consider *past* what He calls *past* and perceive as *done* what He declares *done*. In this way we harmonize our convictions with the divine pronouncements, enabling His almighty power to execute His promises in our lives.

*Acquaint now yourself with Him [**agree with God** and show yourself to be conformed to His will] and be at peace; by that [you shall prosper and great] good shall come to you.*

Job 22:21 AMPC

PART FOUR

In this section we explore the unquantifiable possibilities of a life that is filled with all the fullness of God.

Filled with All the Fullness of God

That you may be filled with all the fullness of God

Ephesians 3:19

A Heritage of Fullness

You've probably heard of the illustration about water in a glass cup used to assess perspectives. Is the glass half-filled or half-empty? According to the illustration, those who see a half-filled glass are probably optimists, while those who see the glass as half-empty are most likely pessimists—as in, how come they focused on the empty portion and not on the filled?

Believers are spared this exercise in the New Testament. Ours is a faith of fullness, which fills us with boundless optimism—a living hope that is anchored on the unfailing promises of a faithful God. A child of God is too blessed to be pessimistic. Even a cursory look at Scripture shows that our God is a God of fullness; He desires that His children walk in His fullness. Indeed, the New Testament is filled with references to being "filled," "full," and "overflowing".

"Filled" appears 59 times in the New Testament (KJV, all in the paraphrases and quotes below). Consider the following references:

- Those who hunger and thirst for righteousness will be *filled* (Matthew 5:6).
- Many persons were *filled* with the Holy Spirit (Luke 1:41, 67).
- God *filled* the hungry with good things and sent the rich away empty-handed (Luke 1:53).
- Jesus grew and became strong in spirit, *filled* with wisdom; and the grace of God was upon Him (Luke 2:40).
- When Jesus multiplied the bread and fish and fed the multitudes, they all ate and were *filled*; even the baskets were *filled*! (John 6:11-13).
- On the day of Pentecost, the apostles were *filled* with the Holy Spirit; even the sound from heaven, as of a rushing mighty wind, *filled* the whole house where they were sitting. Thereafter, they were continually *filled* with the Holy Spirit (Acts 2:1-4; 4:8, 31).
- They *filled* Jerusalem with their doctrine (Acts 5:28).
- Believers were *full* of goodness, *filled* with joy, *filled* with all knowledge (Romans 15:14), *filled* with comfort (2 Corinthians 7:4), and *filled* with the fruits of righteousness, which are by Jesus Christ, to the glory and praise of God (Philippians 1:11). They were also "*filled* with the knowledge of his will in all wisdom and spiritual understanding" (Colossians 1:9).
- God's temple was "*filled* with smoke from the glory of God, and from his power" (Revelation 15:8).

Similarly, the words "full" and "fullness" abound in the New Testament.

- Jesus was *full* of grace and truth, and out of His inexhaustible *fullness* we receive grace upon grace (John 1:14, 16). "For it has pleased [the Father] that all the divine *fullness* (the sum total of the divine perfection, powers, and attributes) should dwell in Him permanently." (Colossians 1:19 AMPC).
- Stephen was *full* of faith and power, and did great wonders and signs among the people (Acts 6:8). Likewise, Dorcas was "*full* of good works and alms deeds which she did" (Acts 9:36 KJV); Barnabas "was a good man, and *full* of the Holy Ghost and of faith: and much people was added unto the Lord" (Acts 11:24 KJV).

- Believers are to walk in the *full* assurance of understanding (Colossians 2:2), the *full* assurance of hope (Hebrews 6:11), and the *full* assurance of faith (Hebrews 10:22). They are not to have these precious treasures in trickles, but in their fullness. They are to seek the wisdom that is from above, which is "first pure, then peaceable, gentle, and easy to be entreated, *full* of mercy and good fruits," and they rejoiced with "joy unspeakable and *full* of glory" (James 3:17; 1 Peter 1:8 [both KJV]).
- Wherever Paul went, he went "in the *fullness* of the blessing of the gospel of Christ" (Romans 15:29).

Thus, both the Lord and the believers in Scripture were full of the Holy Spirit, and with joy, power, faith, mercy, good works, knowledge, and all wisdom. As a consequence of the fullness they bore, they *overflowed* with thankfulness, joy, and generosity. They walked in the fullness of supernatural power—something many believers know so little about.

However, the most amazing fullness to which believers are called is to be *filled with all the fullness of God* even while here on earth—to be indwelt by and filled with God Himself, even as the Lord Jesus was! This is mindboggling, but, as we shall see in this section, it is the clearly revealed heritage of every child of God. Speaking of the Lord Jesus Christ, Colossians 1:19, quoted earlier, emphatically declares that "it has pleased [the Father] that all the divine fullness (the sum total of the divine perfection, powers, and attributes) should dwell in Him permanently" (AMPC). The astounding thing is that it has also pleased the Father that we, joint heirs with Jesus Christ, should likewise be filled with the same fullness that fills Him—that the Body should be filled with the same fullness that fills the Head!

Filled with All the Fullness of God

"For this reason I bow my knees to the Father of our Lord Jesus Christ, from whom the whole family in heaven and earth is named, that He would grant you, according to the riches of His glory, to be strengthened with might through His Spirit in the inner man, that Christ may dwell in your hearts through faith; that you, being rooted and grounded in love, may be able to comprehend with all the saints what is the width and length and depth and height – to know the love of Christ which passes knowledge; *that you may be filled with all the fullness of God.*

Now to Him who is able to do exceedingly abundantly above all that we ask or think, according to the power that works in us, to Him be glory in the church by Christ Jesus to all generations, forever and ever. Amen" (Ephesians 3:14-21 NKJV).

From Paul's prayer for the Ephesian believers above, a host of precious insights emerge.

The Father of Our Lord Jesus Christ . . . Our Father

The Father God is referred to as the Father of our Lord Jesus Christ. But He is not only the Father of our Lord Jesus Christ, He is also the Father of every believer. We share the same Father as our Lord Jesus. We belong to the same family. The same One who is Father to Christ is also Father to us.

This foundational truth is taught everywhere in the New Testament, and it is one of the reasons the Jews persecuted Jesus Christ, and the Church afterwards. Christ called God His Father, and to the Jews, that connoted equality with God—membership of the same class as the Almighty! Other religions cannot fathom the audacity of Christians in claiming that God is their Father.

The implications of sharing the same Father with Jesus Christ are unspeakable. If God is Father, then He is Father to the uttermost—an infinitely and incomparably better Father than any human parent—one who knows His responsibilities and has ability to fulfill them all.

In The Lord's Prayer, Jesus taught us to pray to "*Our* Father in heaven . . ." (Matthew 6:9). He confirmed this common fatherhood following His resurrection when He said to Mary, "Do not hold on to me, for I have not yet ascended to the Father. Go instead to my brothers and tell them, 'I am ascending to ***my Father and your Father***, to my God and your God'" (John 20:17).

Exclusive Privileges

The entire ministry of the Lord Jesus was to bring us, His brethren, into His own exclusive privileges: He died and rose to bring us, by grace, into all He was by right. Where He stood alone by merit, His finished work brought in His brethren by redemption. He wasn't content to be the Man in the glory, so He gave His life to bring many sons to glory (Hebrews 2:10). Blessed be His Name!

Here are several exclusive privileges Jesus had that He has graciously shared with us, His brethren:

- **Sonship**: Jesus was the only begotten Son of the Father; God was His Father—exclusively. But He doesn't monopolize the Father, as He has every right to. He shares the Father with us, His brethren! We now have the same Father as Jesus Christ: as Jesus called Him "Holy Father" when He prayed (John 17:11), so we too can now say, "Our Father . . ." when we pray. We too have been begotten by the Father: "Blessed be the God and Father of our Lord Jesus Christ, who according to His abundant mercy ***has begotten us*** again to a living hope through the resurrection of Jesus Christ from the dead." (1 Peter 1:3 NKJV; see also James 1:18).
- **The Beloved:** Jesus is the beloved Son of the Father (see Matthew 3:17). In Him we are *equally beloved* by the Father: the Father loves us as He loves Jesus Christ! "***See what an incredible quality of love the Father shown to us,*** that we would [be permitted to] be named and called and counted the children of God! And so we are!" "I in them and You in Me; that they may be perfected and completed into one, so that the world may know [without any doubt] that You sent Me, and [that You] ***have loved them, just as You have loved Me***" (1 John 3:1 AMP; John 17:23).
- **Eternal Life:** Jesus Christ now imparts the same eternal life He had exclusively with the Father (John 1:1-4) to all who trust in Him.

He has given us His own life: "My sheep hear My voice, and I know them, and they follow Me. And *I give them eternal life,* and they shall never perish; neither shall anyone snatch them out of My hand" (John 10:27-28 NKJV). "Even when we were dead (slain) by [our own] shortcomings and trespasses, *He made us alive together in fellowship and in union with Christ; [He gave us the very life of Christ Himself, the same new life with which He quickened Him,* for] it is by grace (His favor and mercy which you did not deserve) that you are saved (delivered from judgment and made partakers of Christ's salvation)" (Ephesians 2:5 AMPC).

- **Righteousness:** Jesus is the Righteous One (Acts 3:14-15), but because of His finished work we have now become the righteousness of God: "For our sake He made Christ [virtually] to be sin Who knew no sin, so that in and through Him we might become [endued with, viewed as being in, and examples of] the righteousness of God [what we ought to be, approved and acceptable and in right relationship with Him, by His goodness]." (2 Corinthians 5:21 AMPC).

- **The Indwelling**: Just as Jesus was indwelt by the Father (John 14:8-11), so are we: "Anyone who confesses (acknowledges, owns) that Jesus is the Son of God, *God abides (lives, makes His home) in him* and he [abides, lives, makes his home] in God." (1 John 4:15 AMPC).

- **Access:** Jesus had exclusive access to the Father: no one can come to the Father except through Christ (John 14:6). He has now granted us direct access to the Father in His name: "In that day you will no longer ask me anything. Very truly I tell you, my Father will give you whatever you ask in my name. Until now you have not asked for anything in my name. Ask and you will receive, and your joy will be complete. . . . In that day you will ask in my name. *I am not saying that I will ask the Father on your behalf.* No, the Father himself loves you because you have loved me and have believed that I came from God" (John 16:23-24, 26-27; see also Ephesians 2:18). We can come boldly to the throne of grace (see Hebrews 4:16).

- **Heirs:** Jesus was the singular heir of the Father, but He has now made us joint heirs. Everything that belongs to the Father was His, but He now shares His inheritance with us: "Now if we are children, then we are heirs—*heirs of God and co-heirs with Christ,* if indeed we share in his sufferings in order that we may also share in his glory" (Romans 8:17).

- **Holiness:** Jesus is the holy Son of God (Acts 4:27, 30), but He has now imputed and imparted His holiness to us, making us a holy nation, a royal priesthood, and a peculiar (unique and special) people (1 Peter 2:9–10).

- **Peace:** Jesus is the Prince of Peace (Isaiah 9:6), but He has given us His own peace: the same peace that He Himself enjoys and exudes. He took the chastisement that brought us peace—not such peace as the world gives, but the peace that He Himself enjoys. He has become our peace (Ephesians 2:14)! Now the peace of God, which surpasses all understanding, keeps our hearts and minds in Christ Jesus (Philippians 4:7). In John 14:27 Jesus said, ***"Peace I leave with you; My [own] peace I now give and bequeath to you.*** Not as the world gives do I give to you. Do not let your hearts be troubled, neither let them be afraid. [Stop allowing yourselves to be agitated and disturbed; and do not permit yourselves to be fearful and intimidated and cowardly and unsettled.]" (AMPC).

- **Wisdom:** Jesus Christ is the wisdom of God (1 Corinthians 1:23–24). However, redemption has now made it possible for Jesus to become our wisdom; He is wisdom to us and for us in all affairs of life. He fills us with wisdom through His Word and the Holy Spirit. This is so real that the Bible actually declares that we have the mind of Christ (1 Corinthians 1:30; 2:16).

- **The Light of the World:** Jesus is the Light of the world—a great light (see John 8:12), but He has given us His nature, which is light, and declares us to be the light of the world: "***You are the light of the world.*** A city set on a hill cannot be hidden." "For you were once darkness, but now ***you are light in the Lord***. Walk as children of light" (Matthew 5:14; Ephesians 5:8).

- **Reconciliation:** Jesus came to reconcile the world to God; now He has given us the same ministry that He Himself fulfilled: the ministry of reconciliation. As He was the Father's ambassador, we are now His ambassadors! "All this is from God, who reconciled us to himself through Christ and ***gave us the ministry of reconciliation:*** that God was reconciling the world to himself in Christ, not counting men's sins against them. And he has committed to us the message of reconciliation. We are therefore Christ's ambassadors..." (2 Corinthians 5:18–20).

- **The Holy Spirit**: As Jesus was filled with and anointed by the Holy Spirit (Acts 10:38), so has He given to us to be filled with the same Holy Spirit who filled and anointed Him. We now have the very same Holy Spirit who filled and led Christ throughout His earthly life: "And if the Spirit of him who raised Jesus from the dead is living in you, he who raised Christ from the dead will also give life to your mortal bodies because of his Spirit *who lives in you*." "By this we come to know (perceive, recognize, and understand) that we abide (live and remain) in Him and He in us: because *He has given (imparted) to us of His [Holy] Spirit*." (Romans 8:11; 1 John 4:13 AMPC).

- **The Faithful Witness**: Jesus is the faithful witness (Revelation 1:5), but He has also commissioned us to be His faithful witnesses: "But you will receive power when the Holy Spirit comes on you; and *you will be my witnesses* in Jerusalem, and in all Judea and Samaria, and to the ends of the earth" (Acts.1:8).

- **Authority**: Jesus has all authority in heaven and on earth (Matthew 28:18), but He has delegated that authority to us, His Body: "*I have given you authority* to trample on snakes and scorpions and to overcome all the power of the enemy; nothing will harm you" (Luke 10:19).

- **His Name:** The Father exalted Jesus and gave Him the name that is above every name (see Philippians 2:9–11), but Jesus didn't keep His name, with all its boundless power, to Himself: He gave that name to His Church: "And these signs will accompany those who believe: *In my name* they will drive out demons; they will speak in new tongues; they will pick up snakes with their hands; and when they drink deadly poison, it will not hurt them at all; they will place their hands on sick people, and they will get well" (Mark 16:17–18).

- **Conqueror**: Jesus Christ conquered Satan, sin, death, and diseases, but He didn't keep His victory to Himself; He gives us the victory: "But thanks be to God, who gives us the victory [as conquerors] through our Lord Jesus Christ" (1 Corinthians 15:57 AMP).

"Yet in all these things we are more than conquerors and gain an overwhelming victory through Him who loved us [so much that He died for us]" (Romans 8:37 AMP). We too have become overcomers through our faith in the overcomer who indwells us.

- **His Glory:** Jesus has given us the glory that the Father gave Him. "I have given to them the glory and honor which You have given Me, that they may be one, just as We are one; I in them and You in Me, that they may be perfected and completed into one, so that the world may know [without any doubt] that You sent Me, and [that You] have loved them, just as You have loved Me" (John 17:22–23 AMP). The following comment on this Scripture by Charles H. Spurgeon in his devotional *Morning and Evening* (entry for June 30) captures the wonder of what Christ has done for us:

   Behold the superlative liberality of the Lord Jesus, for he hath given us his all. Although a tithe of his possessions would have made a universe of angels rich beyond all thought, yet was he not content until he had given us all that he had. It would have been surprising grace if he had allowed us to eat the crumbs of his bounty beneath the table of his mercy; but he will do nothing by halves, he makes us sit with him and share the feast. Had he given us some small pension from his royal coffers, we should have had cause to love him eternally; but no, *he will have his bride as rich as himself, and he will not have a glory or a grace in which she shall not share*. He has not been content with less than making us joint-heirs with himself, so that we might have equal possessions. *He has emptied all his estate into the coffers of the Church, and hath all things common with his redeemed.* There is not one room in his house the key of which he will withhold from his people. He gives them full liberty to take all that he hath to be their own" (Emphases added).

- **Resurrection:** Jesus Christ is the *first begotten* from the dead (Revelation 1:5); we also are guaranteed resurrection from the dead: "But the truth is that Christ has been raised from death, as the guarantee that those who sleep in death will also be raised" (1 Corinthians 15:20 GNT).

- **His Throne:** Jesus is enthroned at the right hand of the Father, but He doesn't sit there alone: He shares His throne with His Body. For all eternity, the Head and His Body sit enthroned together! God "raised us up together with Him and *made us sit down together [giving us joint seating with Him]* in the heavenly sphere [by virtue of our being] in Christ Jesus (the Messiah, the Anointed One)." "To the one who is victorious, I will give the right *to sit with me on my throne*, Just as I was victorious and sat down with my Father on his throne" (Ephesians 2:6 AMPC; Revelation 3:21). We have *joint seating* with Christ! Since we are in Him, He sits enthroned *with us within Him!*

- **Everything:** All that belongs to Christ now belongs to the believer; He holds back nothing from His Church: "So then, no more boasting about human leaders! *All things are yours*, whether Paul or Apollos or Cephas or the world or life or death or the present or the future—*all are yours*, and you are of Christ, and Christ is of God" (1 Corinthians 3:21–23).

This is astounding. You will notice that the list is nearly endless. Jesus shares everything with us! Everything that belongs to Christ now belongs to us because we belong to Him. Who would dare to lay claim to the exclusive privileges of Jesus Christ, if not that His grace has brought us into all that was His alone?

Jesus and His Brethren

Jesus calls us "brethren"—"my brothers and sisters" (John 20:17, GW). "Both the one who makes people holy and those who are made holy *are of the same family*. So Jesus is not ashamed to call them brothers and sisters. He says, 'I will declare your name to my brothers and sisters; in the assembly I will sing your praises'" (Hebrews 2:11–12).

It is remarkable that prior to the Cross and His glorious resurrection, Jesus called believers disciples and servants; He called them friends. But after He rose from the dead, having secured our redemption, He called them brethren! He said to Mary, "Go . . . to my brothers and tell them, 'I am ascending to my Father and your Father, to my God and your God'" (John 20:17). Now He is the firstborn among many brethren (Romans 8:29)! We have become partakers of His divine nature and are born of His Spirit. We are members of the family of God. And since the Father is fair and impartial to His family, He is all He is to each of the brothers and sisters in the family.

We share the same Father with Jesus Christ. Meditate on this statement until it settles in your spirit. You are not an orphan; you are born of God, a member of His family.

Anyone who has the same Father as Jesus Christ cannot be like those who do not. Our case is different—made so by the Father we share. Hallelujah! According to Proverbs 17:6, the glory of children is their father: "Children's children are the crown of old men, and the glory of children is their father" (NKJV).

Fatherhood determines pedigree, genetics, characteristics, access, provisions, inheritance, and many other things. Children must receive genetic material from their fathers—and believers have received God's very own divine nature—the God kind of life. God's seed—His principle of life, the divine sperm—abides in the believer (see 1 John 3:9 AMPC). We have been born of God. This is solid reality, not just a nice verse in an old holy book. We are God's children here and now and will be for all eternity.

"His divine power has given us everything we need for a godly life through our knowledge of him who called us by his own glory and goodness. Through these he has given us his very great and precious promises, so that through them you may participate in the divine nature, having escaped the corruption in the world caused by evil desires (2 Peter 1:3–4).

Since we have the same Father, and all children receive inheritance from their father, we too have become joint heirs with Jesus Christ. "The Spirit you received does not make you slaves, so that you live in fear again; rather, the Spirit you received brought about your adoption to sonship. And by him we cry, '*Abba*, Father.' The Spirit himself testifies with our spirit that we are God's children. Now if we are children, then we are heirs—heirs of God and co-heirs with Christ, if indeed we share in his sufferings in order that we may also share in his glory" (Romans 8:15–17).

The implications of the above are astounding. Jesus Christ is no longer the exclusive and singular heir of God the Father. He was that before He went to the Cross, but what He enjoyed alone He decided to make the common heritage of all members of the family! As mentioned earlier, He brought us to be His joint-heirs, fellow heirs, and co-heirs—to the praise of the glory of His grace which He lavished on us, according to the good pleasure of His will!

Who but Christ could do this for another? What heir of a king or billionaire would make a way for nobodies to share his heritage? Would such heirs not use a battalion of lawyers to protect their heritage and give out handouts and peanuts to others? But it pleased Christ not only to make us joint heirs, but to pay the gruesome price to secure the heritage for us. He made us co-heirs with Himself of all that was His alone.

If God were to die today, all the joint-heirs would be involved in sharing His estate!

No heir could corner God's estate alone. But since the immortal God cannot die, He took on flesh and died, so the testament (His will) could become operative. Thus, we don't have to wait for God to die to enjoy our inheritance—He died (and was raised to glorious new life) already!

Every believer, then, must investigate this divine inheritance to which we are joint heirs. What are the riches of the glory of this inheritance that belong to the saints in light? They are ours—as much ours as they are Christ's. Glory to His Name!

Jesus has given us as much access to the Father as He Himself enjoys. It would be improper for members of a family to be denied access to their Father or to have their access limited by another member of the family. So He made a new and living way when He tore the curtain, thereby granting us unlimited access to walk and talk with the Father. We can now come boldly to the throne of grace and find mercy to help us in our time of need.

The Whole Family in Heaven and Earth

We see again from Paul's prayer that we are part of a family that spans heaven and earth. The Father of our Lord Jesus Christ has children in His family in both heaven and earth. Note that hell is excluded, for none of His true children are there.

We are on earth, but we are part of a larger family that embraces heavenly citizens. And it is the will of God that His family on earth should not be shortchanged simply because they are not yet in heaven. Therefore He has placed the same Spirit who rules in heaven into our hearts, that we may enjoy a foretaste of heaven even while we walk on earth. He even taught us to pray, "Your kingdom come, your will be done, on earth as it is in heaven" (Matthew 6:10).

No wonder Andrew Reed was not afraid to pray (in the hymn "Spirit Divine"),

Come as the dove—and spread Thy wings
Thy wings of peaceful love
And let Thy church on earth become
Blest as the church above

It could never be the intention of a father that his children at home should be provided for while those in transit should be forlorn and bereft. No. The Father of whom the whole family in heaven and earth is named has made provisions for His family on this side of eternity to reign as kings in life, by giving us everything that pertains to life and godliness. He has blessed us with every spiritual blessing in the heavenly places—even while we are on earth! The purpose of these blessings is so that we can enjoy the heritage of the family to which we belong—all purchased by the finished work of Jesus Christ.

Jesus taught us to pray that the Father's will be done on earth "as it is in heaven," not "when we get to heaven." This implies that He desires that we, His family yet on earth, will enjoy the boundless possibilities of His blessed will prior to our arrival in heaven, where we will reunite with the rest of the family. This way, His family both in heaven and on earth can enjoy His will, with none shortchanged.

"For it is through Him that we both have a [direct] way of approach in one Spirit to the Father. So then you are no longer strangers and aliens [outsiders without rights of citizenship], *but you are fellow citizens with the saints (God's people), and are [members] of God's household*, having been built on the foundation of the apostles and prophets, with Christ Jesus Himself as the [chief] Cornerstone" (Ephesians 2:18-20 AMP).

Strengthened with Might through His Spirit in the Inner Man

We see the revelation of the Indwelling in Paul's prayer for the Ephesians, that they might be strengthened with might by the Holy Spirit in their inner man: "May He grant you out of the rich treasury of His glory to be *strengthened and reinforced with mighty power in the inner man* by the [Holy] Spirit [Himself indwelling your innermost being and personality]" (Ephesians 3:16 AMPC).

What a prayer! What can move a person who enjoys this mighty inner reinforcement that the Holy Spirit can impart? Notice that this inner strength and reinforcement are consequences of the Indwelling.

Picture yourself enjoying such a blessing. You look quite ordinary on the outside. You seem like a regular human being to those that see and relate with you—at home or in the workplace. But what they cannot see is that there is an almighty Spirit inside you, indwelling your innermost being and personality, reinforcing you with mighty power. Spiritually speaking, you are much more impenetrable and immovable than reinforced concrete. There is dynamic power infusing you with strength from inside. You are ready for anything and everything. You can do all things through Him who strengthens you.

The indwelling of the Spirit means that the Holy Spirit can do in us everything He did in Christ, or in Paul or Peter or John. We are all members of the same Body, and we were all baptized into that Body by the same Spirit. We have one Lord, and one Father, the Father of our Lord Jesus Christ. To Peter's shock and amazement, Cornelius, a Gentile, received the same Spirit that Peter and the other apostles received! Thus, the Spirit we received is not inferior in person, character, quality, or quantity to the One the apostles received in the upper room on the day of Pentecost. Why should He be less in us than He was in them? Why should He do less in us than He did in them?

That Christ May Dwell in Your Hearts by Faith

"May Christ through your faith [actually] dwell (settle down, abide, make His permanent home) in your hearts! May you be rooted deep in love and founded securely on love" (Ephesians 3:17 AMPC).

Here Paul prays that the Ephesians will enjoy the reality of the indwelling Christ—that Christ would actually dwell, settle down, abide, and make His permanent home in their hearts—by faith. This is to be the actual experience of the believer: we are to go through life conscious of the fact that Jesus Christ in all His fullness actually lives in us.

Our faith in Him causes us to accept this reality. The more strongly we believe it, the more real His indwelling will be to us. It is not that our believing creates a nonexistent reality, i.e., that we are trying to believe something that is not real in the hope that it will become so. No. Our believing His indwelling acknowledges the existing reality of His presence in us and enables us to walk in that reality. Paul is praying that we will embrace the Spirit-revealed truth of His awesome presence in us.

Imagine for a moment that this is true. And it is indeed true. Imagine that somewhere in the depths of your person lives another Person. Jesus Christ, the Son of God, actually dwells in you. He abides in you. He is making His permanent home in you. He is not a visitor, dropping in occasionally from the heights of heaven to spend time with you during your "quiet time" and then racing back through space to His throne on high. No. He lives in you. You are His home. Christ is in you! And He is all He is inside you! It is not a portion of Christ who lives in you. All of the risen, exalted, glorified Christ lives in you.

Now face life with this reality. Believe it in increasing measure and with ever-increasing conviction. You cannot be stranded in life. The indwelling Christ is more than enough for anything and everything you can ever encounter. You can do all things through Christ who strengthens you—and keep in mind that He is not strengthening you from outside. He is reinforcing you with His mighty power *from within your spirit!* Christ is in you, and He is your hope of glory for all time and eternity.

Rooted and Grounded in Love

Notice that Paul's prayer that the Ephesians be *"[deeply] rooted and [securely] grounded in love"* is directly consequent upon the reality of the indwelling Christ. The only way to grow in love is to grow in Christ, for the love of God has been shed abroad in our hearts through the Spirit of Jesus Christ. Growing in love equates to growing in Christ; as you acknowledge His presence and submit to His lordship, He pours more and more of His love into your heart by His Spirit.

It must be hard indeed to walk in love if we have to always source that love from heaven. But what if Love Himself—Love personified—lived in us? Aha! Then all we need do is to let Love have His way, and His boundless love pours out through our spirits to a world in need.

No wonder Paul could love the brethren so much that he yearned for them with the tender mercies and affection of Christ Himself. He even calls God to witness to the truth of what he was saying! Listen to these various renderings of Philippians 1:8:

"For God is my witness, how I yearn for you all with the affection of Christ Jesus" (ESV).

"For God is my witness how I long for and pursue you all with love, *in the tender mercy of Christ Jesus [Himself]!"* (AMPC).

"For God is my witness how much I long for all of you *with the compassion that the Messiah Jesus provides"* (ISV).

Paul could love with the compassion of Christ because of the indwelling Christ. Once upon a time, Saul of Tarsus had no love for anyone—only hate. Then he met the Lord of love on the Damascus road, and everything changed. He was a new creature; old things passed away and everything became new. He was in Christ and Christ was in him. And with the very love of the Messiah Himself, the former murderer now yearned for, and pursued, other believers with love.

The indwelling Christ makes it possible for every aspect of His life, character, and Person to flow through us. He is living His life in us—full and free. His love, wisdom, grace, humility, and power can all flow through us as we acknowledge His presence and give Him room to work.

Jesus Christ has "become for us wisdom from God—that is, our righteousness, holiness and redemption)" (1 Corinthians 1:30). Remember that He is all He is in you. And the fullness of the Godhead dwells in Him: "For in Him the whole fullness of Deity (the Godhead) continues to dwell in bodily form [giving complete expression of the divine nature]. And you are in Him, made full and having come to fullness of life *[in Christ you too are filled with the Godhead* - Father, Son and Holy Spirit – and reach full spiritual stature]. And He is the Head of all rule and authority [of every angelic principality and power]" (Colossians 2:9–10 AMPC).

In Christ you are filled with what fills Christ—the same fullness of the Godhead that fills Christ now fills you—because you are *in* Him! You cannot be in Christ and not be filled with what fills Him. The same verses read in the translation of Kenneth Wuest, "Because *in Him there is continuously and permanently at home all the fullness of absolute deity* in bodily fashion. And you are in Him, having been completely filled full with the present result that you are in a state of fullness, in Him who is the Head of every principality and power."

Rooted and grounded in Christ, we now proceed to know and experience, in ever increasing measure, the breadth, length, depth, and height of His love that passes knowledge. This makes possible another amazing possibility of the Indwelling: we become filled with all the fullness of God!

Filled with All the Fullness of God!

"That you may be filled with all the fullness of God" (Ephesians 3:19 NKJV)

Exactly as he declared it to be the heritage of the Colossian believers in the passage above, Paul prayed that the Ephesian believers be *filled with all the fullness of God!*

Seriously? Did Paul really expect this prayer to be answered—for believers to be filled with *all the fullness* of God? Why, this is exactly true of Jesus Christ Himself—the fullness of the Godhead dwells in Him bodily: "In Christ lives all the fullness of God in a human body" (Colossians 2:9 NLT). It pleased the Father that all of His fullness should dwell in Christ, and now, from Paul's inspired prayers, we see that it also pleased the Father that all of His fullness should dwell in us, Christ's Body, as it does in Christ our Head. Paul's desire was for these believers to enter into the fullness of the Indwelling.

With possibilities such as these, we see why Scripture speaks of the exceedingly great and precious promises of God. This must be one of them. Peter had a close walk with the Master, and he had no other words to describe the infinite heritage we received when we trusted Christ to save us: "For His divine power has bestowed on us [absolutely] everything necessary for [a dynamic spiritual] life and godliness, through true and personal knowledge of Him who called us by His own glory and excellence. For by these **He has bestowed on us His precious and magnificent promises [of inexpressible value]**" (2 Peter 1:3–4 AMP).

Other translations describe these precious and exceedingly great promises as follows:

". . . precious and magnificent promises" (NASB)

". . . valuable and superlatively great promises" (CJB)

". . . absolutely terrific promises . . . your tickets to participation in the life of God" (MSG)

"He has granted us His precious and wondrous promises, in order that through them you may, one and all, become **sharers in the very nature of God**" (WEYMOUTH).

The possibilities of a life *filled with all the fullness of God* are absolutely terrific, superlative, and magnificent. These are exceedingly great and precious promises, and through them we have become sharers in the very nature of God!

Paul's prayer for the Ephesians is now the heritage of every child of God. The Ephesians could not have something that does not equally belong to all believers in Christ.

The Amplified translation provides further insight: "That you may really come] to know [practically, through experience for yourselves] the love of Christ, which far surpasses mere knowledge [without experience]; *that you may be filled [through all your being] unto all the fullness of God [may have the richest measure of the divine Presence, and become a body wholly filled and flooded with God Himself]!"* (Ephesians 3:19 AMPC).

Several dimensions of the prayer emerge: as a believer you are to

- be filled [through all your being] unto all the fullness of God
- have the richest measure of the divine Presence
- become a body wholly filled and flooded with God Himself!

I am to be *filled through all my being*—not just in one area but through every fiber of my being—unto all the fullness of God.

I can have *the richest measure of the divine presence,* not an occasional feeling of God's presence or occasional manifestations of that presence, but the richest possible measure of it. This is to be my default setting—a life in which I am daily and always saturated with the richest measure of the divine presence.

Just like the Lord Jesus, I am to become *a body wholly filled and flooded with God Himself!*

Consider the kinds of prayers this apostle prayed for believers— and the ones believers are praying these days. Who has bewitched us from our incalculable heritage in Christ toward the zealous pursuit of frivolities?

Other translations of Ephesians 3:19 further clarify our portion in Christ:

"I am praying this so that you may be ***completely filled with God***" (GW).

"You will be made complete ***with all the fullness of life and power that comes from God***" (NLT).

"And so be ***filled to the full with God Himself***" (TCNT).

"So that you may be ***made complete in accordance with God's own standard of completeness***" (WEYMOUTH).

"And so at last you will *be **filled up with God Himself***" (TLB).

What will happen to you if you pray these prayers for yourself consistently and then begin to experience the answers? Where will all the mountains and Goliaths and Hamans confronting you be? What will happen to the fears, worries, and anxieties that torment and harass your soul?

Can you imagine the infinite possibilities of *a body wholly filled and flooded with God Himself?*

These possibilities are not to be reserved till we get to heaven. They are ours now—individually and collectively. We can walk in them now. We can experience them now, in ever-increasing measure. How can people who possess these possibilities live at such low levels? Dear Lord, plant our feet on higher ground!

Indwelling Trinity

We see from the foregoing that the Father, the Lord Jesus Christ, and the Holy Spirit—the members of the holy trinity, i.e., the Godhead, indwell the believer. We note the following from Ephesians 3:

Verse 16: Believers are to be strengthened with might in their inner being through His Spirit.

Verse 17: Paul prays that Christ may dwell in their hearts through faith . . .

Verse 19: . . . and that they may be filled to the measure of all the fullness of God.

Since each Person of the trinity is God, the presence of any one of them equates to the presence of all three. If Christ is present in a life, then the Father is present too, because Christ and the Father are one. If the Spirit is present, then Christ is present because the Spirit is the Spirit of Christ. However, this Scripture clearly states the Indwelling presence of each member of the trinity in every believer. The Spirit strengthens us in the inner man, Christ dwells in our hearts by faith, and we are filled with all the fullness of God.

What are the possibilities inherent in carrying the holy trinity inside you? People argue about the trinity and try to fathom the mystery of its meaning, but by far the greatest mystery is that we are indwelt by the trinity. The unfathomable indwells us! The same fullness of the Godhead that resides in Christ has now become the heritage of all those who are in Christ:

"For in Him the whole fullness of Deity (the Godhead) continues to dwell in bodily form [giving complete expression of the divine nature]. And you are in Him, made full and having come to fullness of life [*in Christ you too are filled with the Godhead - Father, Son and Holy Spirit - and reach full spiritual stature*]. And He is the Head of all rule and authority [of every angelic principality and power]" (Colossians 2:9-10 AMPC).

Exceedingly Abundantly Above

Now to Him who is able to do exceedingly abundantly above all that we ask or think, according to the power that works in us (Ephesians 3:20 NKJV).

It would still be stupendous if God were to do what Paul prayed for—for believers to enjoy the inner reinforcement of the Holy Spirit and be filled with all the fullness of God. But Paul didn't stop there. He spoke of the God who is able to do *exceedingly abundantly above all that we ask or think!* Earlier, in Ephesians 1:19, he spoke of *the exceeding greatness of His power toward us who believe.*

What happens when we pray for the fulfillment of *exceedingly great promises* and God does *exceedingly abundantly above all that we ask or think,* according to the *exceeding greatness of His power at work in us?* We are now dealing with exponential possibilities—*exceedingly cubed* (E^3!).

Consider the following equation (it's simple enough, so don't worry if you are not a math guru):

Exceedingly great promise—*our believing prayer*

$\times$

Exceeding greatness of His power—*God's method*

$\times$

Exceedingly abundantly above—*God's response*

$=$

Exceedingly, exceedingly, exceeding, abundantly, above possibilities!

Don't try to remember the equation! Just remember all the instances of *"exceeding"* and *"exceedingly"* we are dealing with here.

Do you begin to get an idea of what belongs to us because we belong to Christ? Church is much more than a gathering on Sunday to clap hands and share some elementary testimonies. We are called to serious stuff. Each of us has unclaimed, exceedingly great and precious promises outstanding in our kingdom accounts. We can know the strength of the Spirit's inner reinforcement; we can be strengthened by His Spirit with power permeating our inmost beings (see Ephesians 3:16, JB PHILLIPS, WEYMOUTH). We can walk in the breadth, length, depth, and height of God's love in ever-increasing measure. We can be *filled with all the fullness of God!*

God can do surpassingly more, unutterably more, and immeasurably more than all we ask or imagine (Ephesians 3:20 GOODSPEED, WILLIAMS, NEB). We must enlarge our hearts.

"I am the LORD your God, who brought you up out of Egypt. Open wide your mouth and I will fill it" (Psalm 81:10).

Indwelling Power

Let's take another look at the power that is operating in us, discussed in Chapter 6 ("The Power That Works in Us").

"Now to Him who, **in exercise of His power that is at work within us,** is able to do infinitely beyond all our highest prayers or thoughts—to Him be the glory in the Church and in Christ Jesus to all generations, world without end! Amen" (Ephesians 3:20–21 WEYMOUTH).

Paul brings his prayer to a close by showing *how* God does what He does in us: by His power at work within us.

In our fixation on externals, believers are focused on what is going to happen to them from outside. They expect God to thunder from heaven, descend in fire or smoke, and attend to their issues. They hope that an angel will descend from heaven with the answers they are expecting. But all the while they neglect the indwelling power.

"Now to the One who is able to do beyond all things, superabundantly beyond and over and above those things that we are asking for

ourselves and considering, ***in the measure of the power which is operative in us,*** to Him be the glory in the Church and in Christ Jesus into
all the generations of the age of the ages. Amen" (Ephesians 3:20-21
WUEST).

Pay attention to what is going on inside you. If you are indwelt by
Christ, this means that the omnipotent Messiah resides in you. That
is where the power is. He desires to do exceedingly abundantly above
all you ask or think or imagine—infinitely beyond your highest hopes,
thoughts, or dreams. But He will do it *according to His power that works
in you*—according to the reality and power of the indwelling One.

You are the temple of the living God; He dwells in you. His saving
power is working in you. His healing power is working in you. His Word
is working in you. His infinite wisdom is at work in you, filling you with
insight, hindsight, foresight, and ability to deal prudently in life. His
superhuman power is at work in you. His creative, innovative Spirit is
at work in you, filling you with revolutionary ideas and groundbreak-
ing solutions. His peace that surpasses understanding is active in your
heart. His omnipotent grace is working in you. In short, the fullness
of all the divine attributes is at work in you, transforming you into the
very image of Christ Himself. This is not hype or vain repetition: it is
the amazing revelation of your heritage as God's dwelling place. And
He will indwell you forever.

You see, "it is God who works ***in you*** both to will and to do for His
good pleasure"(Philippians 2:13 NKJV). God is in you; He is working
in you. He is transforming you from within and empowering you from
within with everything you need for life and godliness.

His Word is working in you to quicken you from inside and impart
His life to your entire being: "the word of God, ***which is effectually at
work in you who believe*** [exercising its inherent, supernatural power
in those of faith]" (1 Thessalonians 2:13 AMP).

In explaining how he was able to handle the kind of explosive ministry he did, Paul himself spoke of God's power at work in Him: "I labor
[unto weariness], ***striving with all the superhuman energy which He
so mightily enkindles and works within me.***" (Colossians 1:29 AMPC).

This is not true of Paul alone; it belongs to every believer. The same
One who lived inside Paul and worked in him is at work in us as well.

And by His unlimited power at work in us, He will do "superabundantly more than all that we dare ask or think [infinitely beyond our greatest prayers, hopes, or dreams], according to His power that is at work within us" (Ephesians 3:20 AMP).

Making It Ours

By including Paul's prayer for the Ephesian believers in Scripture, the Holy Spirit made it the heritage of every believer. This means that we can pray that prayer for ourselves and expect it to be answered in our lives, as much as Paul expected it to be answered for the Ephesians.

We must attend to God's Word in order for it to work in our lives. *We must seek to narrow the gap between our knowledge of God's Word and our experience of that Word.* If we read these exceedingly great and precious promises and move on, they remain on the pages of Scripture. But they were not written just to decorate our Bibles with nice but nonfunctional promises: they were written so they can manifest in our lives. If we stand on Scripture, Scripture will stand for us.

> My son, ***give attention to my words***; Incline your ear to my sayings. Do not let them depart from your eyes; Keep them in the midst of your heart; for they are life to those who find them, And health to all their flesh. Keep your heart with all diligence, for out of it spring the issues of life.(Proverbs 4:20-23 NKJV).

In this passage, we see a process that will make God's Word life to us and health to all our flesh. We must attend to it, incline our hearts to it, and refuse to let it depart from our eyes. We must keep it in the midst of our hearts—incubating it and stoking the inner fire—until it releases its power into our lives.

We can ask, like Rebecca, "If it is so, why am I like this?" (Genesis 25:22 NKJV) That is the kind of question that drives us to transformation. "If these things are possible, why am I living at such a low level? How come I am defeated, downcast, and harassed by the enemy while I have these promises by a God who cannot lie, in His Word that is forever settled in heaven?" When we ask questions such as these, a stirring begins in us that will move us towards enjoying our inheritance.

In the face of these precious promises, we can say with Mary, "Behold, I am the servant of the Lord; let it be to me according to your word" (Luke 1:38 ESV).

To make this amazing heritage yours in practical experience, I recommend the following:

- Read the passage (Ephesians 3:14–21) repeatedly, asking the Holy Spirit for light. Repetition is the key to retention. The more you go over the passage, the more insight you will receive.
- Read the passage from as many Bible translations as possible. This will throw more light on it and help to reveal the full dimensions and possibilities of the God-filled life. Several translations can be found online at the websites www.biblehub.com and www.bible gateway.com, among others.
- Spend time to meditate on the prayer (Ephesians 3:14–21), as well as other prayers Paul prayed for believers (see Ephesians 1:15–23, Philippians 1:9–11, and Colossians 1:9–14, among others).
- Pray these prayers for yourself and others regularly. You can actually read them out loud directly from your Bible. Personalize them while you pray, inserting "me" or "I" or "we" where appropriate. These prayers can also be prayed for other believers, as well as by congregations in churches or fellowships.
- As you pray these Scriptures, feel free to pray both in your understanding and in the Spirit—as God stirs your heart.
- Memorize the prayer from your preferred translation of the Bible so you can pray it even if you don't have your Bible with you.
- Confess the truths contained in these Scriptures. Faith speaks—we believe, therefore we speak (see 2 Corinthians 4:13). As you speak them over your life and over other believers, your faith will grow, enabling you to enjoy your full inheritance in Christ.
- Take practical steps of faith as the Lord directs you.

These things will not work automatically. However, if we follow the process and keep at it, we will increasingly come into the place of knowledge, insight, and maturity that will establish us in our inheritance. The measure of attention we give to these realities will determine the levels at which we will operate in them.

And He (Jesus) said to them, Be careful what you are hearing. *The measure [of thought and study] you give [to the truth you hear] will be the measure [of virtue and knowledge] that comes back to you* - and more [besides] will be given to you who hear (Mark 4:24 AMPC).

Stirring Up the Power

"That is why I would remind you to *stir up (rekindle the embers of, fan the flame of, and keep burning) the [gracious] gift of God, [the inner fire] that is in you* by means of the laying on of my hands [with those of the elders at your ordination].For God did not give us a spirit of timidity (of cowardice, of craven and cringing and fawning fear), but [He has given us a spirit] of power and of love and of calm and well-balanced mind and discipline and self-control" (2 Timothy 1:6-7 AMPC).

As Paul encouraged Timothy, I wish to encourage and challenge you: attend to the power that is within you. Stir it up!

There is a river running deep within your spirit, whose streams shall make glad the holy place of the tabernacles of the Most High. God is in the midst of you [see Psalm 46]. The same One who sits enthroned in heaven lives in your heart.

Out of your innermost being will flow rivers of living water—and many will drink and be refreshed. Life and blessing will break out wherever that river flows.

There is a Spirit in you, and He is not a spirit of timidity, cowardice, or craven fear. He is a Spirit of power, of love, and of sound mind. But He will remain dormant in you as long as you neglect His mighty power that is at work in you.

There are divine deposits buried deep inside you. They need to be stirred up. There are embers that need to be rekindled so the inner fire that God put in you can burst into flame. As you do, you will walk in the realities of the Indwelling. This was how the Christ life was designed to work in the believer. You will walk on earth with the eternal One walking in you, His Spirit pouring strength into your inner man, His love glowing in your spirit—until you are filled with all the fullness of God.

> *"Now to Him who is able to [carry out His purpose and] do superabundantly more than all that we dare ask or think [infinitely beyond our greatest prayers, hopes, or dreams], according to His power that is at work with us, to Him be the glory in the church and in Christ Jesus through all generations forever and ever. Amen."*
>
> Ephesians 3:20-21 AMP

PART FIVE

Responding to and Maximizing the Indwelling

17

Nonstop Gratitude

"Add Prayer! Add Thanksgiving!"

I was praying recently and heard these Spirit-inspired words rising from deep within my heart: *"Tinye ekene! Tinye ekene! Tinye ekene!"* I immediately recognized them: they were from my native Igbo, the language of the Ibo people of southeastern Nigeria. *"Tinye ekene!"* means "Add thanksgiving!" Some years ago, a similar word had come from the Lord, instructing *"Tinye ekpere!"* meaning "Add prayer!" The Lord was instructing us to add prayer to the work—to ensure that the prayer base of the ministry matched its growth. For a ministry to outstrip its prayer base is dangerous; the Lord was calling us to greater intercession for the greater things He was doing and desired to do in the ministry.

It is impossible to ignore the recurrent emphasis on continual thanksgiving and praise to God for all that He has done for us in Christ. It's everywhere in the New Testament. We must add thanksgiving—in limitless doses—to our Christian life!

Grateful Hearts

Gratitude and praise are the logical responses of the regenerated human spirit to the ceaseless mercies of God, and especially for the Indwelling. They burst out spontaneously from the grateful hearts of the redeemed. It is impossible to see the wonders of our redemption and the unsearchable riches available to us in Christ and not be moved to heartfelt and continuous gratitude for the grace that changed our damnation to salvation. We are all eternally indebted to God's grace—it is a debt we could never repay. The least we can do is bring a continual sacrifice of thanksgiving, giving glory to His name.

Our entire Christian life is to abound with nonstop gratitude and to overflow with thanksgiving. "So then, just as you received Christ Jesus as Lord, continue to live your lives in him, rooted and built up in him, strengthened in the faith as you were taught, and *overflowing* with thankfulness" (Colossians 2:6-7). This does not speak of an occasional word of thanks but of an overflow of thankfulness.

Thanksgiving is not something we should do sporadically but something that should continually overflow from the rivers of living water bubbling up in our spirits. The realities of the Indwelling and all other amazing benefits of our redemption should call forth deep gratitude to God from our inmost beings.

We are to come before Him with thanksgiving: *"Enter his gates with thanksgiving and his courts with praise; give thanks to him and praise his name.* For the LORD is good and his love endures forever; his faithfulness continues through all generations" (Psalm 100:4-5).

We are to thank Him for His indescribable gift (see 2 Corinthians 9:15).

We are to continually give "thanks to the Father, who has qualified [us] to share in the inheritance of his holy people in the kingdom of light" (Colossians 1:12).

We are to thank Him at all times, in everything, and for everything: *"Give thanks in all circumstances*; for this is God's will for you in Christ Jesus" (1 Thessalonians 5:18).

"Speak to one another in psalms and hymns and spiritual songs, [offering praise by] singing and making melody with your heart to the Lord; *always giving thanks* to God the Father for all things, in the name of the Lord Jesus Christ" (Ephesians 5:19-20 AMP).

"And whatever you do, whether in word or deed, do it all in the name of the Lord Jesus, *giving thanks* to God the Father through him" (Colossians 3:17).

We are to thank Him for giving us the victory through our Lord Jesus Christ: "But thanks be to God, who gives us the victory [as conquerors] through our Lord Jesus Christ" (1 Corinthians 15:57 AMP).

We are to thank Him for the triumphant life we have in Christ, and for spreading the fragrance of His person, presence, and power through us: "But thanks be to God, who always leads us in triumph in Christ, and manifests through us the sweet aroma of the knowledge of Him in every place" (2 Corinthians 2:14 NASB).

All our prayers are to be supercharged with thanksgiving: "Devote yourselves to prayer, keeping alert in it with an attitude of thanksgiving" (Colossians 4:2).

"Do not be anxious about anything, but in every situation, by prayer and petition, *with thanksgiving*, present your requests to God. And the peace of God, which transcends all understanding, will guard your hearts and your minds in Jesus Christ" (Philippians 4:6-7).

Complainers and the ungrateful are classed with the unholy, the proud, and blasphemers, and they do not have any inheritance in the kingdom of God (see 2 Timothy 3:2; Jude 1:14-16). What does a true child of God have to complain about? A joint-heir with Christ is too satiated to be grouchy and grumpy. His heart overflows continually with gratitude for God's kindness and grace.

Do and Done

We have reduced thanksgiving to something we offer on special occasions, monthly or annually—with the turkey and other trappings of Thanksgiving. In some churches, believers dance to the altar and present "special" offerings to God—and then the minister prays some special "breakthrough" prayers over them. Others advocate thanksgiving as a surefire way to get God to intervene in our situations.

Some thanksgiving, even if random, is better than none. Ingratitude is a curse. Just as the love of money is a root of all kinds of evil, so is ingratitude. The litany of evils listed in Romans 1:21-32, including pride, idolatry, murder, sexual immorality, and perversion, were all rooted in a failure to gratefully acknowledge God: "Although they knew God, **they neither glorified him as God nor gave thanks to him**, but their thinking became futile and their foolish hearts were darkened" (Romans 1:21).

Eugene Petersen describes the descent into moral and global chaos in dramatic language:

> What happened was this: People knew God perfectly well, but when they didn't treat him like God, refusing to worship him, they trivialized themselves into silliness and confusion so that there was neither sense nor direction left in their lives. They pretended to know it all, but were illiterate regarding life. They traded the glory of God who holds the whole world in his hands for cheap figurines you can buy at any roadside stand.
>
> So God said, in effect, "If that's what you want, that's what you get." It wasn't long before they were living in a pigpen, smeared with filth, filthy inside and out. And all this because they traded the true God for a fake god, and worshiped the god they made instead of the God who made them—the God we bless, the God who blesses us. Oh, yes!
>
> Worse followed. Refusing to know God, they soon didn't know how to be human either—women didn't know how to be women, men didn't know how to be men. Sexually confused, they abused and defiled one another, women with women, men with men—all lust, no love. And then they paid for it, oh, how they paid for it—emptied of God and love, godless and loveless wretches.
>
> Since they didn't bother to acknowledge God, God quit bothering them and let them run loose. And then all hell broke loose: rampant evil, grabbing and grasping, vicious backstabbing. They made life hell on earth (Romans 1:21-29 MSG).

Acknowledging God is far more important than most imagine. It is the vital foundation of the blessed life. A failure to thankfully acknowledge Him—to know that He made us, that we are the work of His hands—and to give Him the appropriate glory due to Him, is at the center of the current chaos in the world.

But our case is different. We acknowledge Him. We thank Him. Without seeing Him, we love Him. And our hearts overflow with gratitude for the abundant and eternal life He has given us.

In sending Christ to secure our redemption, God has already done exceedingly abundantly above all we could ever ask or think. Jesus was not sent because we realized our need and petitioned heaven for a Savior. The loving heart of the Father decided to send the incarnate Son to us before the foundation of the world. And it was His good pleasure to do so. Can we not trust Him who had our welfare in heart from all eternity to meet our every present need?

If someone were to give you a billion dollars but you were yet to receive a car he promised, that would not prevent you from thanking him for the umpteenth time. It would be nice to have the car, but you would never lose sight of the billion dollars in your bank account. He has already done more than enough. Our case is similar—only infinitely more glorious.

The answers to your prayers might not have arrived, but Jesus Christ, the Lord of the universe, God's Indescribable gift, has already arrived in your heart. He dwells in you. When God gave Jesus to you, He gave you everything; His presence in your heart guarantees every blessing for all time and eternity. He is your hope of glory. And that is more than enough.

We might have waited for some things for a long time, but we are not waiting to have our names entered in the Lamb's Book of Life. By the grace of God, they're there already. So we rejoice, not because demons and situations and circumstances are subject to us but because our names are written where it matters most: we are certified citizens of heaven.

The thanksgiving enjoined in the New Testament does not focus on what God will do for us but on what He has already done. He has done more than enough for us in Christ—such that even if all He did was give us Jesus, that would be sufficient reason for our ceaseless gratitude.

"He who did not spare His own Son, but gave Him up for us all—how will he not also, along with him, graciously give us all things?" (Romans 8:32).

Paul's Nonstop Gratitude

Paul couldn't stop thanking God. Gratitude overflows in all his letters. Even in his most difficult moments, he was ceaseless in his thanksgiving. He overflowed in wonder and gratitude to the Lord for saving him and calling him to the ministry. You can feel his heart pulsating with praise in the following verses:

> *I'm so grateful* to Christ Jesus for making me adequate to do this work. He went out on a limb, you know, in trusting me with this ministry. The only credentials I brought to it were invective and witch hunts and arrogance. But I was treated mercifully because I didn't know what I was doing—didn't know Who I was doing it against! Grace mixed with faith and love poured over me and into me. And all because of Jesus.
> Here's a word you can take to heart and depend on: Jesus Christ came into the world to save sinners. I'm proof—Public Sinner Number One—of someone who could never have made it apart from sheer mercy. And now he shows me off—evidence of his endless patience—to those who are right on the edge of trusting him forever.
> Deep honor and bright glory
>   to the King of All Time—
> One God, Immortal, Invisible,
>   ever and always. Oh, yes!"
> (1 Timothy 1:12–17 MSG).

He couldn't stop thanking God for the brethren and the churches—the ones he had established, as well as others. To Timothy he wrote, "*I thank God*, whom I serve, as my ancestors did, with a clear conscience, as night and day I constantly remember you in my prayers" (2 Timothy 1:3).

For Paul, thanksgiving had to come first. He wrote to the Romans, "*I thank God* through Jesus for every one of you. *That's first.* People everywhere keep telling me about your lives of faith, and every time I hear them, I thank him" (Romans 1:8 MSG).

To the Ephesians he wrote, "For this reason, ever since I heard about your faith in the Lord Jesus and your love for all God's people, **I have not stopped giving thanks for you**, remembering you in my prayers" (Ephesians 1:15–16).

He wrote to the Philippians, "*I thank my God* every time I remember you. In all my prayers for all of you, I always pray with joy" (Philippians 1:3–4).

The pattern is repeated in his letters to the Thessalonians and others. Even his letter to the Corinthians, whom he rebuked for their many faults, was prefixed with thanks: "**I always thank my God for you** because of his grace given you in Christ Jesus" (1 Corinthians 1:4). Thanksgiving was his habit. He was following the heavenly pattern, as well as the example of the Lord Himself.

The Heavenly Pattern

Heaven overflows with thanksgiving. It's ceaseless. In the very presence of the One whose gracious kindness sustains all creation, the response of heavenly beings and the redeemed in glory is nonstop gratitude.

The angels, the 24 elders, and the living creatures give glory and honor and thanks to Him who sits on the throne, who lives forever and ever—and they do so forever and ever (see Revelation 4:9).

"And the twenty-four elders who sat before God on their thrones fell on their faces and worshiped God, saying: "**We give thanks to you**, Lord God Almighty, the One who is and who was, because you have taken your great power and have begun to reign" (Revelation 11:16–17).

Gratitude is the music of heaven. It rings through the halls of eternity and reverberates from the hearts of heavenly creatures to the very throne room of God. "All the angels were standing around the throne and around the elders and the four living creatures. They fell down on their faces before the throne and worshiped God, saying: 'Amen! Praise and glory and wisdom and *thanks* and honor and power and strength be to our God for ever and ever. Amen!'" (Revelation 7:11–12).

Supreme Example

The Lord Jesus is our supreme example in the department of thanksgiving. The only One who was qualified to withhold gratitude to any (as the Maker of all things, and worthy of all praise Himself), gave thanks repeatedly.

He gave thanks to the Father when He took the loaves and fishes, which He then multiplied.

He gave thanks at the tomb of Lazarus before raising him from the dead.

He gave thanks when He instituted the Lord's Supper. He gave thanks when He took the bread, and He gave thanks when He took the cup.

And He was amazed at the thanklessness of nine of the ten cured lepers!

> As he entered a village, ten men, all lepers, met him. They kept their distance but raised their voices, calling out, "Jesus, Master, have mercy on us!"
>
> Taking a good look at them, he said, "Go, show yourselves to the priests."
>
> They went, and while still on their way, became clean. One of them, when he realized that he was healed, turned around and came back, shouting his gratitude, glorifying God. He kneeled at Jesus' feet, so grateful. He couldn't thank him enough—and he was a Samaritan.
>
> Jesus said, "Were not ten healed? Where are the nine? Can none be found to come back and give glory to God except this outsider?" Then he said to him, "Get up. On your way. Your faith has healed and saved you" (Luke 17:12-19 MSG)

Where Are the Nine?

It is possible that the ratio of the grateful to the ungrateful is still today one in ten. If that is true, it means that 90% of all "cured lepers" are heavily indebted to heaven.

It boggles the mind how someone can be cured of leprosy and then simply walk off—with no thought of or thanks to the Great Physician! What in the world were they thinking? Maybe going to show themselves to the priests (to certify their healing, according to the law of Moses) was more important to them than returning to Jesus to give thanks.

Sin is infinitely worse than physical leprosy. It is the lethal leprosy of the soul, but Jesus cured us with His blood. Where are the nine? Where are all those whose sins have been washed in the blood of the Lamb? How many of them are continually shouting their praise and gratitude to God for this foremost mercy of forgiveness?

The Lord not only forgives all our sins, but He heals all our diseases. Where are the nine? Where are the beneficiaries of divine health and healing? Are their praises continually ascending to heaven for strength for daily life?

Many are so preoccupied with what God is yet to do for them that good health doesn't seem like something worthy of perpetual gratitude.

Are you among the grateful 10% or the 90%? Interestingly, the grateful leper was a Samaritan—not one of the leprous Jews who were also healed.

The Lord's example calls us to deep and nonstop gratitude. And as with the healing of the ten lepers, it is apparent that heaven does keep records.

What Shall I Render?

Even Old Testament individuals who were chosen and blessed by God overflowed with gratitude for the unmerited mercies that were bestowed on them.

David's heart overflowed in Psalm 103: "Bless and affectionately praise the LORD, O my soul, and all that is [deep] within me, bless His holy name. Bless and affectionately praise the LORD, O my soul, and do not forget any of His benefits; who forgives all your sins, who heals all your diseases; who redeems your life from the pit, who crowns you [lavishly] with lovingkindness and tender mercy; who satisfies your years with good things, so that your youth is renewed like the [soaring] eagle." (Psalm 103:1–5 AMP).

In Psalm 116:12, the psalmist asks a profound question: "What will I give to the LORD [in return] for all His benefits toward me? [How can I repay Him for His precious blessings?]" (AMP)

What shall we render to the Lord for all the benefits of redemption He has lavished upon us in Christ Jesus? How can we repay Him for Calvary, and for the precious blood by which we are saved, by which we overcome the enemy of our souls?

How can we repay Him for the forgiveness of our sins, for healing our bodies, for hope, for courage to face life, for laughter, for love, for joy, for peace?

What can we render to Him for multiplied answers to prayers, for the new songs He puts in our mouths to sing?

How do we repay Him for the wisdom He has poured into our hearts to meet life and to thrive, even in life's hardest places?

Can we possibly pay Him for the glorious gift of His Spirit—His own Spirit—whom He has poured upon us and into us?

The largest offerings, the most relentless service and sacrifice, the loudest Hallelujahs will all fall far short of being sufficient to even begin to show our gratitude for His mercies towards us. As Isaac Watts so aptly stated in the hymn "When I Survey The Wondrous Cross," love so amazing, so divine, demands our souls, our lives, and our all. And even that will still not be enough.

It will take an eternity to begin to fully express the depth of gratitude we owe the Lord for His great goodness to us.

Look again at what God did for us: "But God – so rich is He in His mercy! Because of and in order to satisfy the great and wonderful and intense love with which He loved us, Even when we were dead (slain) by [our own] shortcomings and trespasses, *He made us alive* together in fellowship and in union with Christ; [*He gave us the very life of Christ Himself, the same new life with which He quickened Him,* for] it is by grace (His favor and mercy which you did not deserve) that you are saved (delivered from judgment and made partakers of Christ's salvation). And *He raised us up together with Him* and *made us sit down together [giving us joint seating with Him]* in the heavenly sphere [by

virtue of our being] in Christ Jesus (the Messiah, the Anointed One)"
(Ephesians 2:4-6 AMPC).

God made us alive together with Christ—despite the fact that we were
dead through our own trespasses and sins.

He gave us the very life of Christ Himself, the same new life with
which He quickened Him.

He raised us up together with Christ.

He made us sit down together with Christ, giving us joint seating
with Him in the heavenly sphere. And after giving us joint seating with
Christ, He also made us joint heirs with Him.

The next verse tells us why God did all these wonderful things for
us: "He did this that He might clearly demonstrate through the ages to
come *the immeasurable (limitless, surpassing) riches of His free grace
(His unmerited favor) in [His] kindness and goodness of heart toward
us in Christ Jesus"* (Ephesians 2:7 AMPC).

Notice the words being used to describe God's incalculable kindness to us. His intense love released intense benefits—blessings so great
as to be totally immeasurable—the unsearchable riches of Christ.

Throughout all ages of eternity, God will continue to demonstrate
the immeasurable riches of His free grace. We will be the eternal evidence of the unfathomable, unquantifiable mercies of God. Glory to
His Name!

How do we pay Him back for all these?

The short answer is "No way!" We never could. But at least we can
try. We can do what we can—by bringing heartfelt and nonstop gratitude and praise to Him.

This is why certain declarations should never depart from our
mouths: they rise from our grateful hearts in prayer, in our everyday
speech even while we attend to everyday chores. In church, in the
kitchen, in the bathroom, on the street, while driving, and in a million
other situations, we are to give Him nonstop praise.

Hallelujah! Glory! Glory to God! Thank you, Jesus! Thank you,
Lord! Bless the Lord! Oh, glory!

These are not examples of vain "Christianese" but the sacrifice of
our lips giving glory to His name.

Commensurate Praise

The wonders and benefits of our redemption are stupendous—so much so that they actually seem incredible—if we think deeply on them. There is no way to meditate on our redemption privileges and the wonders of the Indwelling and not marvel at what God has done for us in Christ. We must never lose the wonder; we must never get used to the price of redemption and the glorious inheritance it has brought to us, all purchased by the finished work of Jesus Christ.

I invite you to read the revealed reality of your heritage in the following verses (Ephesians 1:3-8, AMP) with fresh wonder:

> Blessed and worthy of praise be the God and Father of our Lord Jesus Christ *who has blessed us with every spiritual blessing in the heavenly realms in Christ*, just as [in His love] *He chose us in Christ [actually selected us for Himself as His own]* before the foundation of the world, so that we would be holy [that is, consecrated, set apart for Him, purpose-driven] and blameless in His sight. *In love He predestined and lovingly planned for us to be adopted to Himself as [His own]* children through Jesus Christ, in accordance with the kind intention and good pleasure of His will—to the praise of His glorious grace and favor, which He so freely bestowed on us in the Beloved [His Son, Jesus Christ]. *In Him we have redemption [that is, our deliverance and salvation] through His blood*, [which paid the penalty for our sin and resulted in] the forgiveness and complete pardon of our sin, in accordance with the riches of His grace *which He lavished on us*. In all wisdom and understanding [with practical insight] . . .

In Chapter 11 ("The Sense is in The Tense"), we established that we find the true sense of what God says to us by attending to the tense in which He speaks. A close look at the tenses in this passage reveals what God has *already done* for us—He has chosen us, foreordained us, adopted us, blessed us, redeemed us, and then lavished His grace on us. He is not *going to* do these things for those of us who are in Christ: He has done them already—lavishly!

There is nothing stingy about the word *lavish.* It connotes abundance, profusion, and generosity. In reality, the connotation of "to lavish" borders on profligacy, excess, and waste. God cannot be profligate, but you begin to get a sense of the unquantifiable grace that He has *lavished* on us in Christ. Nothing compares to our heritage in Him.

According to the Complete Jewish Bible, the expected outcome of all that God did for us in Christ is "so that **we would bring him praise commensurate with the glory of the grace he gave us** through the Beloved One"; He "guarantees our inheritance until we come into possession of it and thus **bring him praise commensurate with his glory**" (Ephesians 1:6, 14).

The word *commensurate* means "equal in size," "matching," "corresponding to," or "in proportion to." Thus, our praise should be equal in size to the grace He has given us. Our gratitude must be in proportion to His omnipotent benevolence to us in Christ Jesus. They must match.

It is possible to have a mismatch of gift and gratitude. A simple thank you will be sufficient if someone has given you a ride in their car or a gift of $50. But what about sending a text message to thank someone who has given you a house? Are you kidding me? Sounds a little like our casual "Thank you" to Jesus—for saving us from a lost eternity!

What quantity of praise and gratitude could be *commensurate* with the glory of God and to the riches of His amazing grace that He has lavished upon us in the Beloved? Do our praise and thanksgiving match His boundless mercies?

What quantity of praise will be commensurate with the grace that saved us from a lost eternity and made us sons and daughters of Almighty God? Our lives are to express such gratitude to our divine benefactor. Hallelujah!

How much praise is enough to show our gratitude to the One who saved us from an eternity in a lake of fire? At what point would we have praised and thanked Him enough?

What quantity of thanksgiving is commensurate with our names being included in the Book of Life?

How can we thank enough the One who was wounded for our transgressions and bruised for our iniquities—who took the chastisement that brought us peace, and by whose stripes we are healed?

Temporary gratitude is not commensurate with eternal blessings. Occasional thanksgiving is not commensurate with continual and unceasing kindness. We see why our praise and thanksgiving must continually overflow to the Lord—a continual sacrifice of gratitude that is pleasing in His sight.

Our gratitude issues out of a sense of indebtedness: grace has made debtors of us all, and this is a debt we can never repay. We must never cease to be grateful from the depths of our hearts, *both verbally and practically*, for God's indescribable gift to us in Christ Jesus. "Now thanks be to God for His Gift, [precious] beyond telling [His indescribable, inexpressible, free Gift]!" (2 Corinthians 9:15 AMPC)

If the gift is indescribable, the praise and thanksgiving that will be commensurate with the gift must also be indescribable. Indescribable praise? We must yet be a million miles from this standard of nonstop gratitude!

We believers would be all ablaze all our days with praise and thanksgiving if we could continually consider the boundless blessings and benefits of our redemption. We would be wild with praise—like David dancing nearly naked before the ark of God.

David's Example

David knew the impact of God's merciful kindness and grace upon his life. As David and all Israel moved the ark of God to its resting place, he celebrated the God who had taken him from following sheep and goats in the bush to the throne—with great abandon. The story is found in 2 Samuel 6:

"David, ceremonially dressed in priest's linen, danced with great abandon before GOD. The whole country was with him as he accompanied the Chest of GOD with shouts and trumpet blasts. But as the Chest of GOD came into the City of David, Michal, Saul's daughter, happened to be looking out a window. When she saw King David leaping and dancing before GOD, her heart filled with scorn" (vv. 14–16 MSG).

Michal obviously never saw her father, the defunct King Saul, celebrating God's choice of himself as the first king of Israel in this fashion.

If she had, she would have been slow to scorn a grateful recipient of grace. This tells something about Saul. His lack of manifest gratitude for having been chosen by God—a donkey-seeking Benjamite from the least tribe in Israel hiding among the baggage, whom God promoted to the throne of Israel—contributed to his destruction. Now his daughter was treading his ignoble path.

"David returned home to bless his family. Michal, Saul's daughter, came out to greet him: 'How wonderfully the king has distinguished himself today—exposing himself to the eyes of the servants' maids like some burlesque street dancer!'" (v. 20 MSG)

What a way to welcome a husband home—one who was king, for that matter, and was coming home *to bless his family*! Instead of Michal joining the procession and dancing alongside her husband, she stood aloof, peering through a window! All she had for him was scorn as he celebrated God. Her idea of decency and decorum did not make space for extravagant praise for extravagant blessings. She was too dignified to glorify God!

"David replied to Michal, 'In GOD's presence I'll dance all I want! He chose me over your father and the rest of our family and made me prince over GOD's people, over Israel. ***Oh yes, I'll dance to GOD's glory—more recklessly even than this.*** And as far as I'm concerned . . . I'll gladly look like a fool . . . but among these maids you're so worried about, I'll be honored no end.' Michal, Saul's daughter, was barren the rest of her life" (2 Samuel 6:21-23 MSG).

We can learn something here from the man after God's heart. Maybe we could leap and dance some more. We could love a little more extravagantly. We could praise Him more recklessly. We could sacrifice with more abandon—all in praise and gratitude to the worthy One. We could become grateful fools for Christ.

Nothing we can do for Him would ever be commensurate with what He has done for us, but at least we can bring our best to His feet—to the One who has honored us beyond words by redeeming us, by indwelling us—by making His throne in our hearts.

Joy Unspeakable

As we cultivate the habit of nonstop gratitude and praise, our hearts overflow with joy unspeakable—indescribable joy arising from our possession of God's Indescribable gift, our Lord Jesus Christ, within our hearts.

"Though you have not seen him, you love him. Though you do not now see him, you believe in him and rejoice with *joy that is inexpressible* and filled with glory, obtaining the outcome of your faith, the salvation of your souls" (1 Peter 1:8-9 ESV).

Most believers know nothing of the inexpressible joy of which this Scripture speaks, but it's our heritage. Though we have not seen Him, we believe in Him. We love Him because He first loved us. And with His love bubbling up in our spirits, we overflow with gratitude and praise for all He has done for us. We rejoice with joy that cannot be put into words. We are full of glory.

"Without having seen Him, you love Him; though you do not [even] now see Him, you believe in Him and exult and thrill with inexpressible and glorious (triumphant, heavenly) joy" (1 Peter 1:8 AMPC).

There is heavenly joy in our spirits. It is the very joy of the Lord Himself—the joy of the indwelling Lord who resides in us is overflowing from our hearts! And that joy is our strength.

We are possessors of salvation so glorious that the prophets who prophesied of what we now enjoy wondered who could be the recipients of such amazing blessings. The very angels long to take a peep into what we enjoy in Christ. Hallelujah!

This will be a great place to take a praise break. Let your heart overflow with nonstop gratitude. Say something to the Lord to show you are grateful. Do something to show you are grateful. Sing. Shout. Dance. Lift your voice in praise and thanksgiving for your name being included in the Book of Life, for manifold mercies and untold grace, for testimonies of triumph through terrible tests and trials. Praise Him for who He is, for all He's done, and for all He will yet do in your life. Bless the Lord as you have never done before.

Glory to His Name!

18

Embracing the Indwelling

An Anniversary Gift

On a recent trip to Cape Town, South Africa, the wife of the pastor of the church where I was teaching on the Indwelling shared a story that illustrates the condition of many believers. Her husband wanted to give her a grand gift for their 20th wedding anniversary, so he booked a getaway at a fabulous resort, choosing an all-inclusive package. Everything was available—excellent lodging, gourmet food, personal care, and a host of fun activities. When they arrived, they were shown to a gorgeous room and given a pass to every event and service at the resort.

She was, however, wary of accumulating bills and so avoided most of the activities. She declined a massage she was offered. When asked if she wanted manicure and pedicure, she responded that she wasn't interested—that Jesus had "cured" her of everything! She ate the barest meals, while other guests enjoyed the finest dining.

On the morning they were to leave, she ate a simple breakfast. The shock came when they went to settle their accounts: the bill included everything she had carefully avoided at the resort. She protested, but the staff explained that the all-inclusive package covered all the services offered, to which they had been entitled! Whatever miscommunication that was to blame wasn't enough to avoid full settlement of the bill.

Jesus purchased an all-inclusive redemption for us. The package includes every benefit of the Cross, the inheritance of the saints in the light, and the exceedingly great and precious promises of a God who cannot lie. The greatest of all redemption benefits—the Indwelling—is in the package. But whether we acknowledge and maximize our inheritance is another matter altogether. Our response to the glorious reality of the Indwelling will determine how much of its amazing potential we experience and manifest.

Our indwelling by the triune God is real, but we can maximize or minimize it; we can choose to live the "normal" life of mere mortals. How sad it would be at "check out" to discover the astounding possibilities to which our ignorance and unbelief have blinded us. *God has taken up a current, permanent, and irrevocable residence within us.* But we can chose to continue the life of struggle and bare survival, ignoring the exceeding greatness of His power at work in us. Or we can allow Him to live large in us, to use our bodies as His holy headquarters on earth for blessing humanity and advancing His kingdom.

Several principles and practical steps that will enable us to embrace and maximize the Indwelling are discussed in the sections that follow.

Acknowledgment

As we have already seen, we must agree with God. The Indwelling is not a myth; it is reality. "***We know [for a fact] that we are of God***, and the whole world [around us] lies in the power of the evil one [opposing God and His precepts]. And we [have seen and] ***know [by personal experience]*** that the Son of God has [actually] come [to this world] and has given us understanding and insight so that we may [progressively and personally] know Him who is true; and ***we are in Him who is true***—in His Son Jesus Christ. This is the true God and eternal life" (1 John 5:19-20 AMP).

Observe how "we know" is repeated in these verses. This is not guesswork. We are in Him Who is true, and He is in us. We are of God—we are born of Him, and His seed abides in us. We are partakers of His divine nature. We believe and confess that Jesus Christ is the Son of God, and according to 1 John 4:15 God dwells in us and we dwell in God:

"Anyone who confesses (acknowledges, owns) that Jesus is the Son of God, *God abides (lives, makes His home) in him and he [abides, lives, makes his home] in God."* AMPC

A continual acknowledgement of the Indwelling is central to maximizing its possibilities. "I thank my God, making mention of you always in my prayers... that the sharing of your faith may become effective *by the acknowledgment of every good thing which is in you in Christ Jesus."* (Philemon 4, 6 NKJV).

Keep the revelation of the Indwelling in constant view. Confess His presence in your heart. The more you acknowledge His indwelling presence, the more you will experience His manifest presence. Christ is in you, and He is the hope of glory.

Many Infallible Proofs

The Indwelling is not a parable: it is reality. Our acknowledgment of it is based on truth, not fickle feelings or fiction. Acts 1:3 declares that Jesus' resurrection was not a figment of imagination and that He "presented Himself alive after His suffering *by many infallible proofs"* (NKJV), to His apostles whom He had chosen. Likewise, the Indwelling is not a myth. The truth that God lives in you and that you live in Him is confirmed by many infallible proofs—by a multitude of irrefutable, unambiguous, and unbreakable verses of Scripture. Consider the following plain and incontrovertible statements of God's Word:

- "On that day you will realize that *I am in my Father,* and *you are in me,* and *I am in you*" (John 14:20).
- "*Christ in you,* the hope of glory" (Colossians 1:27).
- "The man who does obey God's commands lives in God and God lives in him, and *the guarantee of his presence within us* is the Spirit he has given us" (1 John 3:24 PHILLIPS).
- "All who keep His commandments [who obey His orders and follow His plan, live and continue to live, to stay and] abide in Him, and He in them. [They let Christ be a home to them and they are the home of Christ.] And *by this we know and understand and have*

the proof that He [really] lives and makes His home in us: by the [Holy] Spirit Whom He has given us." (1 John 3:24 AMPC).

- "You realize, don't you, that you are the temple of God, and **God himself is present in you**?" (1 Corinthians 3:16 MSG).
- "Do you not know that your bodies are temples of the Holy Spirit, **who is in you**, whom you have received from God?" (1 Corinthians 6:19).
- "And because you [really] are [His] sons, **God has sent the Spirit of His Son into our hearts,** crying out, Abba! Father!" (Galatians 4:6 AMP).
- "Guard the good deposit that was entrusted to you—guard it **with the help of the Holy Spirit who lives in us**" (2 Timothy 1:14).
- "Test yourselves to see if you are in the faith; examine yourselves! Or **do you not recognize this about yourselves, that Jesus Christ is in you**—unless indeed you fail the test?" (2 Corinthians 13:5 NASB).

The biblical rule is that at the mouth of "two or three witnesses" every truth is confirmed. However, the Indwelling is not a matter of "two or three witnesses": the evidence is overwhelming. It's a proven fact, guaranteed by the very presence of God's own Spirit *within* us. It is the ultimate proof of belonging to Christ: anyone who fails the test of the Indwelling does not belong to Christ. This is the secret of everything in the New Testament. It's God in us, living His life in us, working His wonders in and through us. We must continually acknowledge His indwelling presence.

Preparing the Temple for His Glory

Oftentimes My glory cannot fill My temple because My temple is already filled with other things. My glory cannot manifest as I want it to and as My people desire, because there are things contrary to My glory among My people. If My glory manifests in such an atmosphere, it will consume and destroy.... My glory will not manifest in the presence of the idols of My people, lest I consume them. My glory tolerates nothing contrary to it. Take away the

stumbling block of your vanities. Prepare the way that the glory of the Lord may be revealed, and all eyes see it together. In the interim, I will fill those in whom I can find space for My Spirit. I will flow through those that are ready and use them for my glory.
—A prophetic word received by author

In many passages of Scripture, we read of how God's glory filled His temple (see, e.g., 2 Chronicles 5:12-14; Haggai 2:5-). As we have seen in *The Indwelling*, we are God's temple. However, His glory cannot fill His temple if the temple is already occupied with other things.

It is interesting to note what happened following Jesus' cleansing of the temple: "Jesus entered the temple courts and ***drove out*** all who were buying and selling there. He overturned the tables of the money changers and the benches of those selling doves. 'It is written,' he said to them, ' "My house will be called a house of prayer," but you are making it "a den of robbers." ' The blind and the lame came to him at the temple, and he healed them" (Matthew 21:12-14).

The moneychangers and other merchants had occupied the space in the temple, God's house of prayer, where unceasing prayers were to be made for all nations. Materialism had taken center stage, where compassion for the broken and wounded was designed to reign. But Jesus drove them all out. According to Mark's account of the incidence, Jesus would not even "permit anyone to carry any household equipment through the temple enclosure [thus making the temple area a short-cut traffic lane]" (Mark 11:16 AMPC). People who didn't have God on their minds and had no business in the temple were using the temple for their own agendas—using it as a shortcut traffic lane to shorten their trips to their varied and vain destinations! But Jesus ended all that.

After Jesus chased out the strangers from God's temple, *then* the blind and lame came to Him in the temple and He healed them. The glory of God was let loose in His purified temple. Wonderful things began to happen in a temple that had hitherto been a den of thieves. Heavenly traffic replaced human traffic!

There is no way the glorious realities of the Indwelling can manifest in fullness if our lives are occupied with other things, or if they have become a shortcut traffic lane for all kinds of desires, imaginations, and deeds. The temple needs to be thoroughly cleansed within and its precincts and perimeters secured from every unholy invasion. Then the glory of the Lord will fill His temple.

Undertake a thorough cleaning exercise of your heart-house. If there are things the Lord has been dealing with you about, bring them to His feet in humble surrender. Even our preoccupation with the legitimate cares of this life, our anxieties, and our fears must be swept away so that our hearts may be still and know that He is God. Let His Spirit do a great work inside you, uprooting every desire, affection, or thought that competes with Him for space in your heart. According to Jonah 2:8, if we cling to worthless idols and vanities we forfeit the great grace and blessing God desires to pour into our lives.

Crucified with Christ

"I have been *crucified with Christ* [that is, in Him I have shared His crucifixion]; it is no longer I who live, but Christ lives in me. The life I now live in the body I live by faith [by adhering to, relying on, and completely trusting] in the Son of God, who loved me and gave Himself up for me" (Galatians 2:20 AMP).

Here Paul identifies himself with Christ's death on the Cross: he died when Christ died. On that Cross, the old Paul died; the life he now lived was not that of the old Paul, but of Christ indwelling him, living His life within him. "And he [Christ] died for all, that those who live should no longer live for themselves but for him who died for them and was raised again" (2 Corinthians 5:15).

The death of Paul's "I"—his flesh i.e., his carnal, sinful nature—was foundational to the full manifestation of the Indwelling. Self and Christ cannot be on the throne together. The indwelling Holy Spirit cannot lead us if we are bent on leading ourselves.

Death to self, the flesh, and the world causes the life of Christ to be fully manifest in and through us. Such was the death by which Peter was to glorify God: it would be the death of Peter's lordship over Peter—of Peter directing Peter on what to wear, where to go, what to do, etc. It would no longer be Peter living for himself and leading himself: another would be in charge, leading him where he might not wish to go. But he would willingly yield to being dressed and led by someone other than himself.

Jesus said to Peter, "Very truly I tell you, when you were younger you dressed yourself and went where you wanted; but when you are old you will stretch out your hands, and *someone else will dress you and lead you* where you do not want to go.' Jesus said this to indicate the kind of death by which Peter would glorify God. Then he said to him, 'Follow me!'" (John 21:18–19).

We do not have to wait like Peter until we are old before we reckon ourselves crucified with Christ. The sooner we come to the point where we die daily (like Paul; see 1 Corinthians 15:31), the sooner Christ can reign in us and manifest the astounding potential of His presence.

It is important to note that death to self is not something we achieve—it is something we *believe* and then walk within. It is one of those things already *done* for us, in Christ, which we then experience by faith—by claiming His death as ours. The passage below summarizes it best; I encourage you to meditate deeply on it and to make it yours by faith.

> We were buried therefore with Him by the baptism into death, so that just as Christ was raised from the dead by the glorious [power] of the Father, so we too might [habitually] live and behave in newness of life. For if we have become one with Him by sharing a death like His, we shall also be [one with Him in sharing] His resurrection [by a new life lived for God].
>
> We know that our old (unrenewed) self was nailed to the cross with Him in order that [our] body [which is the instrument] of sin might be made ineffective and inactive for evil, that we might no longer be the slaves of sin.
>
> Even so consider yourselves also dead to sin and your relation to it broken, but alive to God [living in unbroken fellowship with Him] in Christ Jesus. Let not sin therefore rule as king in your mortal (short-lived, perishable) bodies, to make you yield to its cravings and be subject to its lusts and evil passions (Romans 6:4–6; 11–12 AMPC).

All that Jesus did, He did for us. We were condemned with Him, crucified with Him, buried with Him, and raised with Him. So by faith we can lay claim to all He has accomplished. Consider yourself dead indeed to sin, but alive to God.

The death of the old, indwelling sinful nature frees us to be indwelt by Christ and for His life to be made manifest in our mortal bodies.

Living Sacrifice

In line with the foregoing, we are commanded to present our bodies as living sanctuaries a most holy God can indwell.

"I appeal to you therefore, brethren, and beg of you in view of [all] the mercies of God, to make a decisive dedication of your bodies [presenting all your members and faculties] as *a living sacrifice,* holy (devoted, consecrated) and well pleasing to God, which is your reasonable (rational, intelligent) service and spiritual worship" (Romans 12:1 AMPC).

Once we perceive the priceless honor of *hosting* God within our bodies, it is only reasonable that we respond to such an immeasurable privilege by devoting our bodies exclusively to Him. This means we must avoid anything that can defile our bodies or corrupt our minds—sexual immorality of any kind, lust, pornography, substance abuse, greed, etc. Our consecration is not arbitrary; it is consecration with an agenda: we separate ourselves from the common so that the uncommon can manifest freely in us. We are providing *accommodation* for a holy God!

This puts holiness of heart, mind, and body on a whole new plane. The motivation is powerful. Others may do a whole lot of things, but I will not—because God is in the house! I am His temple, and I must be holy because He is holy. His presence is far more priceless than the fleeting pleasures and treasures of this life. Nothing compares with the amazing heritage of His abiding presence.

God told the Israelites, "You must keep your camp clean of filthy and disgusting things. *The LORD is always present in your camp*, ready to rescue you and give you victory over your enemies. But if he sees something disgusting in your camp, he may turn around and leave" (Deuteronomy 23:14 CEV). My body is my "camp" on earth—the tabernacle where my spirit lives. It is also the place of the Indwelling, the camp of the Holy Spirit who lives within me. So my camp must be holy. The Lord is always present in my camp—to deliver me, rout the enemy, and give me unbroken victory. I don't want him to see something disgusting anywhere near me; He might turn around and leave.

The Indwelling is our greatest motivation for holiness. Some have reduced holiness to dogmas, dos and don'ts. They reel out rules for everything and bind heavy burdens for people to bear. But true holiness is love's logical response to the miracle of the Indwelling.

We read these amazing words in 2 Corinthians 6:16, "What agreement [can there be between] a temple of God and idols? *For we are the temple of the living God; even as God said, I will dwell in and with and among them and will walk in and with and among them,* and I will be their God, and they shall be My people" (AMPC). This is the astounding promise of the Indwelling. According to Kenneth Wuest's translation, "What agreement does the inner sanctuary of God have with idols? *For, as for us, we are an inner sanctuary of the living God, even as God said, I will dwell in them in fellowship with them as in a home and I will live my life in and through them.* And I will be their God and they themselves will be my people."

On the basis of this exceedingly great and precious promise—of God indwelling us and living His life in and through us, we are then admonished to "come out from them and be separate, says the Lord. Touch no unclean thing, and I will receive you" (v.17). We are then told in 2 Corinthians 7:1, "Therefore, *since we have these promises*, dear friends, let us purify ourselves from everything that contaminates body and spirit, perfecting holiness out of reverence for God". Our total and uncompromising separation from defilement is rooted in the reality of the Indwelling: we are to be holy because we are heirs of the stupendous promise of the Indwelling. *We are to be the holy homes of the most holy God!*

So we refuse to yield our bodily members as instruments of unrighteousness, to be used as tools for fulfilling the will of the flesh and the devil. By the power of the indwelling Lord, we say No to all ungodliness and live soberly, righteously, and in a godly manner in this present world. We rid ourselves of everything that defiles both body and spirit, perfecting holiness in the reverential fear of our resident Lord. We live in such awe of the indwelling One that we shrink from anything that will defile His temple.

This presentation of our bodies as living sacrifices is our "reasonable" act of worship. Every other response to the Indwelling is unreasonable. It is clearly unreasonable to use a body indwelt by God for something contrary to His character. Genuine worship does not begin until God indwells His temple, and He cannot indwell a shared temple. Some believers are under the fatal illusion that since their spirits are saved it does not matter what they do with their bodies. How can anyone even imagine that it doesn't matter what we do with God's temple, with Him in it?

Scripture clearly warns us, "Do you not know that you yourselves are God's temple and that God's Spirit dwells in your midst? *If anyone destroys God's temple, God will destroy that person*; for God's temple is sacred, and you together are that temple" (1 Corinthians 3:16–17).

"Do you not know that *your body is the temple (the very sanctuary) of the Holy Spirit Who lives within you,* whom you have received [as a Gift] from God? You are not your own, you were bought with a price [purchased with a preciousness and paid for, made His own]. So then, honor God and bring glory to Him in your body." (1 Corinthians 6:19–20 AMPC).

It does matter what we do with our bodies: God currently and permanently lives in them! Our bodies don't belong to us anymore: Jesus Christ purchased them with His blood. His goal was that, just as the Father prepared a body for Him for His work in the world, He would prepare our bodies for the Holy Spirit to indwell, for the Spirit's work in the world (see Hebrews 10:5).

Having consecrated our bodies as God's holy, operational bases, we then proceed to renew our minds to the realities of His indwelling, refusing to be conformed to this world.

"Do not be conformed to this world (this age), [fashioned after and adapted to its external, superficial customs], but *be transformed (changed) by the [entire] renewal of your mind* [by its new ideals and its new attitude], so that you may prove [for yourselves] what is the good and acceptable and perfect will of God, even the thing which is good and acceptable and perfect [in His sight for you]" (Romans 12:2 AMP).

The presentation of our bodies to God must be deliberate and decisive. The reader may wish to pause and perform this sacred dedication at this time. As you consecrate your body to Him, ask Him to come afresh in His fullness and *fill* His temple with His glory.

We must constantly make reference to this dedication in the face of temptation and other external distractions that Satan uses to cheat people out of their indwelling treasure. Our bodies are no longer ours to do with as we please. We are living sacrifices upon God's altar, so we bind the sacrifice with cords of love, reverence, and faithfulness to the horns of the altar (see Psalm 118:27).

Honoring the Presence

As a consequence of presenting our bodies as a living sacrifice on God's altar, we are deeply aware of His presence in us, and we choose to honor that presence. Like a pregnant woman who is indwelt by her baby, we are always conscious of the One we carry within our bodies! We carry the ultimate treasure in our earthen vessels!

An expecting mother is always conscious of the presence of another, i.e., her baby within her. She never loses awareness of it. There are things she can't eat, medicines she can't take, as well as places and activities she avoids. There are other things she has to eat, medicines to take, and appointments to keep. Her indwelling baby even affects her dressing and sleeping posture! She knows she is soon to deliver. The expectation of "someone" who will soon be born keeps her alert to what she's carrying. That expectation heightens as her date of delivery draws near. Without this continual consciousness of her indwelling, she risks a miscarriage or deformation of her unborn child.

People of the Indwelling must honor the Presence they carry. Someone lives in us. We must never forget that even for a moment. Indeed, He is too big to be present but then forgotten! We wouldn't forget if the president of our country were present in our home; and we certainly would not ignore him or her. We wouldn't forget or be negligent if we were carrying a million dollars in cash! Why should we forget that the Lord Jesus Christ Himself lives in us? The fact that we can think of something else while He indwells us is a testament to our unrenewed minds! May the indwelling One continually fill our thoughts!

We are to be in constant tune with the One who indwells us. Our consciousness of His presence should not be only when we pray or study the Bible but a continual awareness that we carry Someone in the sacred chambers of our innermost beings. We are to live in eager expectation of what He will say next or do next and of where He might lead us next. We must continually engage the indwelling One. Only in this way can we readily respond to His leading and thereby experience His mighty works. As earlier stated, the more we acknowledge His indwelling presence, the more we will experience His manifest presence.

God's presence manifests where that presence is honored. As carriers of the indwelling Christ, our words, actions, choices, etc., need to reflect our deepest honor for the omnipotent One who indwells us.

Faith, Not Feelings

The realities of the Indwelling are not physical but are no less real. They are invisible spiritual realities that cannot be experienced by reason or feeling. The Indwelling can only be received and cultivated by faith. The same faith by which we are saved helps us to receive the truth of the indwelling Christ.

In promising the Holy Spirit, Jesus said, "I will ask the Father, and He will give you another Helper (Comforter, Advocate, Intercessor—Counselor, Strengthener, Standby), to be with you forever—the Spirit of Truth, whom the world cannot receive [and take to its heart] **because it does not see Him or know Him**, but you know Him because He (the Holy Spirit) remains with you continually and will be in you" (John 14:16-17 AMP). The primary reason the world cannot receive the Holy Spirit and benefit from His indwelling is quite instructive: because it does not *see* Him. Since the world walks by sight, it does not accept the reality of what it doesn't see. And since (in the world's version of reality) sight must precede knowing, it is unable to welcome and recognize the Spirit whom it cannot see.

Our case as believers is quite different. Our entire Christian life is based on our willingness to accept the reality of the invisible. Without seeing Christ we love Him. Without seeing the Father we believe in Him. We accept the existence of heaven, angels, Satan, and other invisible entities by faith—by accepting the evidence of God's written Word. We are able to welcome the Spirit because "*we walk by faith [we regulate our lives and conduct ourselves by our conviction or belief... not by sight or appearance*" (2 Corinthians 5:7 AMPC).

You see, "faith is the assurance (title deed, confirmation) of things hoped for (divinely guaranteed), and *the evidence of things not seen [the conviction of their reality—faith comprehends as fact what cannot be experienced by the physical senses]*" (Hebrews 11:1 AMP). Our faith enables us to perceive and receive the reality of things that are not revealed to the senses. We know that the triune God indwells us, and we perceive His presence in us as a real fact—a present reality, not a future possibility. We know it is so because we have God's Word on the matter.

Paul prayed for the Ephesian believers, asking that God "grant you out of the rich treasury of His glory to be strengthened and reinforced with mighty power in the inner man by the [Holy] Spirit [Himself indwelling your innermost being and personality]. *May Christ through your faith [actually] dwell (settle down, abide, make His permanent home) in your hearts!* (Ephesians 3:16-17 AMPC). There is no other way Christ can dwell in our hearts except through faith.

Faith accepts the testimony of Scripture. It agrees with every verse we have encountered in *The Indwelling*, thereby making each a reality in the life of the believing one. We do not walk by feeling or by sight but by faith. This means that we may not *feel* the indwelling Father, Son, and Holy Spirit, yet we *know* they indwell us. We do not need to see wind, rain, or fire to know that we are the temples of the Holy Spirit. We simply believe—with ever-increasing conviction rooted in the infallible Word of God—that the Father, Son, and Holy Spirit indwell us. As our conviction of these realities increases, the manifestations of the Indwelling will also abound in us.

Paul knew the realities of the Indwelling. Indeed, much of the truth we have encountered in this book was revealed to Him by the Spirit and written down as Scripture. He lived by faith, not by feelings or sight; he declared: "I have been crucified with Christ and I no longer live, but Christ lives in me. *The life I now live in the body, I live by faith in the Son of God*, who loved me and gave himself for me" (Galatians 2:20).

The faith that acknowledges the Indwelling and makes it real comes from the Word. "So then faith comes by hearing, and hearing by the word of God" (Romans 10:17 NKJV). We believe that this faith is stirring in your heart as you read *The Indwelling*. The more we apply ourselves to these truths, the more faith we will have in their veracity.

"My son, give attention to my words; incline your ear to my sayings. Do not let them depart from your sight; keep them in the midst of your heart. For they are life to those who find them and health to all their body" (Proverbs 4:20-22 NASB).

Give continuous attention to the truths of the Indwelling. *The Indwelling* is much more than something to read and put aside: it is a revelation of your inheritance in Christ. Incline your ear to these sayings of Scripture. Don't let them out of your sight. Read, meditate, and pray these truths deep into your spirit. Never lose sight of who you are in Christ, nor of who He is in you. *Christ in you* is the hope of glory; therefore, keep your eyes on the indwelling Christ. Keep these undeniable truths in the center of your heart. They will be life to every fiber of your being, and that life will flow through you—in increasing measure—to impact and bless many.

The Opening of the Eyes

The unfolding of the realities of the Indwelling will come in answer to heartfelt prayer for insight—for the opening of our eyes. Paul prayed for the Ephesian believers that

> The God of our Lord Jesus Christ, the Father of glory, may grant you a spirit of wisdom and of revelation [that gives you a deep and personal and intimate insight] into the true knowledge of Him. . . And [I pray] *that the eyes of your heart [the very center*

and core of your being] may be enlightened [flooded with light by the Holy Spirit], so that you will know and cherish the hope [the divine guarantee, the confident expectation] to which He has called you, the riches of His glorious inheritance in the saints (God's people), and [so that you will begin to know] what the immeasurable and unlimited and surpassing greatness of His [active, spiritual] power is in us who believe. These are in accordance with the working of His mighty strength" (Ephesians 1:17-19 AMP).

These were believers, yet Paul prayed that God would give them "a spirit of wisdom and revelation in the knowledge of Him." He prayed that their "inner vision may be flooded with light" (BARCLAYS), that they may receive "that inner illumination of the spirit" (PHILLIPS), so that they may know "the superabounding greatness of His inherent power to us who are believing ones" (v. 19 WUEST). There was *inherent power* within and for these believers, but they needed their eyes flooded with light to *know* it.

We too need our eyes enlightened to see the possibilities contained in the call we received when we answered the One who called us to His glory and virtue. We need this "spirit of wisdom and revelation [of insight into mysteries and secrets] in the [deep and intimate] knowledge of Him." Without this, we will be carrying Yahweh and His unlimited power in our bodies but never know it. We will be like Jacob:

"Jacob woke up and said, "The LORD is here! He is in this place, and I didn't know it!" "*Certainly,* the LORD is in this place, and I didn't know it!" (Genesis 28:16 GNT; GW). Jacob named the place of this encounter Bethel, meaning the house of God.

You are God's house. You, believer, are His temple. We have provided many infallible scriptural proofs to this assertion in *The Indwelling*. The Indwelling is not an idea or an illusion: it is sober reality. Indeed, without it you would not be a Christian at all (see Romans 8:9). He lives in you and you live in Him. How tragic it would be to wake up in the blazing light of eternity and, with the benefit of perfect eternal hindsight, look back to the small, limited life you lived on earth and then exclaim, "Yahweh was inside my heart, but I didn't know it! I was *carrying* God inside me, but I lived like an ordinary human being! The Healer was in me, but I didn't know it! The One who stilled the storm and calmed the raging waves was in me, and I was petrified by fear and harassed by worry!"

There was no question as to whether or not God was at Bethel. Certainly, surely, the Lord was there. Yahweh Himself, not just angels, was personally present. But Jacob didn't *know* it. How could he benefit from, or maximize the presence of the eternal, omnipotent Lord of the universe when he didn't even know He was there? How can we maximize the infinite possibilities of the Indwelling if we don't *know* it? There are billions of dollars in unclaimed dividends and inheritances because the owners don't know about their existence. So they live in penury while they are the heirs of great wealth. They need their eyes opened!

The Lord Himself resides in your heart: "**God himself has taken up residence in your life**" (Romans 8:9 MSG). It is not an angel that lives in you, but Jesus Christ Himself. You need to know it and walk in the reality of it. You carry omniscient omnipotence within you: the Father of our Lord Jesus Christ, Christ Himself, and the Holy Spirit indwell you. But until you *know* it, you will live a limited, small, and defeated life—the sad but unwarranted lot of billions of believers.

Continue to pray this prayer Paul prayed for the Ephesians—for God to give you the spirit of wisdom and revelation in the knowledge of Him, and for your eyes to be flooded with light—until you come to an experiential knowledge of this glorious reality. It will change everything.

Wonder

We must never lose the wonder of the Indwelling. God dwells in you. Jesus Christ is in you, and He is your hope of glory. The Holy Spirit indwells you. You are born of God and have overcome, because greater is He who is in you than he who is in the world.

These are not "normal" things we can get used to. There's nothing casual about a life indwelled by God.

We marvel at the wisdom of God, and we are astounded at His grace that will make Him take up actual residence inside us, His creatures.

Out of our wonder will proceed worship—the unrestrained out-pouring of our lives to God in loving surrender, humble adoration, praise, and obedience born out of a revelation of His Person and His love for us. We bow in awe in His presence; we break out in vibrant praise at His goodness; we celebrate His unlimited grace and kindness to us in Christ.

Communion: Engaging the Indwelling One

An unbroken fellowship—nonstop communion—with the Lord of the Indwelling will cause mighty manifestations of His presence and power in and through our lives.

In the Old Testament, we see a wonderful picture of what happens in the place of communion with the Lord. The holy garments of the high priest were designed by God Himself and made according to the pattern He gave to Moses on the mountain. One of the items of clothing was known as the breastplate: it was attached to the ephod. On it were mounted 12 precious stones with the name of one tribe of Israel inscribed on each. The high priest wore the breastplate right over his heart. A description of the intricate patterns and actual production of the high-priestly garments can be found in Exodus 28 and 39.

The 12 stones on the breastplate seemed ordinary until the high priest entered the holy of holies. There, the Shekinah glory and brightness of Almighty God shone on them; then all those 12 precious stones came alive, throwing off amazing colors of dazzling brilliance. Each tribe of Israel (represented by a stone on the high priest's breastplate) glittered in splendor *in the presence of God!* Nowhere else could the 12 tribes of Israel shine as they did in the holy of holies!

Similarly, outside the inner sanctuary people of the Indwelling seem quite ordinary—like precious jewels in minimal light. But when they come to the throne of grace in communion with the Lord, the glory of the Lord enthroned in heaven connects with the glory of the indwelling Lord—in a blaze of light, life, and power. Deep begins to call to deep, and waves of glory flood the soul (see Psalm 42:7). The exceeding greatness of His power that is at work in us (by which He is able to do exceedingly abundantly above all that we ask or think) begins to work wonders within us, and wonders without, which manifest beyond our closets. As we seek Him secretly in private communion, He rewards us openly with "awesome deeds in righteousness" (Psalm 65:5 NKJV)—amazing manifestations of His grace and power.

I encourage you to spend time with the Lord, to cultivate solitude with Jesus—to sit at His feet, gaze on His face, and receive His Word. Being with Him will transform you and make you a wonder to many. It did that for the apostles—"uneducated non-professionals," "unlettered and obscure men," "illiterate persons, untrained in the schools," and "uncultured persons and mere outsiders"—they brought wonder and astonishment to the Sanhedrin because of the mighty miracles God performed through them (Acts 4:13—TLB; ROTHERHAM; WEYMOUTH; MOFFAT translations). Here's how Kenneth Wuest translates this record of the consequence of spending time with Jesus Christ:

"And viewing with a practiced eye the free and fearless confidence of Peter and John as manifested in their uninhibited and unreserved manner of speaking, and comprehending the fact that they were without formal education and that they were not professional men but laymen, they began to wonder and kept on wondering, and they began to recognize them as those who were with Jesus" (Acts 4:13).

If you spend time with the Lord, it will show. Your secret times in His presence will manifest in your private and public walk and work. Peter and John were characterized as unlearned and ignorant, but they obviously knew something the Sanhedrin didn't know. Being with Jesus will help you know the things that matter most in life. It will cause you to experience the full potential of His indwelling presence.

Devote extended periods of time to study and meditation in the written Word. You will see things you have never seen before. The Lord will open your eyes to behold wondrous things out of His Word. And He will do things in your life that you never imagined possible.

Spend time in fellowship with the Holy Spirit in prayer. One of His sacred responsibilities is outlined in 1 Corinthians 2:12: "Now we have not received the spirit [that belongs to] the world, but the [Holy] Spirit Who is from God, *[given to us] that we might realize and comprehend and appreciate the gifts [of divine favor and blessing so freely and lavishly] bestowed on us by God"* (AMPC).

God gave us His Spirit so that we can know, understand, appreciate, and apprehend the blessings He has lavished on us. Without the help of the Holy Spirit, we will be "blessed with all spiritual blessings in heavenly places in Christ Jesus" but live like orphans in earthly places. We will not walk in the reality of our kingdom heritage. As you commune with the Holy Spirit, He will make the amazing blessing of the Indwelling real to you. Ask Him to maximize His temple—to make the most of you as His habitation and operational base, to bring maximum glory to the Father. Ask Him to do all that He did in our Lord Jesus Christ in you and through you.

> My people thirst in the middle of The River because they do not engage the indwelling One. My people seem helpless like orphans while they have the omnipotent Helper within, because they do not engage the indwelling One. When will you be wise? Come to the waters. Come to the waters . . .
> —Prophetic word received by author

Don't neglect the fellowship of God's people—in corporate worship and in fellowship with brothers and sisters of the burning heart. The same One who indwells us individually also indwells us corporately. As we seek Him together the reality of His indwelling is made manifest.

Walk in Love

"Dear friends, let us love one another, for love comes from God. Everyone who loves has been born of God and knows God. Whoever does not love does not know God, because God is love" (1 John 4:7-8).

The love of God has been shed abroad in our hearts by the indwelling Holy Spirit (see Romans 5:5). As we walk in love, we experience deeper dimensions and manifestations of the Indwelling.

"No one has ever seen God; but *if we love one another, God lives in us* and his love is made complete in us. This is how we know that we live in him and he in us: He has given us of his Spirit. And we have seen and testify that the Father has sent his Son to be the Savior of the world. If anyone acknowledges that Jesus is the Son of God, God lives in them and they in God. And so we know and rely on the love God has for us. ***God is love. Whoever lives in love lives in God, and God in them***" (1 John 4:12–16).

Notice the plain statement of this Scripture: though no one has seen God at any time, if we love one another God lives in us, and we in Him. The God whom no one has seen indwells us—if we love one another! We carry the invisible, invincible One within! We haven't seen Him but He lives in us. But the day hastens when we shall see Him who now indwells us. Oh the wonder of this astounding heritage!

Love makes it possible for God to dwell in our hearts and is indeed the proof of His indwelling. "If we love one another, God dwells deeply within us, and his love becomes complete in us—perfect love! . . . God is love. When we take up permanent residence in a life of love, we live in God and God lives in us" (1 John 4:12, 16 MSG). Permanent residence in a life of love! What a beautiful thought!

Another reason to love one another is that the same One who indwells us also indwells the brethren. We see Christ in every believer. Thus, whatever their status, race, sex, age, etc., we love them. It's not about them, what they have, or where they're from—it's about the One they carry within. What a powerful motivation to love and serve God's people!

Imagine what would happen if believing spouses—beneficiaries of the Indwelling—would continually see Christ in each other. This would change everything! Unfaithfulness would be unthinkable. Abuse would be unimaginable: Abuse someone with Christ inside? Beat up a wife whose body is the temple of the Holy Spirit? Insult a man who is carrying Christ within? That would be absurd! Christ's presence would overshadow every shortcoming, change the tone of our communication, and multiply our consideration for each other. Respect would be constant, for it would be a matter of honoring the indwelling One in our spouses. The beauty of His indwelling presence—a fragrance like no other—would envelop our spouses and our homes! Imagine the possibilities of raising our children in such an environment, saturated with love. Oh, how the Indwelling answers the deepest needs of humanity.

We can now understand how Jesus could say to the righteous on the last day, "I was hungry and you gave *me* something to eat, I was thirsty and you gave *me* something to drink, I was a stranger and you invited *me* in, I needed clothes and you clothed *me*, I was sick and you looked after *me*, I was in prison and you came to visit *me*" (Matthew 25:35-36). The righteous would wonder when they had done such things for Him. "The King will reply, 'Truly I tell you, whatever you did for one of the least of these brothers and sisters of mine, you did for me'" (v. 40.). The King would then condemn the unrighteous for not having done these things for Him because they failed to do them for the least of His brethren. How could these things be?

The Indwelling holds the key to understanding this Scripture. Jesus was indwelling even the least of His brethren when the righteous gave them a drink, took them in, clothed them, or visited them in prison. He was in His temple when the righteous blessed that temple! Therefore they did these things to and for Him. The King was inside the least of His brethren when the unrighteous failed to do these things; in failing to do these things for the least of His brethren, they failed to do them for the King who indwelt them! They saw and treated them as the least, but they never saw the King they carried within!

Saul of Tarsus must have been shocked to learn the identity of the real person he was persecuting: "As he neared Damascus on his journey, suddenly a light from heaven flashed around him. He fell to the ground and heard a voice say to him, 'Saul, Saul, why do you persecute me?' 'Who are you, Lord?' Saul asked. 'I am Jesus, whom you are persecuting,' he replied" (Acts 9:3-5). Saul was persecuting the Church, members of the Body of Christ and beneficiaries of Christ's indwelling. Jesus was so united with His Church that persecuting the Church, "the least of His brethren," was exactly the same as persecuting Christ Himself!

May you see Christ in people. That would change the way you treat them. You would cherish them, serve them, and pour out your life in love for them. And in doing this for them, including the least of His brethren, you would be doing it for the King Himself. And the King will surely reward you!

Love like never before. Love as though you've never been hurt. See the world through Christ's eyes. Let His compassion flow through you to bring healing to the wounds of a bleeding world. This is impossible in our own strength, but it will be Him loving through us.

Listen Inside

As you grow in the revelation of the Indwelling, you will learn to listen *inside*. This is because that is where the Holy Spirit—the One who leads God's children—resides.

Be still and know that He is God.

Listen as you pray.

Listen as you study the Word.

Listen as you walk.

Listen as you work.

We must even listen *as we talk!*

The indwelling Spirit speaks all the time; if you listen you will learn to recognize His voice and follow His leading. And He will lead you to green pastures and still waters of rest and refreshment.

Through the Holy Spirit's leading, you will learn the proper protocols of carrying divinity in humanity. He will keep you balanced in the Word and away from dangerous extremes and false assumptions. While we enjoy the Indwelling, we are still humans, not God. We must still care for our bodies, rest, refresh, exercise, and eat right. We accept responsibility to care for His temple, which we are. We must lovingly care for our families and attend to our work: indeed, these become platforms for revealing the Indwelling Lord and spreading the fragrance of His presence. His Spirit interprets the Word to our hearts in a balanced way. We grow to become deeply spiritual but not spooky or phony. We are real and relatable even as we carry divinity in our earthen vessels.

To listen effectively, we have to learn to cut out the noise. The din from the world outside has a way of distracting our hearts and drowning out the voice from inside. Satan still uses the external to corrupt the internal and collect the eternal. We must guard our hearts. We must still our souls to hear the still, small voice. While we use technology and the media, we must not allow them to possess or overcharge our hearts or quench the still, small voice of the Spirit. We must wean our hearts from the world and its flashy perishables to focus on the indwelling treasure.

Act in Faith

As an heir of the indwelling, your case is different from that of the rest of humanity who do not have what you have. You cannot be stranded in life. Your Helper, the great Spirit of the eternal God, resides in you. There is nothing He cannot handle. He is your Comforter, Counselor, Helper, Advocate, Intercessor, Strengthener, and Standby (see John 16:7 AMP).

As you commune with Him, listen to what He tells you from deep within (and in line with God's written Word). Then act in faith.

When He prompts you to lay your hand on the sick and pray for them, do it.

He will prompt you to speak of Jesus to others—to invite them to partake of this glorious indwelling. Do it.

Preach the Word. Lift up your eyes and behold a lost world in desperate need, waiting for the only message that can save. They surround you on every side. And you bear words that can bring eternal life; indeed, you carry the Life Himself within you! He desires to flow into other hearts—that they too may have eternal life—but He can only do it as you preach the Word. How shall they believe in a Savior they've never heard about, and how will they hear without a preacher? (see Romans 10:13-15). According to Titus 1:2-3, God's promise of eternal life is manifested through preaching. You are God's co-laborer, His sent one. He desires to save, heal, and bless a broken world through you. As you preach the gospel and carry His power to the lost, the oppressed, and the broken-hearted, you will see mighty manifestations of the indwelling One. He will work through you to will and to do of His good pleasure.

If He sends you to the ends of the earth, go; He will go with you. The power of His Holy Spirit was not given for us to sit around and just enjoy church, but so that we can be His witnesses—in Jerusalem, Judea, Samaria, and the uttermost ends of the earth. Go with Him to His harvest fields to reach the lost for whom He shed His precious blood; His signs and wonders will *follow* you as you go.

He will tell you to let go of past hurts and wounds inflicted by others; do it. Trust Him to heal your heart. Your future in Christ is incomparably better than all that has happened in your past.

If He puts a great business idea in your heart, take the necessary steps to actualize it. Remember that He made Bezalel a master craftsman. He can make you a business magnate. He can help you write software and develop digital applications. He can give you innovative solutions to global problems. He can make you anything—nothing is impossible with Him.

He may ask that you surrender something precious to you. As soon as you ascertain that He really is the one speaking, do what He says. Don't quench or stifle His voice. Remember, He cannot ask you to surrender something unless He has something better and greater in view. Trust Him and step out in faith.

Many people of the Indwelling do nothing with the omnipotence that resides inside them. They are perpetually waiting for something to happen from *outside*. But that is not how the victorious life was designed to work. The exceeding greatness of His power is at work in you.

Your Words Matter!

In the light of the Indwelling, it will be improper for heirs of such a heritage to speak in a manner contrary to God's presence, power, and superhuman ability at work in them. In Chapter 15 ("Agree With God"), we saw the importance of saying what God says and putting it in the right tense.

You can no longer say what others say. They speak from the evidence of the senses, but our case is different. We have the testimony of His Word and the witness of His Spirit. We know what the world does not know. We have what others do not have. We belong to a kingdom they know nothing about. Our case is different.

God warned Isaiah, "Do not call conspiracy [or hard, or holy] all that this people will call conspiracy [or hard, or holy]; neither be in fear of what they fear, nor [make others afraid and] in dread" (Isaiah 8:12 AMPC).

In other words, don't call it what they call it. Don't say hard when they say hard. Don't say hopeless when they say hopeless, and don't say impossible when they say impossible. Don't label something great, beautiful, or awesome just because they label it great or beautiful or awesome. Call it what God calls it.

You are not supposed to talk like those who do not have Yahweh residing in them. Your case is different. You are His temple, and that includes your mouth, which should show forth His praises.

Jesus is called the high priest of our confession (see Hebrews 3:1). True Christianity is a confession of certain facts issuing from conviction in the heart. Without this, one cannot be saved—you must believe in your heart that God raised Jesus from the dead and confess with your mouth that Jesus is Lord in order to be saved (see Romans 10:9-10). We have the spirit of faith; we believe, and therefore we speak. And we speak according to what God has spoken—according to His Word.

I invite you to speak out the following statements:

I believe that Jesus Christ is the Son of God; therefore God dwells in me and I dwell in God.

The Spirit of the One who raised Christ from the dead dwells in me.

Greater is He who is in me than he who is in the world.

I can do all things through Christ who strengthens me.

By the stripes of Jesus Christ I have been healed.

Jesus took my sins and my diseases; therefore I refuse to carry what Christ has carried on my behalf.

My God shall supply all my need according to His riches in glory by Christ Jesus.

The Lord is my Shepherd; I do not lack.

I am more than a conqueror through Him who loved me.

God is the strength of my life. Whom shall I fear?

The Lord is my helper; I will not be afraid. What can man do to me?

God has not given me a spirit of fear, but of power, of love, and of a sound mind.

The more you speak like this—with conviction and in harmony with the undeniable facts of the Indwelling—the more you will walk in victory.

Twice I Have Heard

"Once God has spoken; *twice* I have heard this: that power belongs to God" (Psalm 62:11 NASB). Here we have an indication of how to hear when God speaks. He speaks once, but we must hear more than once. We must hear twice—yes, continually—if we are to truly comprehend and apprehend what He says.

You see, *you cannot fully hear God in one hearing.* When God speaks, there is eternity in everything He says. Whatever God says is as endless as He is. His words issue from the depths of His person and are as deep as He is. To expect to read or listen to them once and presume to understand or master them is the height of presumption. This is a major reason the Word of God does not take root in our hearts. His Word must continually ring in our hearts.

Consider this instruction Jesus gave to the disciples: "And He said to them, Be careful what you are hearing. ***The measure [of thought and study] you give [to the truth you hear] will be the measure [of virtue and knowledge] that comes back to you*** - and more [besides] will be given to you who hear"(Mark 4:24 AMPC).

The emphasized part of this Scripture is a vital key to maximizing the Indwelling. *The measure [of thought and study] you give [to the truth you hear]—this truth of the Indwelling—will be the measure [of virtue and knowledge] that comes back to you.* And more will be given to you—if you commit to hearing it continually. Most believers give small, sporadic measures of thought and study to the great truths of holiness, healing, the anointing, answered prayer, etc., and then expect mighty manifestations of virtue and power in these areas. It doesn't work that way.

Let the truths of the Indwelling never depart from your eyes. Keep them perpetually in view. In every conflict, in every situation, never forget that you are possessed by the Holy Spirit, by the Lord Jesus Christ, and by the Father Himself. You are not an empty vessel. You are not a regular guy on the street: you are God's temple in which He currently and permanently dwells. There is nothing ordinary about a person carrying God inside.

One of the ways you can do this is to keep this book close by, and read it often. There is nothing disposable about these truths. They are not something to hear and then move on to something else. There is nothing more central and crucial to the triumphant life than the revelation of the indwelling.

Another way to keep these truths in view is to teach them or study them with others. *The Indwelling* can be used for family devotions, church or fellowship Bible studies, by men's or women's groups, etc. Deeper insights will emerge as you share the revelation of the Indwelling with others. Just as when the Lord fed the multitudes, the bread of life will multiply as you break it and share with others. God will use you to feed many and help them to enter into the fullness of their inheritance in Christ.

If you will give increasing measures of thought and study, prayer and meditation, and unbroken attention to the reality of the Indwelling, you will begin to change from one degree of glory to another. And don't forget that when degrees change, possibilities change too. With increasing degrees of glory, things that were impossible become difficult but possible—then easy, then expected, and finally guaranteed. You will experience the transformational upward spiral that comes from encountering truth. You will come to experience for yourself the God who is able to do "superabundantly, far over and above all that we [dare] ask or think [infinitely beyond our highest prayers, desires, thoughts, hopes, or dreams]" —according to His power that is at work in you (Ephesians 3:20 AMPC).

You will experience the exceeding greatness of His power toward us who believe. You will become a channel of untold blessings to untold multitudes.

You will be filled—with all the fullness of God!

Amen. So be it.

19

Jesus at the Door:
Experiencing the Indwelling

An old rabbi used to say to his people, "Repent before the day you die."

"But," they said to him, "Rabbi, we know not the day of our death."

"Then," he answered, "repent today."

This story was told by Dr. Clarence McCartney in his famous sermon "Come Before Winter."[15] The grace of God is available now—in this day of salvation and mercy. Receiving that grace by humble repentance and faith in the finished work of Jesus Christ on Calvary will make the Indwelling possible in your life—with all its unending benefits.

From reading *The Indwelling*, we see why *receiving* Jesus is so vital: "Yet to ***all who did receive him***, to those who believed in his name, he gave the right to become children of God" (John 1:12). Only by your receiving Him can He indwell you and thus impart His life and nature into you. Only by receiving Him can you come to share in His inheritance.

Jesus gave a firm promise to come and dwell inside you, if you will open the door. He said, "Here I am! I stand at the door and knock. If anyone hears my voice and opens the door, ***I will come in*** and eat with that person, and they with me. To the one who is victorious, I will give the right to sit with me on my throne, just as I was victorious and sat down with my Father on his throne" (Revelation 3:20–21). When He indwells you, you will walk in close fellowship with Him; He will give you the right to sit with Him on His very throne, reigning with Him in life as an overcomer.

Time will soon give way to eternity. Now is the moment of action—to repent from your sins and come to Jesus Christ for salvation. No matter what you have done, come to Him as you are, and He will receive you with wide open arms. Let Him do in you what you can never do for yourself: He will cleanse you, take away the stony heart from you, give you a new heart, and put His Spirit within you.

Here is a prayer you can pray from your heart to let Him in:

"Heavenly Father, thank you for loving me and for sending Jesus to save me. I acknowledge that Jesus Christ is the Son of God. I believe He rose from the dead. Lord Jesus, forgive all my sins. Come into my heart and make me a new person inside. I receive you now. Break sin's power over my life. I invite you, the Father, and the Holy Spirit to come in and dwell in me as you have promised. Help me to know and experience the reality of your indwelling. Reveal yourself continually to me in your Word and by your Holy Spirit. Fill me with all the fullness of God. Thank you for answering my prayer. In Jesus' Name, Amen."

If you have prayed this prayer earnestly from your heart, then trust that God has done what He has promised to do. You are now a beneficiary of the Indwelling. Read your Bible daily, pray regularly in the Name of Jesus, and attend a Bible-believing fellowship of born again Christians. Read The Indwelling over and over again until these great truths settle in your heart. Don't forget to open your mouth wide to appropriate the other blessings God has for you—to maximize the amazing possibilities of the Indwelling. And remember to share this wondrous good news with others, so they too can receive Him and become partakers of the indwelling.

For further fellowship and resources, or to share your experience with The Indwelling, connect with us on the following platforms:

Websites: www.eternityministries.org, www.ferdinandnweke.com and www.theindwelling.net

Facebook: www.facebook.com/drferdinandnweke and www.facebook.com/eternityministries

Subscribe to our YouTube channel, www.youtube.com/burningtruthtv, where we teach on these great truths of God's Word.

Notes

1. http://dictionary.cambridge.org/grammar/british-grammar/prepositions

2. http://www.thefreedictionary.com/indwell. Accessed 20th May 2017.

3. https://en.wikipedia.org/wiki/Intel. Accessed 18th February 2018.

4. https://en.wikipedia.org/wiki/Intel. Accessed 5th May 2017.

5. http://www.wholesomewords.org/biography/bwatts3.html; Accessed 6th May 2017.

6. Brian Tracy, *Change Your Thinking Change Your Life* (Hoboken, New Jersey: John Wiley & Sons, 2003), p. 52.

7. https://www.theguardian.com/technology/2018/jun/09/apple-first-company-valued-at-1-trillion. Accessed 9th June 2018.

8. https://en.wikipedia.org/wiki/Apple_Inc. Accessed 18th February 2018.

9. http://biblehub.com/commentaries/jfb/mark/5.htm. Accessed 6th May 2017.

10. Strong's Hebrew and Greek Dictionaries, E-Sword Electronic Bible Study Software; Rick Meyers.

11. https://m.facebook.com/notes/evangelist-reinhard-bonnke-official-page/jesus-in-your-eyes/10150200064642270/

12. Ferdinand Nweke; *Divine Protocols—Principles & Protocols of God's Kingdom Government*, book and audio teachings (Bauchi, Burning Books, 2013). This resource is available at www.eternityministries.org.

13. https://www.google.com.ng/webhp?sourceid=chrome-instant&ion=1&espv=2&ie=UTF-8#q=tense&*. Accessed circa 25th March 2017.

14. Ferdinand Nweke, *Overflowing Grace*, book and audio teachings (Bauchi: Burning Books, 2013). This resource is available at www.eternityministries.org.

15. http://www.preceptaustin.org/come_before_winter. Accessed 20th May 2017.

Acknowledgments

I acknowledge the Father of our Lord Jesus Christ, the Father of glory, for life, for eternal life, and for the priceless privilege of the Indwelling. Only He could have thought up such an astounding design. Only He could love such as us, to such an astonishing degree. All glory to Him alone!

I bless the Name of the matchless One, Jesus Christ the Son of God, who made the design of the Indwelling implementable by paying the Price that made it possible. Thank you, Lord!

And I thank the blessed Holy Spirit, the indwelling Helper who inspired these truths and continues to make them real, in ever-increasing measure, in and through our lives.

I thank my publisher, Tim Beals of Credo House Publishers, for believing in the message of *The Indwelling* and employing his wealth of experience—in line with Credo House's commitment of "Bringing Words to Life"—to make it available to the world. My gratitude also goes to my editor, Donna Huisjen, and to the book designer, Klaas Wolterstorff, for their painstaking work on *The Indwelling*. Their attention to detail is incredible! And to Verna Kokmeyer, a publishing industry veteran, I express my heartfelt gratitude for connecting me to the amazing team at Credo House.

I thank Greg and Kathy Kelley of World Mission for their treasured friendship and partnership in the gospel. Their passion for those who have never known the love of Christ is relentless and infectious. Thanks too for the foreword, Greg. And thanks for receiving me into The Kelley Clan!

My gratitude also goes to the board, management, and staff of Eternity Ministries for their untiring labor in ensuring that we maximize Calvary together and multiply these truths by every means possible. I'm honored to serve God with such a unique team of sold-out souls. Femi Reis, our IT Administrator and Team Lead for Global Advance at Eternity Ministries, deserves mention by name: thanks, Femo!

And to my wife, Nnenna, and our children—a trillion thanks for your immeasurable love and encouragement. I celebrate you! Journeying through life with you has made both the tempests and the triumphs as memorable as ever. I love you guys more than words can tell!

"Now to Him who is able to do exceedingly abundantly above all that we ask or think, according to the power that works in us, to Him be glory in the church by Christ Jesus to all generations, forever and ever. Amen." Ephesians 3:20-21

About Eternity Ministries

E ternity Ministries exists to help all live in time with eternity in view, by prioritizing eternal realities over the temporary things of this life. We seek to maximize the finished work of our Lord Jesus Christ on Calvary by preaching the gospel of the kingdom of God and by mobilizing, training, and igniting leaders and nationals across the nations to take the gospel to all, especially among unreached peoples. We welcome the partnership of all those who desire to see the earth filled with the knowledge of the glory of the Lord, as the waters cover the sea.

eternityministries.org